W9-BEY-311

DECORATING ON THE CHEAP

BY MARY GILLIATT

WITH SUSAN ZEVON & MICHAEL W. ROBBINS

PHOTOGRAPHS BY TOM YEE
ILLUSTRATIONS BY WILLIAM RUGGIERI

WORKMAN PUBLISHING
NEW YORK

Copyright © 1984 by Mary Gilliatt
All rights reserved.

No portion of this book may be reproduced—mechanically, electronically, or by any other means, including photocopying—without written permission of the publisher. Published simultaneously in Canada by Saunders of Toronto, Inc.

Library of Congress Cataloging in Publication Data
Gilliatt, Mary. Decorating on the cheap.
1. Interior decoration—Handbooks, manuals, etc.
I. Zevon, Susan. II. Robbins, Michael W. III. Title.
NK2115.G426 1984 747'.1 82-40499
ISBN 0-89480-353-0
ISBN 0-89480-354-9 (pbk.)

Book design: Paul Hanson with Susan Aronson Stirling

Workman Publishing Company
1 West 39 Street
New York, New York 10018
Manufactured in the United States of America
First printing May 1984
10 9 8 7 6 5 4 3 2 1

To my patient family, with love.

ACKNOWLEDGMENTS

I am particularly grateful to certain people who have helped so much on a very complicated project—i.e., giving precise and thoughtful recipes that do not blind the amateur with science, and telling me about potential sources to photograph.

So my very real gratitude goes to Barbara Plumb who first initiated this book, to Sally Kovalchick, James Harrison, Paul Hanson, Wendy Palitz, and Susan Stirling who worked so long and hard and gracefully to get it right. To Marilyn Bethany who so kindly gave me a whole list of sources to follow up; to Tom Yee for his enthusiasm and sensitive eye; to Susan Zevon who did so much of the original compiling; to Michael Robbins and William Ruggieri who slaved on the carpentry; to Jocasta Innes and her book *Paint Magic* who almost singlehandedly changed the face of 1980s walls; and to all the people who so patiently let us photograph their homes and dug up notes on how they achieved it all.

CONTENTS

INTRODUCTION 7

THIRTY GREAT SPACES

ALL-IN-ONE LIVING 11

BREAKING OUT OF THE BOX 12

AN EYE FOR BARGAINS 14

DUAL-PURPOSE DOMICILE 16

FAMILY PLANNING 17

LOFTY DRAMA 18

NOUVELLE MODULARITY 21

THREE-DIMENSIONAL PAINTING 22

STEPPED-UP SPACE 24

PUMP HOUSE MEWS 26

AD HOC AT HOME 28

TRIUMPH D'AUTOMAT 30

SONOTUBES REVISITED 32

A ROOM OF THE PAST 33

SPLIT IMAGE 34

THE ARTFUL LODGER 36

OUTSIDE IN 39

PUNCTUATING A PERIOD 40

SPACE EX MACHINA 42

COUNTRY AIR 44

BACK TO BASICS: BLACK & WHITE 46

LUMINOUS ALLURE 48

ROOM FOR ALL REASONS 50

AN ARTIST'S FANTASY 52

DARK ELEGANCE 54

A WRITERS' RETREAT 55

SIMPLE HARMONY 56

DRESS CIRCLE 58

TREASURES LOST & FOUND 60

VERNAL HIGH TECH 62

THE WORKBOOK

WALLS & CEILINGS 64

FLOORS 66

FURNITURE 69

LIGHTING 70

POPULAR PAINT TECHNIQUES 72

COVERING WALLS & CEILINGS 73
- PAINTING WALLS & CEILINGS 74
- PAPERING WALLS & CEILINGS 81
- COVERING WALLS WITH FABRICS 84
- COVERING CEILINGS 86

FIXING UP FLOORS 87
- FINISHING FLOORS 88
- PAINTING FLOORS 90

UTILIZING LIGHT 97

BUILDING THE BASICS 107
- SIMPLE BOXES 110
- PLATFORMS 115
- BOOKCASES & SHELVED UNITS 121
- PARTITIONS 128
- TABLES, COUNTERS & MISCELLANEOUS PROJECTS 133
- SAM NEUSTADT'S MODULAR SYSTEM 139

FURNISHING SPACE 143
- REFURBISHING FURNITURE 145
- TRANSFORMING CASTOFFS 148

SOURCE GUIDE 153

INDEX 163

INTRODUCTION

I came to—or, perhaps more accurately, fell into—designing interiors through writing about them. This means that I have had to put my precepts into practice, and vice versa, because for many years my writing and designing have been totally intertwined, the one feeding the other. Because of my writing and reporting I have had the good fortune to see the work of many designers as well as to visit many nondesigner homes on both sides of the Atlantic. These opportunities have inevitably given me a good across-the-board perspective on what is happening in domestic decoration.

The most interesting thing that seems to be happening just now is a very stylish form of "making do." Time and again nowadays, furnishings thrown out on the street or the garbage dump, hand-me-downs or junk pieces of furniture, and bargains from tag sales are being retrieved or bought for next to nothing and fixed up by the keen-eyed. Floors, walls, and ceilings are being given new looks (and sometimes new functions) with original or rediscovered money-saving do-it-yourself ways with paint, glazes, and applied decoration. Inexpensive substitutes are being found that work as well and look just as good as costly items and techniques. This is a whole new thing in a world that lately has become accustomed to the expendable, the throwaway.

This trend may in some ways be attributed to the high cost of everything (rising prices always have the effect of encouraging ingenuity and improvisation), but lately improvisation and imaginative recycling seem to have become an art form in and of itself. This ingenuity, combined with high-tech stand-bys (new or recycled industrial, hospital, and restaurant equipment; photographic paraphernalia; all manner of "out of place" decorative pieces), has produced a fresh and lively style that is not so much a movement as an attitude, a way of looking at things and putting them together. It is the sort of look that manages to turn impersonal rooms into highly individual environments—and it can be achieved in varying degrees and various ways by anyone. Best of all, it is usually remarkably cheap.

For a long time I have, at least in my mind, equated decorating with cooking. Just as you can make a dish memorable and distinctive by the judicious use of seasonings, herbs, and spices; just as you can vary classic dishes with your own improvisations and innovations, so too can you alter rooms with dashes of color, mixtures of pattern and texture, and interesting and original variations on almost every theme. And just as the same foodstuffs are available to everyone to be put together in whatever way they choose, the same materials are available to everyone for room decoration. In both cases identical ingredients can achieve either standard, commonplace results or new and exciting effects. Because of this decoration/cookery connection, I thought that it would be useful to give how-to-do-it directions in this book in something like a recipe format.

Some recipes are remarkably simple, others more complex and ambitious. The real common denominator is that everything in this book is cheap to carry out or capable of being adapted or applied inexpensively.

The key to the kind of decorating I'm talking about is finding the confidence to do your own thing, therefore a large section of this book is devoted to showing interiors by people who have found that confidence. Techniques in general are discussed and particularly good ideas are cross-referenced to a workbook section. The workbook contains clear recipes for building tables, shelves, platform beds, and other furniture as well as for easy-to-do decorative finishes for walls, floors, and furniture. There are also hints about good-looking low-cost lighting. General decorating problems are discussed: how to work on a budget, and how to take best advantage of the space you have. Tips are given on how to cheer up rentals or any temporary accommodation without leaving an expensive present behind for the landlord when you move on. You will learn how to pep up walls, floors, ceilings, windows, and furniture without having to rob a bank; how to recognize a "find" in junkyards, flea markets, yard sales (you will find a source guide, with listings of off-price stores from coast to coast that will be handy in your bargain hunting); how to make interesting and useful items out of quite ordinary and often unexpected everyday objects. And how inexpensively to transform a space into something that looks as if it cost thousands of dollars. It really is airs on a shoestring, not necessarily because one has a shoestring budget, but because of the sense of achievement in making something out of almost nothing.

I always find it interesting that so many people ask how much decorating a house, an apartment, or just one room is likely to cost. The answer is, of course, that it could cost as much—or as little—as they make it cost, which is what this book is all about.

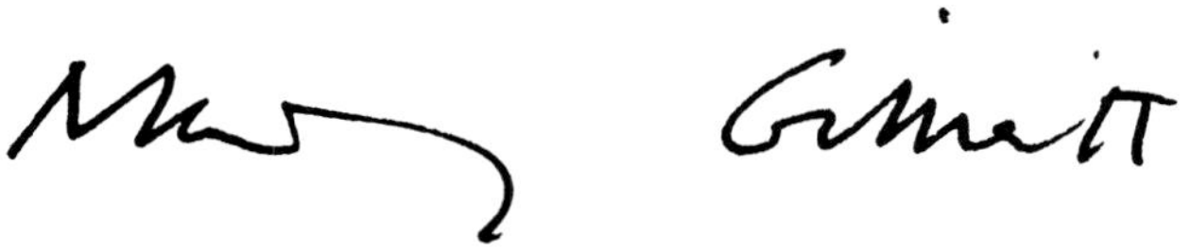

THIRTY GREAT SPACES

ALL-IN-ONE LIVING

The basic requirements—eating, sleeping, working, sitting, storage—are handily attended to in Jamie Roper's 15-by-20-foot one-room city apartment. This versatility is achieved by an arrangement of pared-down, multipurpose elements, most notably banquettes. The color scheme is kept simple—important in a limited space: black and pale aqua is accented by the bare bricks of the chimney wall, the brick red pillows, and the Afghan throw. The ornate frame of the antique mirror complements the severity of the clean-lined furniture, and the metal blinds set off the room's many contrasting textures.

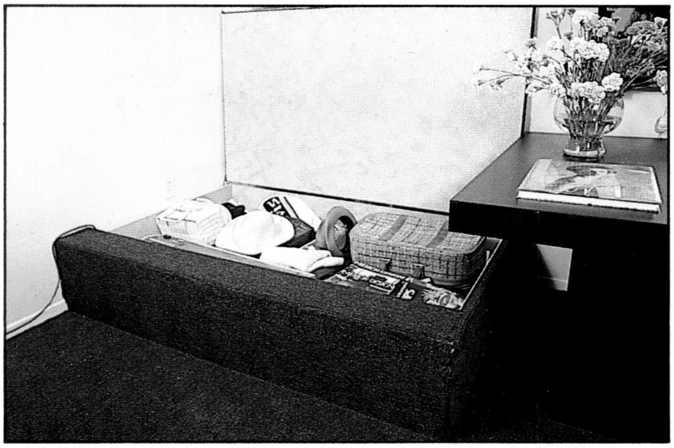

VERSATILE BANQUETTES. Banquettes, for sitting and sleeping, have lift-up lids for storage. ◆ *RECIPE, SEE PAGE 112.* Their bases are covered in the same charcoal gray industrial carpeting as the floor; the polydacron mattresses and large rectangular pillows are covered in inexpensive cotton duck. The table, from an unpainted-furniture store, is covered with black plastic laminate; a similar—less costly—effect could be obtained with paint.

BREAKING OUT OF THE BOX

Susan Zevon's living room (12 by 20 feet) was a typical post-World War II design with all the problems of the period: narrow shoe box-like space; one long shallow window; minimal detailing; and the usual jumble of radiators and air-conditioning machinery. Architect Samuel Neustadt saw the space and built his model for it in an actual shoe box. He suggested that flush doors—$450 worth—be painted, carpeted, and topped with cushions to transform it into a place of platformed orderliness with room for a guest bed, generous seating, and dining and study areas.

AN URBANE VISION. The wall above the seating unit was mirrored to ensure that either the Manhattan skyline itself or its reflection would be seen from both sides of the seating area. Bookshelves above both the mirror and the window give equal emphasis to the view. Also, the banquettes were angled to take advantage of the view.

A MENTIONABLE STUDY. A minuscule triangular study is formed by hollow-core doors set at right angles. Behind them, a desk top, bookshelves, and filing space are all made from sawed-off sections of doors.

DOOR ENCORE. Edges of hollow-core doors were reinforced and used for angled platforms, divan banquette seating units, built-in storage, partitions, and bookshelves.

STIR-FRIED LIGHT. The lid of a steel wok, relieved of its usual culinary duties, makes a functional dining room light shade. ◆ *RECIPE, SEE PAGE 104.*

LEAFING IT. Hollow-core doors were used for the dining table and as an extension to the table to seat eight. When not in use, this extension (not visible in photo) is hung as a triangular piece of sculpture.

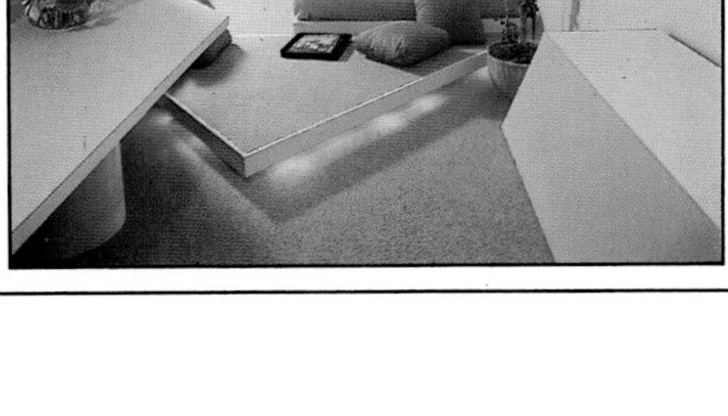

YULE GLOW. This platform is transformed at night into a festive floating island by suspending concealed strings of Christmas tree lights beneath it on cup hooks. ◆ *SEE PAGE 117.*

AN EYE FOR BARGAINS

Actress Leslie Roberts' homey four-room Greenwich Village apartment is an illustration of what can be done for little money but a lot of ingenuity, clever improvisation, and elbow grease. Leslie Roberts searched through junkyards and thrift shops, haunted auctions, pounced on furnishings abandoned on streets, and snatched up discards. Once she'd gathered a core of furniture, she stripped, painted, polished, and re-covered. The result: highly personal rooms as comfortable as they are colorful.

THE ART OF SCAVENGING. Most of Leslie Roberts' furniture was either bought for pennies, or just simply found abandoned. She spotted the chest of drawers pictured below and a corner cupboard on a street corner and carted them home for minor overhaul: stripping down, sprucing up. The best bargain was the iron bedstead with brass insets. Purchased for less than $1, Leslie Roberts scrubbed it, de-rusted it, painted it white, and buffed the brass insets to a high shine.

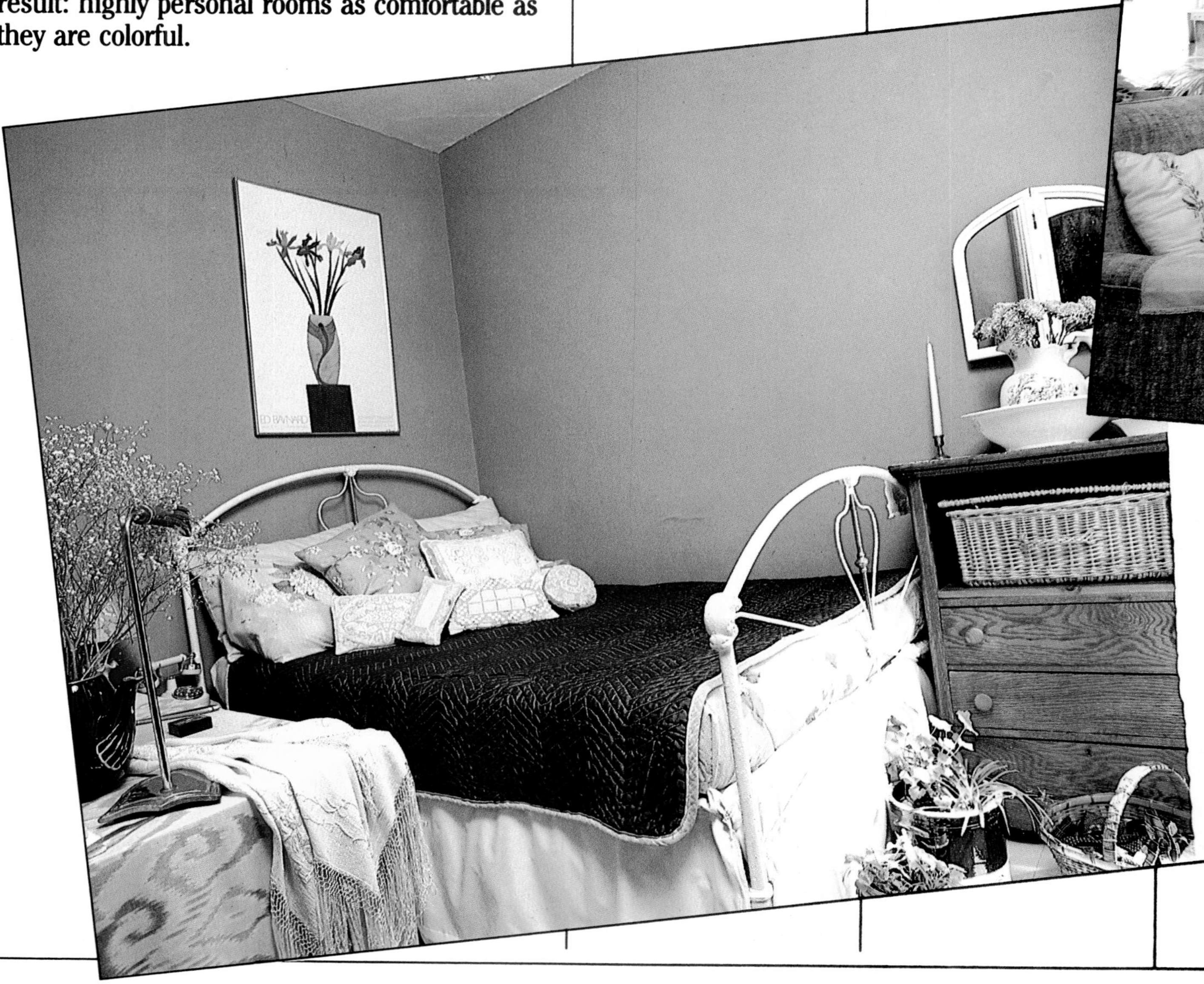

MOVERS' QUILTS. Designed originally to protect household goods while moving, the actress seized the potential of these chic fabrications—as covers for the bed and the sofa bed, and even as a sitting room rug.

FIREPLACE FORGERY. There was no real fireplace in Leslie Roberts' apartment, so she built her own ersatz one. Flanked by a slipcovered chair and a comfortable rocker, this excellent deception—made from plywood and ceramic tiles—becomes a focal point for the living room and gives off its own kind of old-fashioned warmth.

◆ *RECIPE, SEE PAGE 137.*

DUAL-PURPOSE DOMICILE

For reasons, of both economy and convenience, more and more professionals are choosing to work at home, which has made combining working and living spaces a new domestic art. In his one-room L-shaped apartment (12 by 15 feet), which has windows at either end, designer William Machado managed to separate living, working, and sleeping areas with a commendable lack of clutter or contrivance.

DIVIDE AND CONQUER. This white laminate-covered unit, which neatly divides off the space, contains shelves behind one door and a Murphy bed behind the other two. When the bed is down, the doors provide a bit of privacy for sleeping.

DOUBLE DESK. Positioned directly beneath a large window, the ample, handsomely proportioned desk/work table suitable for two persons—or two jobs—was made from three large pieces of plywood, all covered with black plastic laminate: one piece for the top, one for the end panel/support, and one (not visible in photo) running lengthwise under the center for further support. Black metal file cabinets fit snugly beneath.

WELL-TAILORED WALLS. Covered panels, all of an equal width and height, give a feeling of uniformity and continuity to the room. Some panels are hinged and serve as actual doors to conceal storage spaces and a small bathroom, while others simply hang to complete the smooth unbroken look. The panel covering is inexpensive unsized artists' linen. Leather tabs are almost invisible "doorknobs." ◆ *SEE PAGE 85.*

FAMILY PLANNING

A familiar family dilemma in a time of soaring housing prices: how to accommodate an additional child when moving isn't an economic option. Designer/architects Robert Kliment and Frances Halsband came up with an interesting solution for this small—only 1,200-square-foot—apartment. The problem was handily solved by constructing a fanciful pedimented divider wall across a standard-size (11-by-7-foot) bedroom. For $2,500, Kliment and Halsband carved out a nursery, an entrance hall, and a sliver of a room for an older child.

BROTHER'S DOMAIN. A well-organized almost nautical compactness—complete with bunk bed and desk—characterizes this 8-by-7-foot room for older brother. The main dividing wall is at left in photograph.

INFANT POST-MODERNISM. The new baby's room (10 by 11 feet) is on one side of the divider; on the other side a wall divides the remaining space into the older child's bedroom/study and a hall.

The back panels of the bookshelves in the pedimented wall were made from fabric-covered Homosote. ◆ *SEE PAGE 125.*

LOFTY DRAMA

Though few apartment dwellers will complain of excessive square footage, surprisingly enough some find that too much space can be as hard to arrange as too little. For a 3,800-square-foot Manhattan loft, designer Mark Hulla managed to make the seemingly limitless and cavernous area appear intimate and warm. In lieu of the barnlike atmosphere common to many loft conversions, Hulla created the illusion of a series of rooms. Two rows of structural columns marching down the length of the space frame "islands" for separate dining and seating groups and at the same time unify the entire loft. Another divide-but-not-overpower architectural feature is the wall that partitions off the bedrooms. The wall stays well below the high vaulted ceiling, thus maintaining the feeling of openness.

CASTING FOR JUNK. Virtually all the furnishings in this loft were secondhand or fashioned from junkyard items. All the rattan-look furniture (actually maple made to resemble rattan) is from a secondhand shop. Eight armchairs and a card table with four additional chairs came to under $1,000.

PALLETABLE. Mark Hulla has made couches, visible in the photographs here, from industrial pallets, the wooden platforms designed for fork-lift loading.

◆ *RECIPE, SEE PAGE 148.*

Cushions are foam rubber covered in comfortable corduroy. Pallets can be wood stained, or, as they are on the floor of the roof garden (not shown), allowed to weather to a silvery patina. Brown and white cowhide rugs were purchased from a leather goods wholesaler whose skins normally are sold to garment manufacturers.

PURE THEATER. The visual focal point and the central space divider of this loft was a fabulous street find: a stage-set window of unusual presence and charm. It is suspended from the ceiling by transparent 50-pound-test monofilament fishing line.

STAGE FLOOR. The design of this floor, an interesting variation on the usual checkerboard, combines white-painted squares with unpainted ones in a free-form arrangement. The squares on the floor coordinate with the rectangular panes of the stage-set window. ◆ *SEE PAGE 90.*

TURNING THE TABLES. For one coffee table, Hulla reversed a familiar decorative touch by using stacks of coffee table books for the base under a slab of glass; another table (see top photo, page 18) was created by two trash finds: a wooden crate and a glass top polished by a glazier. The use of simple glass tops makes possible the creation of any number of imaginative coffee tables. ◆ *SEE PAGE 149.*

BEDTIME STORY. This bedroom, and another, were set off from the main area by a wall constructed of stock materials, principally 4-by-8-foot standard drywall. Steps to each room, which can be seen in the photo at left, heighten the feeling of separation. The bed ($100), iron pitchfork ($10), and oak trunk at the foot of the bed ($75) were found in a flea market.

NOUVELLE MODULARITY

Architect Samuel Neustadt, who designed Susan Zevon's "shoe box" apartment (page 12), is also responsible for the modular system in this 25-by-13-foot one-room apartment. The main component is a six-foot-high unit that divides the space. On one side is a queen-size bed and a wardrobe; the other side converts into a handy drop table which serves as a desk and a dining table. A low side table and a coffee table flank the central unit. All components were made from plywood, painted a high-gloss Pompeii red and secured with metal rods. Total cost of construction, start to finish, was *under* $250.

SPACE DIVIDER. The system neatly separates the apartment into a dining area on one side and a bedroom on the other.

MORE THAN A DOOR. The hinged door of the wardrobe beside the bed can be opened at night to lend a feeling of privacy and coziness.

A HOLDING PRINCIPLE. All the components in this system are constructed in the same ingenious way. Plywood panels were first painted, then fitted together with steel rods placed inside lengths of hollow aluminum tubing. The steel rods are held in place by visible nuts on the exterior side; the tubes act as spacers and functional design elements on the interior side.

◆ *RECIPES, SEE PAGES 139–142.*

DROPPING BY. The drop table, two feet wide by four feet long, is perfect for an elegant dinner for four, or a desk for working at home. Inside the unit, ordinary vinyl-coated baskets become drawers for storage.

THREE-DIMENSIONAL PAINTING

For an unbelievable budget of less than $600, designer Bill Engel managed to totally refurbish and decorate his 13-by-30-foot studio apartment; his prime ingredients: paint, found objects, furniture—and a remarkable talent for imaginative improvisation. First, he removed handrails from the stairs and sleeping loft to open up the space and reduce it to basic forms. Trained as an artist, Engel then considered his apartment as a three-dimensional painting. The basic interior shell was kept white, but an array of colors was used in a playful way to give emphasis to architectural details. A dominant structural column in the living room was painted a striking flat gold. Additional carefully thought-out accents were provided by repainted old furniture.

PLAY OF LIGHT. Much of the apartment's charm comes from the lighting, which includes a blue fluorescent behind the bed, a pink fluorescent that gives a wash of color behind the microwave, an Abolite dome light above the table, and two drafting lamps for reading and working.

CULINARY CUBISM. Below, through the use of bold color, with the ease of a painter on canvas, Engel turned what might have been a lackluster kitchen into a dramatically geometric space.

A PICTURESQUE STUDY. Bill Engel's work space (above) is defined by a long low telephone table made of three pieces of plywood and painted white and robins-egg blue. ◆ *RECIPE, SEE PAGE 133.* A pink telephone cord becomes the ultimate finishing touch.

OLD AND NEW. Engel found a pair of discarded but solid doors. From these he constructed a platform in the sleeping loft, painted the base a pale lavender, and added an inexpensive foam rubber mattress. Some captain's-style chairs, a present from a friend, were given an unusual asymmetry with contrasting bold and pastel colors. The metal slat partition is a cast-off vertical blind.

GRATE FINDS. The top of the double-duty table is an old subway grating; the base is made from a discarded metal grid that was once a trash can holder, which Engel painted. On top of the table are an old cafeteria tray and baker's rack found outside a neighborhood pizzeria. Rolls of no-seam paper propped against the wall complete the post-modern look.

BAR FORMICA. The long plastic laminate shelf, which serves as a bar/bookcase/sideboard, was found outside a construction site and cut down to fit. It is supported on stacked metal milk crates.

STEPPED-UP SPACE

Architects Louis Muller and William Murphy of New York City have made a reputation for manipulating small spaces to the best possible advantage. In this one-bedroom apartment for Peter Blaustein, they created a number of eminently adaptable ideas: ramps, platforms, seating wells, and partitions at various levels. As in other such minimalist concepts, the architectural planes become the furniture and vice versa. A basically neutral color scheme—grays, creams, and beiges—unifies this multifaceted interior landscape. All is accented by plants, green pillows, gleaming metal blinds, and a cleverly painted two-tone cornice.

LEGERDEMAIN. In both the living room and bedroom, windows were awkwardly high. To solve the problem, Muller and Murphy raised the floor, which then seemed to increase the amount of light and also made the windows themselves seem larger. The effect was further enhanced by mirroring the reveals and side pilasters. Now in both rooms their client has an eye-level view of Manhattan's skyline.

LIVING WELL. By raising the floor and constructing various levels, two separate wells or pits were created—one for dining and one, near the window, for lounging. A raised platform, accessible by a ramp, serves as both divider and backrest. ◆ *RECIPES, SEE PAGES 115–116.*

LOW MAINTENANCE, HIGH TECH. At right, carpeted plywood forms the base for the platform bed and the partitions. An angled and carpeted wall, with shelves and working surfaces on one side, separates the raised sleeping area from the lower study space. An additional lower partition at the foot of the bed conceals a television.

DEPTH PERCEPTION. The architects painted the cornice area with soft beiges and a frosty green, which not only lends an illusion of interesting detailing, but also draws the eye down the room toward the window.

LIGHTMOTIF. New floor, ramps, and platforms were kept free of the walls wherever possible. In the resulting recesses, Plugmold® strip lighting, easily installed to use existing outlets, gives soft indirect illumination to the walls.

◆ *SEE PAGE 101.* The shallow cone-shaped "light fixture" suspended over the dining table by an almost invisible filament is actually a reflector. A recessed light, set flush in the center of the marble tabletop, shines light up; the reflector casts it back onto the table.

SOFT TOUCH. Plenty of plump pillows add that finishing flair.

PUMP HOUSE MEWS

In Brooklyn Heights, architect John Gillis bought an Edwardian pump house, at one time a pumping station for the fire department. Gillis converted the whole building into six separate apartments, like six houses in a row, keeping one for himself. In doing so, he created a charming small private "mews." The large space in Gillis' own two-story home incorporates a host of clever and resourceful uses for wooden dowels and ideas for lighting and display. Much of the work was done by Gillis himself; many of the constructions can be easily reproduced by any reasonably handy home carpenter.

HALLWAY WALLS. On the facing walls of the upstairs corridor, unframed prints, drawings, and photographs are displayed on a versatile, inexpensive metal system. At the far end of the hallway Gillis uses a wooden dowel to make a railing.

ZIGGURAT BOOKCASE. Gillis created an interesting three-dimensional illusion by designing curved and angled asymmetrical shelves for this grand bookcase. Supports for the individual shelves have a ziggurat pattern.

ROMANTIC CANOPY. With a splendid length of antique Venetian lace, Gillis sculpts the empty space above his bed.

DISPLAYS TO SPEAK OF. One long wall—used for displaying pictures and prints—demonstrates Gillis' extraordinary knack for imaginative woodwork and lighting. Here the "shelves" are long wooden dowels, milled at the lumberyard to make both a flat surface to support prints and a notch underneath to conceal lights: strings of Christmas tree bulbs pressed into year-round service.

WOOD WORKING. Gillis used lengths of extra-thick plywood (actually ¾″ plywood glued together and rounded at the front corners) to make an efficient and sturdy desk-and-shelf arrangement. The work surface rests on a pair of file cabinets; some handy pigeonholes lend an old-fashioned touch. All is physically and visually held together by columns made from groupings of dowels.

TOWEL DOWELS. In the bathroom, Gillis demonstrates another use for wooden dowels: here, against an airy background of dotted bathroom tiles, they are used for hanging towels.

AD HOC AT HOME

Julia McFarlane is one of the owners of Manhattan's Ad Hoc Housewares, a well-known source for innovative high-tech accessories, storage systems, and kitchen and bath hardware. For her one-room apartment, which measures a scant 14 by 22 feet, she clearly knew where to get most of the furnishing components and how to make them work for her. But she called Yann Weymouth, an architect with Redroof Design, to help her plan the limited space.

MIRROR, MIRROR ON THE . . . The room had certain amenities to begin with: a fireplace, high ceilings, and nice windows. To make the room look bigger, Weymouth suggested the infallible method of mirroring the walls on either side of the fireplace—a major, but well-spent, portion of the available budget.

CURTAINS WITH A TWIST. To bypass the expense and formality of conventional window treatments, an unusual wigwam-like effect is used here: two 10-foot-long bamboo poles are propped against each window frame; 9-by-12-foot painters' drop cloths are knotted in two corners and draped from the tops of the poles. They can be moved sideways in either direction to control light and are unusually decorative as well.

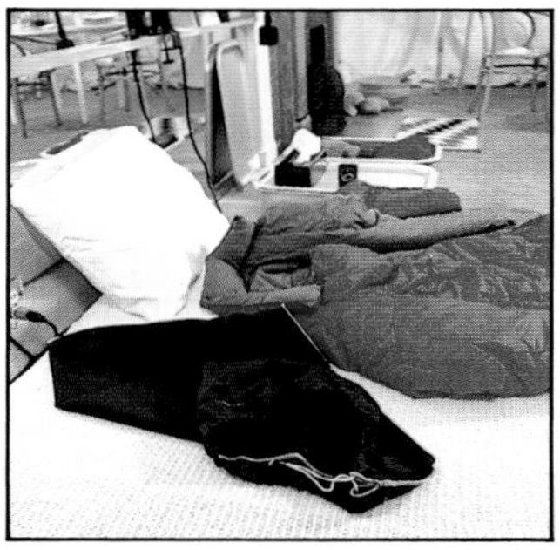

UP WITH DOWN. What to do with down coats in the summer? No closet seems big enough. McFarlane has a simple solution: stuff them into black laundry bags and use them as floor pillows.

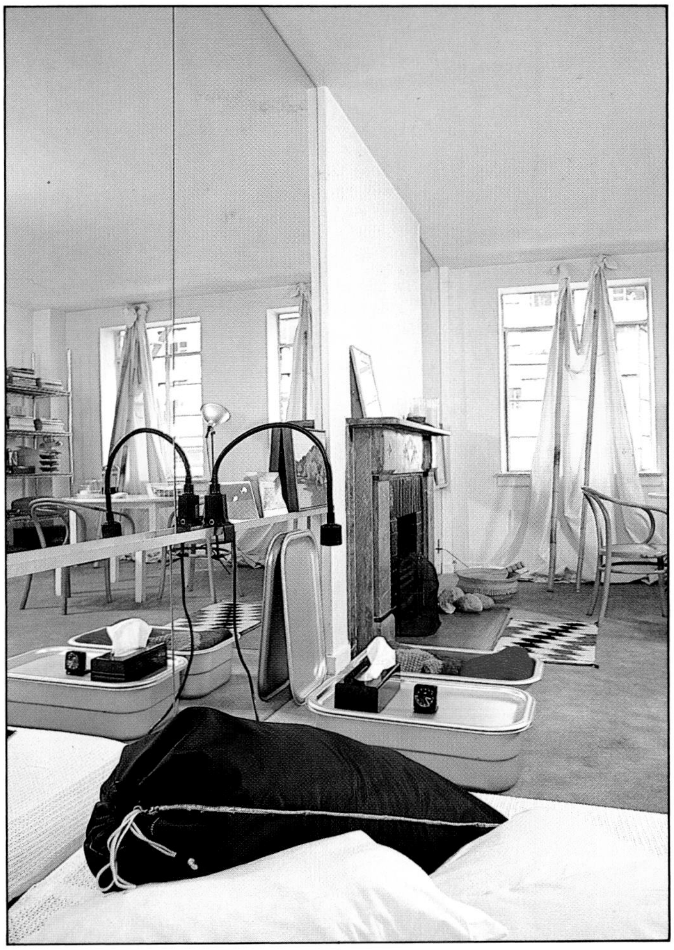

HIGHLY TECHNICAL. Architect Weymouth mounted Metro wire shelving along the entire length of one of the longer walls. This unit, which can be seen in the mirror, holds books, odds and ends. On the mirrored wall, a four-inch strip of aluminum channel bolted into the mirror supports a lamp and is used for display. Other high-tech furniture solutions: the two bedside "tables" are actually aluminum restaurant bins, normally used for holding and stacking dirty dishes. The lid of the bin is sold separately as a serving tray.

TRIUMPH D'AUTOMAT

Designer Charles Hughes captures the ambience of the 1950s in his two-bedroom New York City apartment by imaginatively arranging a wonderful collection of inexpensive components. Industrial dishwasher trays, cafeteria chairs and canisters, a metal restaurant stacking cart, stainless serving ware, and a prominent twirling postcard rack all work to create an overall mood reminiscent of a postwar Automat.

RAINBOW ROOM. Chairs, only $3 apiece, were picked up in a second-hand store, and the dining table was assembled from a circular black plastic laminate top set on a base sold by restaurant supply stores. Rows of anodized aluminum tumblers and pitchers glow in front of the rosy warmth of unrolled photographers' paper.

TOPS IN DINING. An ordinary backyard barbecue grill becomes a centerpiece for the circular table; and round stainless steel pot tops from an odds and ends bin on the Bowery become dining plates.

ALTERED STATES. To set off his period decor, Hughes ingeniously uses backdrops made from rolls of seamless photographers' paper. The rolls come in dozens of stunning colors and are mounted on adjustable tension rods. Walls look clean, crisp, subtly shaded—and the spare rolls propped around the place look more sculptural than cluttered.
◆ *SEE PAGE 82.*

PHOTO FINISH. Here in Hughes' living room, a photographer's reflector light amusingly clamped to a classical bust shines on the no-seam "wallpaper." An aluminum tension rod, usually used to support seamless paper, is put to use as an indoor laundry line.

SIMPLE SOLUTIONS. A stand-out so-simple coffee table is a thick sheet of cut and polished glass set atop a wooden cube. ◆ *RECIPE, SEE PAGE 110.* Garden chairs can be made to coordinate with different wall colors simply by changing their canvas slings.

PLAYBACK. Continuing with a playful retro look, this bedroom, extremely spare in its decor, includes: a large metal storage unit from an office furnishings store; wall-to-wall industrial carpeting; simple foam cushions upholstered inexpensively in cotton duck and used both for sleeping and seating.

SONOTUBES REVISITED

The imposing cylindrical forms dominant in this two-room New York City apartment (as well as in the Pesketts' loft on page 52) are known as sonotubes. Made of fiberboard and used for casting concrete columns, they were adapted originally for use in commercial interiors. But designer Joan Regenbogen was among those to see their potential versatility in residential interiors as well: as storage containers, display cases, room dividers, tables, columns, and other architectural elements.

TUBULAR TABLE. Sonotubes were sliced in half, wrapped in carpeting, and set on top of each other to form the base of this console table. ◆ *SEE PAGE 150.* Its curved lines act as a foil to the straight lines of a nearby coffee table.

◆ *RECIPE, SEE PAGE 113.*

REVOLVING AMUSEMENT CENTER. In her client's living room, Regenbogen used sonotubes to create an unusual freestanding display case that she calls an "amusement center." To make it, each cylinder was cut in half lengthwise, covered in plastic laminate, wired for concealed lighting, and mounted on a turntable. When closed, a dramatic wall of multicolored undulated curves is created. ◆ *SEE PAGE 151.*

A ROOM OF THE PAST

In 1976, designer Tim Romanello moved into this 18-by-13-foot apartment on Manhattan's East Side. At that time, because he needed an apartment primarily for entertaining and for sleeping, he designed this cozy, unified space with ample seating and a certain formal flair. A few years later Romanello began working at home, and so he redesigned the apartment (see page 50) to suit his new needs. Both designs demonstrate a remarkable talent for high style that functions efficiently—and that can be created on a relatively low budget.

UP SHADES, DOWN SHADES. Standard pull-down shades were installed on the windowsill to pull *up*, allowing for maximum privacy and maximum light. Also worth noting: the multifunctional construction, made from plywood at minimal cost, serves as backs for the banquette, as a headboard for the bed (in the foreground), and as storage for bulky suitcases and other unsightly belongings.

MOVING ON. The essential design ingredient here was the unusual and abundant use of neutral-colored movers' padding. Dozens of square yards of it covered everything—the wide banquette, foam cubes, throw pillows, the futon-like sitting/sleeping pad, and even the floor—creating a simplicity and a unity to the scheme. Total cost of the "upholstery:" $350.

FELICIANO

EAST SIDE. The tatami-like effect of the padding on the floor, as well as the arching bamboo trees and Noguchi rice-paper lamp, add to the room a quiet oriental feeling.

SPLIT IMAGE

The problem in designing separate living and sleeping quarters in this boxy, 20-by-30-foot one-room apartment was that there was only one window. The owner, a psychologist, likes to entertain, yet wanted a sleeping area that wasn't submerged in total darkness. Designer Janice Gewirtz with Lewis Winthrop—both of Interspace Design, Inc.—came up with an interesting solution: an angled partition wall pierced with a precisely positioned semicircular opening to allow maximum light without sacrificing a sense of privacy. They also saved scarce space with upbeat storage concepts and multipurpose furniture.

GYM CLASS. Tucked away in a corner, these slim gym lockers from the American Pressed Steel Corp. in Brooklyn were painted white; the compartments are just the right size for shirts, sweaters, or underclothes, and they keep everything neat and tidy.

ANOTHER OPENING. Besides allowing light to pass through, the half-circle interior "window" is a stylish focal point. ◆ *RECIPE, SEE PAGE 132.* The table in front of it—seen at right—when pulled away from the partition wall, easily seats six and also acts as an occasional desk.

HUNG UP ON WHEELS. Turning a bicycle into a piece of sculpture is one of the designers' resourceful solutions to limited storage space; suspended from the ceiling by a chain, in front of a brilliant yellow panel, the bike becomes sculptural pop art. The remaining wall space is almost totally utilized for shelving. The top shelves are filled with books and other objects; the lowest shelf serves as a work surface.

BASED ON LUNCH. Stainless steel bases for the table in front of the half-circle window were manufactured as bases for luncheonette tables. Available from L & B Products in the Bronx, they are a cheap substitute for what can be a costly item.

WINDOW SEATING. To further create the illusion of space, an eclectic mixture—at left—of velour sofa, a Chippendale-style chair, and versatile director's chairs is positioned on an area rug in front of the large picture window. The long vertical blinds on the window add linear diversity.

THE ARTFUL LODGER

The problem with the old-fashioned 1,300-square-foot New York City apartment of the Tom McHugh family was not its size, it was that the apartment's space was inefficiently laid out. By removing four partition walls, architect/inventor McHugh created an open, airy loftlike space, while at the same time retaining the best of the original structure: the bedrooms. The space now serves—in the best sense—as a family room. At one end is an office with books and other working materials stashed behind a louvered screen. The bedrooms, one for young Michael, the other for his parents, provide visual and acoustical privacy. Thus Tom McHugh has artfully solved the lodging dreams of his whole family.

LESS THAN MEETS THE EYE. As a result of a few well-thought-out features, the McHughs' family room appears larger than it actually is. The Knoll foam-cube furniture is simple, movable, and low. The wall hangings—pictures and mirrors—also are placed low, and the bleached floor further lightens and unifies the space. ◆ *SEE PAGE 90.* Visual "islands" over either of the two tables can be created by moving the pendant light wired to an electrical track (see also below). On the walls, playful ornate bedroom mirrors add sparkle and reflected light.

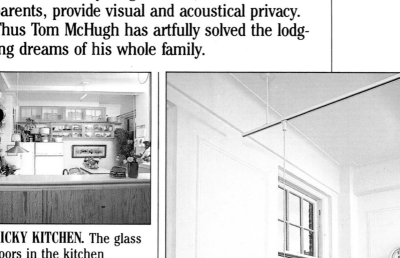

KICKY KITCHEN. The glass doors in the kitchen originally hung on built-in cabinets on one of the apartment's now-removed walls. The doors were stripped to their natural wood, then hung horizontally on specially built plywood "boxes" to form cupboards.

A FAMILY TABLE. McHugh made the top for the small, low table between the windows out of peach-colored laminate and wood. He then mounted the top on a sawed-down and painted cast-iron restaurant table base. Surrounding the table are sunny yellow "knock-down" canvas-covered tubular chairs.

DO-IT-YOURSELF TABLE. The generous-size handmade plywood table is large enough for working drawings and plans and can be used for dining as an alternative to the smaller table by the windows. Supported by a fiberboard sonotube at one end and attached to the wall at the other, it defines the office space.

◆ *RECIPE, SEE PAGE 134.*

Books, files, working materials, and a drawing board are neatly concealed behind louvered doors made into a hinged folding screen.

CHILD'S PLAY. To make a play area for their son, Michael, the McHughs arrange their Knoll foam cubes as a safety barrier; the floor is efficiently "carpeted" with movers' padding. Michael's little chair, in the foreground, was designed and made by Tom McHugh from an old refrigerator carton.

ONE-PIECE BEDROOM. For less than $400, Tom McHugh designed and constructed this bedroom unit (above), which contains storage space, a desk, shelves, a closet, and—on top—a bed. The unit can be taken apart into smaller sections, fortuitously enough since it has now survived moving to three different apartments.

STEPPING UP. On one side of the McHughs' bedroom unit, steps lead up to the bed. Behind them, the inside of the unit provides ample space for hanging clothes and other storage. The opposite side forms a desk unit with sliding-door storage cabinets from an unpainted-furniture store.

SKY HIGH. Just below the sky blue ceiling in the entrance hall, shelves for storing books and slides make good use of otherwise wasted space. A mirror on one wall opens up the area. Covering the light fixture, a Japanese rice paper shade hovers like a cloud.

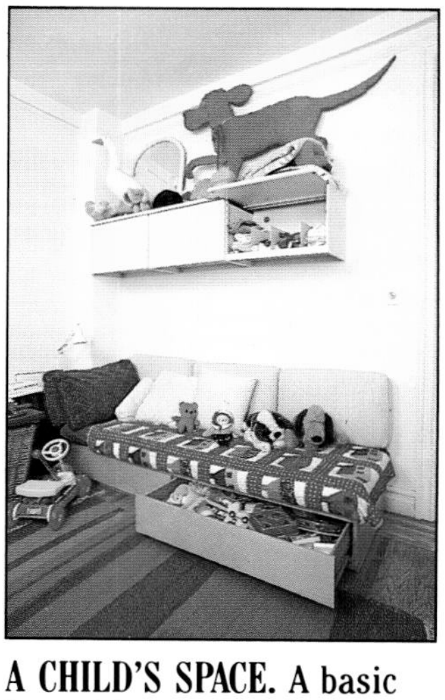

A CHILD'S SPACE. A basic box with two built-in drawers is used for a guest bed as well as for storage.

◆ *RECIPE, SEE PAGE 114.*

On the Knoll office system cabinets, Tom McHugh's own handmade plywood dog and a Gladdy Goose lamp wired with a dimmer switch to serve as a night-light, keep Michael good company.

OUTSIDE IN

There are splendid trees on the street outside this tiny two-room apartment in Manhattan. Young designer Ken Sanden, creating his own space, took full advantage of this rent-free bonus by echoing the greenery inside with masses of plants. Sanden then painted the living area to subtle graphic effect: lovely soft gray walls are complemented by brilliant sunny yellow trim; a high-gloss white ceiling captures the leafy design of the outside foliage in shadowy patterns.

SCALING UP. Three bookcases of different heights shield the sleeping alcove from the living area. Their enclosing angle and open shelving effectively create a separate sleeping zone without visually dividing the small space. ◆ *RECIPE, SEE PAGE 124.*

TAKING PANES. By gluing vertical "mullions"—actually short pieces of wooden molding—to the standard double-hung windows, Sanden creates a warm Colonial look. In lieu of buying costly shutters, he built wooden ones by hinging pine boards.

TOUR DE FRAME. Both the windows and the display niche in one corner of the living area are framed in shades of yellow. To make the niche, Sanden removed the door from what had been a closet, added glass shelves, strip lights, and then framed the doorway in a one-inch border of glittering gold leaf. This yellow framing unifies the room and draw's one's eye toward the windows—a trick to maximize the room's sunlight.

PUNCTUATING A PERIOD

For an astoundingly low $1,600, designer Austin Chinn managed to decorate this 12-by-19-foot studio apartment for client Robert Fitzgerald. The budget was maintained by shrewd shopping for the various components, chosen for period of design, versatility, low prices, and for harmonization with a background enriched more by color and texture than expensive ornamentation. The curtains, which came first, recall the 1930s and set the mood. The furnishings––from the neoclassical-style painted wooden coffee table to the Art Deco standing lamp and contemporary shelving units—reflect the eclecticism of the Thirties. At the same time, the furnishings serve multiple purposes: the pink-painted Parsons table at the end of the bed serves as nightstand, buffet, desk, and dining table for up to six. The platform bed conceals storage space and doubles as a sofa. The result of the whole seems nostalgic, coordinated, complete.

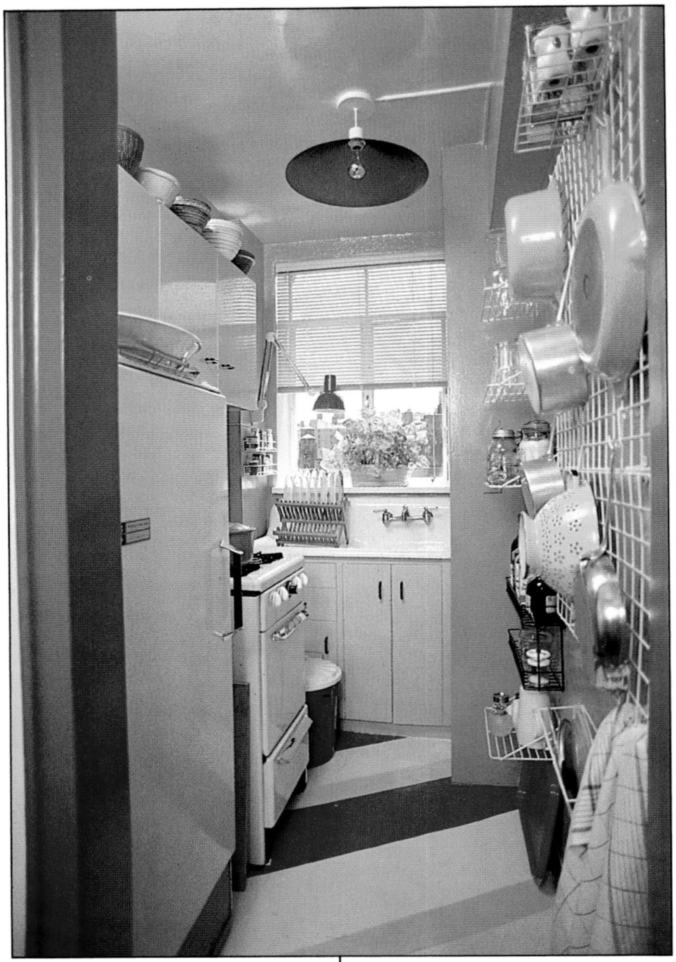

IN KEEPING. The metal utility shelves in this room are perfectly at home in their Art Moderne surroundings. Used for books and stereo equipment, they were bought second-hand, scrubbed down and painted with shark's-tooth gray oil-base enamel.

DIAGONAL DIVERSITY. To enlarge the narrow kitchen visually—facing page—Chinn engagingly painted the floor in diagonal stripes of various widths, each a different color. ◆ *SEE PAGE 90.* A floor-to-ceiling vinyl-coated wire storage system provides not only narrow split-level storage but also versatility and accessibility: cooking utensils, canned goods, and other kitchen essentials are all within easy reach.

STREAMLINED. In the raised entrance, an Art Deco chest flanked by two Breuer-style chairs creates a period space within a space. Complementary second-hand treasures in the living area (see below) include a vintage armchair and a Deco floor light, stripped down to its basic metal structure.

CENTERING CURTAINS. The curtains, oddly enough the most expensive item in the apartment budget, have a floral print specifically chosen to provide a unifying color scheme for walls and upholstery; cornices around the living room were painted the same deep red as the baseboard and door molding to better define the space. In the foreground, a specially designed platform bed has built-in space for books and bedside belongings.
◆ *RECIPE, SEE PAGE 120.*

SPACE EX MACHINA

New York City-based architect Gerald Allen had a real problem: how to turn a tiny 7-by-14-foot room into a sleeping and working area. For less than $1,000 Allen constructed for this space what he calls his "bedroom machine"—which functions as study, bedroom, dressing room, and library. Allen further enhanced the feeling of spaciousness by installing a suspended track lighting system; in addition, a checkerboard pattern of mirror tiles was applied to one section of the ceiling. The most expensive decorating touch is a valuable antique chandelier—lending grandeur to the room.

HOME SCENE. This desk was made simply by laying a piece of plywood on top of two 28-inch-high and 24-inch-deep file cabinets. The cabinets cost about $60 each, and the plywood about $30. The books above and the walls on either side create a compact work space.

CUISINE SMART. Hanging food preparation equipment, above, nearly covers one wall of the kitchen. This not only gives the tiny space a great deal of storage, but it also helps disguise the poor condition of the old wall. This wall is painted deep blue, another clever way to disguise its condition.

CUISINE ART. Diagonal stripes of varying widths, reminiscent of the supergraphics of the 1960s, were painted on this wall to distract from the diminutive size of the kitchen. The skylight is framed with track lighting and hung with plants to make the small space luxuriant.

WORLD OF ONE'S OWN. Gerald Allen's bedroom machine—facing page—was made from two-by-fours, formed just like standard wall construction, and then covered with plywood. Resplendent scarlet corduroy is secured to the wood with wheat paste, like wallpaper. The bookshelves, hung by standard brackets and tracks, span the space between the bed structure on one side and a floor-to-ceiling panel on the other.

◆ *SEE PAGE 126.*

MAKING TRACKS. The suspended homemade track lighting above Allen's bedroom machine was made of Plugmold®, with outlets at regular intervals. The total cost of this imaginative fixture was about $125, less than half what it would have cost ready-made. ◆ *RECIPE, SEE PAGE 101.*

CHECKERBOARD HIGH. Inexpensive mirror tiles are arranged in a checkerboard pattern on a purple-painted ceiling. Since the ceiling was unusually bumpy, mirror tiles were attached with mastic adhesive normally used for vinyl wall tiles. ◆ *SEE PAGE 86.*

COUNTRY AIR

Designer Caroline Bowyer was lucky enough to acquire a spacious 1,800-square-foot loft in lower Manhattan. Her greater fortune, however, was in having architects for parents. The senior Bowyers designed a series of storage units that define—without enclosing—living, sleeping, dining, and work areas. Walls are washed in fresh white paint; ceiling beams are highlighted in a deep natural finish. Many furnishings reflect Caroline Bowyer's love of country things. The result is an inviting ambience enriched by the best of two worlds: the open architectural planes of spacious city loft living, and the warmth and comfort of a more rustic style of life.

DECOROUS WALLS. Throughout her loft, Caroline Bowyer's walls hold an eye-catching array of rich graphic devices, from posters and prints—even framed menus—to the cluster of lapel buttons on the bulletin board in her work area.

SCAVENGING SAVVY. Money for modern classics—such as the Wassily chair—was saved by finding and refurbishing other pieces from garage sales and junk shops. The unusual sloping Victorian divan was stripped and varnished, then upholstered in deep blue velvet for about $250; a coral-covered rattan couch was snatched up for $15; a pair of ratty director's chairs were painted black and refitted with new canvas backs and seats; the commercial standing ashtray was purchased for only $1.

THE GREAT DIVIDE. One of this loft's most useful storage units is a freestanding divider which separates the sitting area from the entrance hall. It was designed around some previously owned bookcases. Glass shelves at each end are for collections of objects.

OLD AND NEW. A wrought iron bedstead and a handsome antique quilt contrast comfortably with a sleek, handy room divider in the sleeping area. The bottom half of the divider has cabinet space on the other side for household storage.

BACK TO BASICS: BLACK & WHITE

Bruce Bierman, artist, weaver, and designer, believes firmly that on a stringent budget a spare, contemporary look is best, with furnishings and design elements unified wherever possible. For his own 50-by-21-foot apartment he found black the answer to this unity—it is generously used throughout, and serves as an excellent foil for the rich, dense colors of his woven tapestries. Black is used for carpeting, upholstery, furniture, and is occasionally contrasted with white: in the black and white vinyl tile floor of the dining area and in the all white coffee table. One wall is lined with cardboard tubes covered in Bierman's woven fabrics in a spectacular spectrum of graduated colors.

SHOWCASE KITCHEN. Straightforward painted plywood shelves hung by tracks and brackets on a high-gloss white brick wall hold colorful kitchenware and draw the eye to an orderly, simple, and spacious kitchen area.

◆ *SEE PAGE 126.*

BORN-AGAIN BREUER. Marcel Breuer's tubular S-shaped chairs, those classics of modern interiors, are covered in long black pillowcases, concealing their somewhat ragged condition. The table is lacquered—glossy black, of course.

LOW (BUDGET) SEATING. Ordinary box springs and mattresses for sitting and sleeping are slipcovered in black cotton, then lavishly strewn with slipcovered pillows for comfort.

WALK RIGHT IN. Clothes perfectly arranged in a two-tier walk-in closet appear as sumptuous and colorful as the fabric lineup on the wall of the dining area.

SPECIAL EFFECTS. In addition to the color and texture provided by tapestries and fabrics, Bierman uses other engaging elements as accents: three matched round mirrors above the seating area create a shipboard "porthole" effect; and a large white cocktail table seems to hover a few inches from the floor.

ABLE TABLE. The design of the coffee table is one of many adaptations of the basic box. Other easy-to-make variations include drawers, platforms, storage chests, and even bookcases.

LUMINOUS ALLURE

For an all-inclusive $9,000, Bill Engel tackled his parents' basic builder's ranch house in Minnesota and totally transformed it. Outside, he painted the house black with cobalt blue ductwork and added a concrete entry ramp. Inside, he installed a reflective glass brick wall to separate the living area from the bedroom; camouflaged odd-shaped walls by using stretched colored canvas to diversify their form; and laid down a mixture of dark gray industrial carpet and gray Pirelli tiles. Finally, he enlivened the whole space with lighting, ranging from colored fluorescents—creating a kaleidoscopic nocturnal glow—to theater spots above the sofa.

LOOKING IN. Engel took out the original nondescript door and replaced it with a modern version in clear glass, adding, for visual interest, a pink-sprayed oak pole.

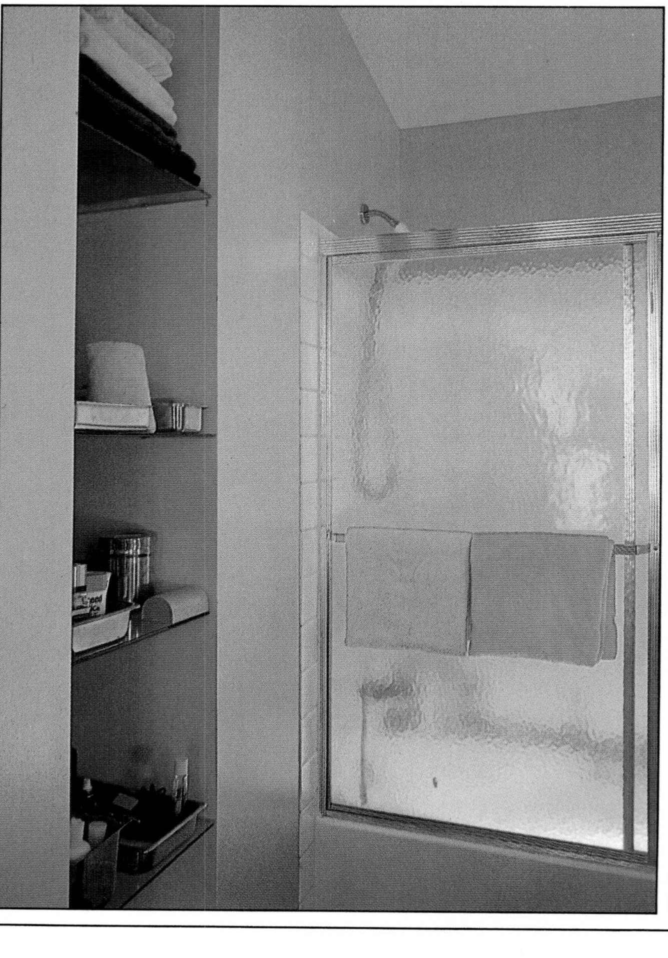

BATHED IN LIGHT. Engel painted the open storage area in the bathroom (left) a deep pink and made $1/4''$-thick glass shelves appear to float by supporting them with almost invisible small metal pins. At right the lights on either side of the bathroom mirror were made from items actually fabricated for industrial use. ◆ *RECIPE, SEE PAGE 102.* The sink, a one-piece unit of cultured marble was given a coat of gleaming black epoxy paint. A bright magenta spotlight under the sink provides an extra touch of drama.

REFLECTIONS. A basic wooden rectangular box—from an unpainted-furniture store—is mirrored, with a slender triangle spray painted flat black on one side. This "edge" intentionally repeats the oblique angle of the stretched pink canvas above the glass room divider. The inset above shows the house at night.

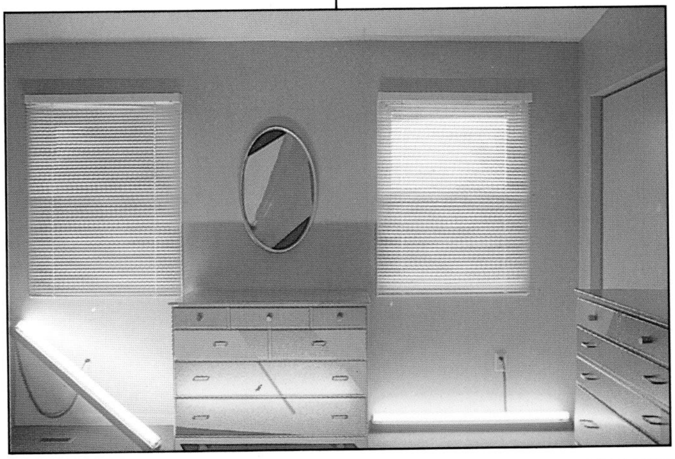

FLUORESCENT FRAMEWORK. In the bedroom, two interestingly painted 1950s dressers are flanked by fluorescents. An oval mirror offsets the horizontal lines of the aluminum blinds.

ROOM FOR ALL REASONS

When Tim Romanello began to work at home, he redesigned his 18-by-13-foot apartment (see page 33) to maximize its living and working space with minimal expense and effort. The centrally placed platform bed/sofa acts as an inventive room divider: with plump bolsters, it divides the room into two separate areas—a living room on one side and a dining area on the other. At night it serves as a king-size bed. Elegant shelves and storage cupboards contain books, television, and stereo equipment. And a cherry Biedermeier table, the most valuable piece in the room, serves as both dining surface and desk. The success of the overall design lies in the simplicity of the individual components.

PANELS OF CANVAS. In his entrance hallway, Romanello uses easy ingredients to create a decor suggestive of the clean, dramatic simplicity of an art gallery. The louvered doors shielding the kitchen and opening into the living room were replaced with floor-to-ceiling panels of artists' canvas that slide on tracks in the ceiling. ◆ SEE PAGE 131. Track lighting and a drafting table complete the look. The same artists' canvas is used for Roman shades in the living room (right). When shades are pulled and door panels shut, the effect is one of uninterrupted, enveloping space.

OFF-WHITE SPECTRUM. Romanello orchestrates a calm neutral color scheme to offset his seasonal shifts of color and fabrics. The walls and ceiling are painted a high-gloss cream color, an inexpensive substitute for lacquer. The floor is covered in natural straw sisal matting. (Diving board matting, a cheaper version, looks just as nice.) A neutral shade of canvas is used to cover the bolsters and the mattress.

ROOM FOR ALL SEASONS. This room's mood is ingeniously changed from season to season by swapping heavy fabrics in winter for lighter materials in summer. In winter two slipper chairs show off their Kilim-rug upholstery and the wicker chair its wool paisley. Beneath the secondhand gilt mirror is an assemble-it-yourself Parsons table covered by wool paisley and a piece of soft leather. For summer, the two slipper chairs are transformed with no-sew slipcovers: a sheet is stretched over the back and seat, then tightly knotted at both sides. The wicker chair is covered in chintz, and the Parsons table is draped in lightweight canvas.

BED AND BOLSTER. Platform beds are less obtrusive and more versatile than most other styles of beds; and they can be surprisingly easy to make. For the price of the building materials, one can build a bed that will serve as a back-to-back sofa. The total cost will be less than the price of one store-bought king-size bed. ◆ *RECIPE, SEE PAGE 118.*

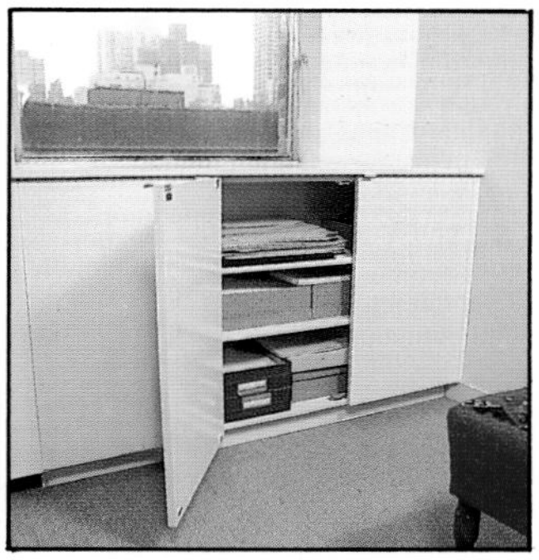

CLEANER CLUTTER. Under the windows at the end of the room, built-in cabinetry contains handy shelving at both sides and, in the middle, conceals an unsightly radiator.

AN ARTIST'S FANTASY

English artist Stan Peskett, now relocated in California, used his extensive 2,000-square-foot loft space in Manhattan as a "canvas," giving full three-dimensional rein to his imagination and inventiveness. Peskett likes "art that functions; objects that you can use but that have other levels." The surreal loftscape that he—and his wife Roanne—created is offset by painted walls of dream settings suggesting Egyptian-columned exteriors; furnishings and decorative elements are, as he terms it, "extraordinary ideas from ordinary ingredients; found objects transformed into playful works of art that also function as furnishings as well." The effect is an art lover's dream: actually *entering* an abstract painting, much like Alice in Wonderland.

A WAY WITH PAINT. Another Peskett specialty: rescuing old pieces of furniture and patiently applying layers of lacquer for high-gloss revitalization. Two familiar 1950's butterfly chairs were given a stunning look with new covers sewn by Roanne Peskett and the frames spray painted. The floor also was painted in large marbleized squares, then polyurethaned for durability and easy maintenance. ◆ *SEE PAGE 93.*

DRESSING ROOM PRIVACY. Painted screens form a convenient dressing room; a sailcloth curtain completes the privacy. Clothes are hung on utilitarian cloakroom racks or stacked on industrial shelving. Screens were made by stretching artists' canvas over wooden frames, then painting them in abstract designs. ◆ *RECIPE, SEE PAGE 128.*

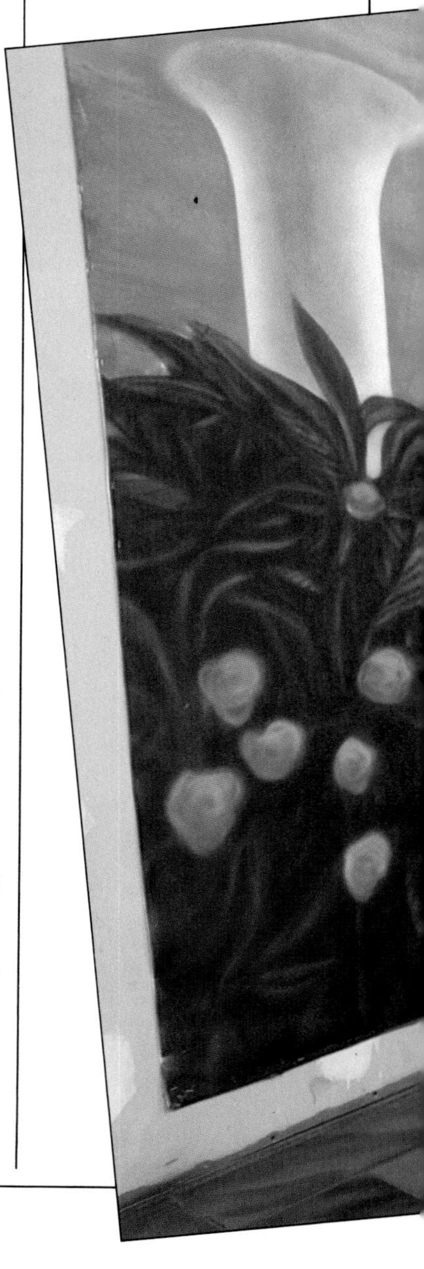

LOTUS COLUMNS. Stan Peskett's fanciful mural, seen at right, is entitled "Paradise Garden," and features an arcade of the brilliantly painted columns that he uses in so many forms. The old garden swing, here charmingly out of context, was spray-painted with blue lacquer. Foam cushions were covered in artists' canvas, stretched tight, soaked with water, painted, ironed, and finally Scotchgarded.

TOPS IN TABLES. The Pesketts specialize in tables made from cut-down sonotubes, the fiberboard forms used for casting concrete columns. The tabletops are plywood; bases bound with stretched canvas, primed, painted with acrylic, and sprayed with sealer.

◆ *SEE PAGE 152.*

The work of art propped against the wall is an alternative dining table top.

DECO ECHO. In addition to the low sonotube tables, Peskett makes these tall sonotube columns that have Moderne appeal. For a New York gallery installation in 1981, he grouped ten of them together; the name of the presentation: "Twilight Shrine."

DARK ELEGANCE

Compare this 12-by-20-foot studio belonging to Richard Lamley to that of Susan Zevon (see page 12); they are not only on the same New York City block, but are the same basic size and shape—a lesson in the variety of design solutions. Lamley's was designed by Elizabeth Winchester with the prime requirement an atmosphere of easy comfort for evening entertaining. For warmth, designer Winchester lacquered walls and storage units a rich brown, nicely offset by wall-to-wall camel-colored carpeting. Space and light have been judiciously augmented by the large panel of mirrors above the cabinets. The total effect is inviting and subdued.

CUSTOM CABINETRY. The 18-foot storage unit extending from under the windows and at right angles down one side, was made by Richard Lamley himself, though he had never before attempted such ambitious carpentry. Standard stock shutters were the principal ingredient; the cost of materials was $350. The unit contains a pivoting TV, a bar, and a miscellany of decorative objects.

VALANCE LIGHTING. The lighting in Richard Lamley's apartment is carefully planned to create a serene atmosphere. Above the windows, extending across the width of the room, a pine valance conceals and shields the glare from a row of spotlights. This recessed lighting reflects off the aluminum slat blinds and from the mirrors over the storage unit for a dazzling jewel-like effect.

SENSUAL SEATING. The neutral tones of the lush carpeting, chairs, and modular seating units act as a foil to the dark walls. To make the most of the floor area, seating units were backed to the wall and arranged in a deep, wide U-formation.

A WRITERS' RETREAT

In an apartment for two novelists, designer William Machado built a trapezoid-shaped office into one corner of the living room by constructing a projecting wall and then closing off the new space with large angled doors mirrored on one side. When doors are closed, they reflect shelves of books and make the living room seem larger; open, the imposing floor-to-ceiling panels give added architectural perspective to the room. Living and office space are demarcated by different floor coverings: beige carpeting for the living spaces; black rubber for the office.

CANNY CONCEPT. A narrow storage closet for canned goods (above) was built on one side of a wide hallway near the kitchen. ◆ *SEE PAGE 127.*

STORAGE IDEAS. In the kitchen, bars of formed black metal make excellent pot and saucepan racks. One corner of a hallway (above, left) was converted into a wine closet incorporating a standard wine rack and separate shelves for bottles and glasses.

ELEGANT SHELVING. Floor-to-ceiling bookshelves in the living area are a basic design with adjustable shelves. ◆ *RECIPE, SEE PAGE 123.* Clamp-on lights with green glass shades provide easy examination of titles. The study/office walls are fitted with an L-shaped work counter and a shelf above.

SIMPLE HARMONY

For an all-inclusive $2,000, architect Richard Oliver managed to decorate and furnish his small apartment, which consists of a 14-by-21-foot main room, a 7-by-15-foot kitchen, and a 7-foot-square alcove. The price is as appealing as the uncluttered look so flawlessly achieved. Seating and storage are brilliantly combined in a central L-shaped unit. The foam mattresses and pillows are covered in emerald green cotton, which is handsomely complemented by the strong Chinese yellow of occasional tables. Additional storage is provided by a large plan file which doubles as a bedside table.

DINING OUT. In this alcove, the wooden floor, stripped of its original varnish, then sanded, waxed, and polished to glowing clarity, enhances the small space.
◆ *SEE PAGE 88.*

HIDE-A-BIKE. Most rooms are full of dead space, and only habit prevents us from seeing the storage potential in them. Here a bicycle is tucked underneath an easy-to-make plywood kitchen counter, which also serves as a general work surface.
◆ *RECIPE, SEE PAGE 135.*
The kitchen cart with the tomato red base, actually a tool chest on rubber wheels topped with butcher block, provides excellent storage space.

ALL-PURPOSE BANQUETTE. The L-shaped, furniture-grade plywood seating unit, the dominant piece in the main room of the apartment, is backed by storage cabinets for stereo equipment, files, and books. Seating sections double as sleeping places. Critical to the success of the design was Richard Oliver's decision to keep the dimensions of the components slightly under-scaled. The depth of the cushions and the height of the seats are less than furniture makers would make them. And the bookcases were kept low, to make the ceiling look higher. ◆ *RECIPE, SEE PAGE 136.*

DRESS CIRCLE

Interior designer Franklin Salasky (of Bentley, LaRosa and Salasky) decided that fashion designer Bonnie August's colorful collection of clothes and shoes should be a decorative focal point of her New York apartment—a solution both personally and professionally fortuitous. Ms. August's array of attire clearly provides more color, pattern, and texture than any decorator's showroom. For this storage/display, Salasky used Metro shelving for the entire length of the bedroom for shoe racks, shelves, and hanging clothes. For closed storage, Salasky removed old doors on existing closets to install lightweight canvas curtains on hospital tracks. The color of the walls and ceiling, a soft pink, was carefully selected to complement Bonnie August's own complexion. The floor was treated with a transparent raspberry-colored stain.

CLASSICAL CLOSETS. Two closets, fronted with canvas curtains from Capital Cubicle Company in New York, frame the doorway. The pilasters and double cornices suggest a neoclassical feeling.

SHOWTIME LIGHTING. In the dressing area (right) a long row of low-power bulbs creates a dramatic horizon line. ◆ *RECIPE, SEE PAGE 100.* The dressing table is Metro shelving topped with black glass.

VISIBLE WARDROBE. For the open storage system spanning one wall (right), Salasky used Metro shelving, which is chic, versatile, and—with the assistance of a rubber hammer—painless to install. Shelves and rungs on top and bottom are arranged so that they sandwich and frame clothes and also provide ample storage space for boxes, bags, and shoes.

HANDMADE MISCELLANY. Bonnie August loves unusual collectibles. Displayed on top of her dressing table are miniature face brooches and hand-painted papier-mâché dolls.

BEYOND HARVARD. Using a standard Harvard frame, Salasky designed a bed with specially constructed matching curved head- and footboards. A flouncy dust ruffle conceals the frame beneath. The life-size hand-painted wooden lamb is for seating—as well as for conversation.

TREASURES LOST & FOUND

A cache of high quality arched windows was among the major finds of two inventive loft-dwellers for their 2,400-square-foot space in lower Manhattan. The couple shares an admiration for things not necessarily cheap, but visibly aged. When, one lucky afternoon, they spotted the windows in a sidewalk dumpster, they took them home and utilized them to imaginative effect. All the furnishings and design details in the loft are evidence of a keen eye and a comprehension of the infinite variety and value in treasures lost and found.

HOME SCREEN. Hinged drywall panels make a handsome, movable five-section dividing screen and give this space definition and perspective. ◆ *RECIPE, SEE PAGE 130.* On each fold of the screen, postcards—different views of the same subject—are arranged in neat strips.

WINDOWS ROMANESQUE. In the loft's central space, the found windows are used for their original purpose and also mounted against the brick wall, lighted for a trompe l'oeil effect. Finally, more windows are used (not shown) between this space and the bedroom.

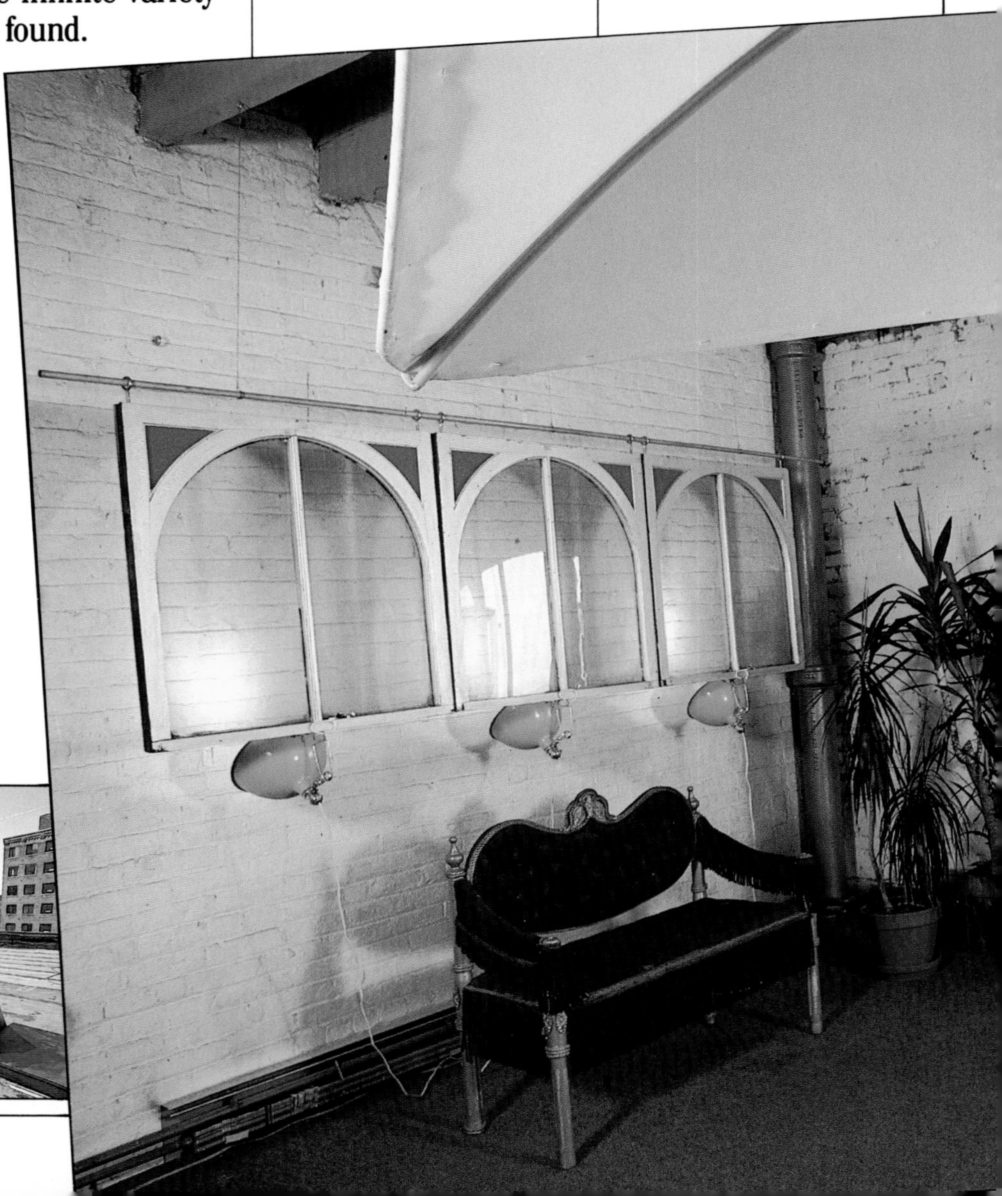

LEITMOTIF. Outside on the roof, the arched windows form a clerestory-style skylight.

COUNTERS OF A NEW KIND. One-of-a-kind kitchen cabinets were made from packing boxes found on the street outside a nearby cheese warehouse. Using metal wall studs and ceramic handles, these boxes were transformed into an inexpensive, functional storage system as flexible as it is eye-catching.

SIDEWALK CACHET. This "still life" captures the loft's appeal. The Victorian chest—abandoned in poor condition by previous owners of the loft—was stripped, refurbished, and painted a soft pale gray. Decorative objects, likewise, were serendipitous finds: old bottles have become vases; an old motorcycle chassis a thoroughly modern sculpture.

VERNAL HIGH TECH

Faced with a somber warren of small rooms on the garden level of their home in London, Nick and Charlotte Frazer resolved to knock down several partition walls to form one large kitchen/dining/family room. In the center of the kitchen is a sleek and efficient island stove unit with built-in shelves for storage. Green linear accents against white walls and cabinets give the kitchen high-tech pizzazz, while at the same time imbuing the space with a garden freshness. The spotless white ceramic tiles—and the green grouting—further enhance the feeling.

CORD CHANDELIER. Over the butcher block dining table hangs a smashingly original pendant light fixture. The lights hang from coilcord, tech-look electrical cord designed to resemble the spiral cord of a telephone. ◆ *RECIPE, SEE PAGE 103.*

FANCY FAN. The exhaust fan above the stove is concealed within a large, curved green pipe rather than the standard stark hood. Above, flanking the pipe, wine racks are placed on a shelf supported by spindly metal rods.

DIVIDING RODS. Besides supporting the shelves, the rods work visually as a room divider and, as one of the room's key geometric elements, they unify the space.

THE WORKBOOK

WALLS & CEILINGS

Besides experimenting with the rainbow of paint colors now on the market for walls and ceilings, many people are trying their hand at decorative treatments previously known only to designers. There are also dozens of other ways to achieve striking effects: putting up simple molding, hanging fabric or wallpaper, exhibiting prints or personal collections. Wall hangings might include rugs, screens, macramé, quilts and bedspreads. Or, for that matter, hat collections, keys, buttons, pretty plates, an arrangement of theater stubs. The fact is that almost anything, given some imagination and thoughtful arrangement, can be made to look interesting on a wall.

SPOON-FULL. Designer Veva Crozer applied a brown glaze over a peach-colored base for her dining room wall. The garden border at the bottom of the wall was then stenciled in white, gray green, and barn red. ◆ *RECIPE, SEE PAGES 76 AND 80.* The showstopper is a dazzling arrangement of antique silver soup spoons.

COUNTRY WARMTH. The small-patterned burgundy wallpaper is perfectly suited to the 19th-century Block Island summer retreat of Peter and Shirley Wood. A similarly impressive effect could be achieved by stapling inexpensive patterned fabric to the wall. ◆ *SEE PAGE 84.* Equally at home is a truck spring (found at the town dump), which holds fireplace equipment and a long-handled spoon.

COLLECTIBLES. Walls are a wonderful background for collections of all kinds, providing a place for storage as well as display. In their study, Odessa and Bill Bourne hung their antique American farm tools and kitchen equipment in a beautifully spare composition.

SHIRR ENERGY. This dining room was given a rather grand aspect by the simple solution of shirred fabric on the walls. ◆ *SEE PAGE 84.* Shirring is just one of the ways one can use fabric to good effect on walls.

STENCILING. Above, in her kitchen, designer Veva Crozer stenciled a charming animal motif (see inset) along the border around the ceiling, and a leafy pattern around the doorways. ◆ *RECIPE, SEE PAGE 80.* If stenciling itself seems formidable, Veva Crozer suggests a simplified technique that involves making a stenciled outline. ◆ *SEE PAGE 80.*

CONNECTIONS. Some of the best stencils are inspired by fabrics used elsewhere in the same room. In this bedroom, the colors and shapes of the stenciled border echo the pattern of the early-American quilt on the bed. Fabric is used on the ceiling for a snug and comfortable feeling. Ceilings can be softened with fabrics in much the same way as walls.

FLOORS

Many home decorators have more difficulty deciding what to do with floors than with the other five surfaces of a room combined. As a result, work on floors is often postponed or forced out of mind completely. This is too bad, for paint stores are stocked with a wide range of easy-to-apply floor finishes that look great and aren't expensive. There are, of course, the transparent stains, dyes, and varnishes that give a classic look to a room. There are also painted floors. Paint on floors—part of a long American and British interior design tradition that had in recent decades been looked down on—again is happily being seen as offering many creative and interesting possibilities. Not to mention that floorcloths, the carpetlike expanses of canvas with freehand or stenciled designs—also popular in days gone by as a cheap substitute for rugs—are once again enjoying a well-deserved vogue.

ABOVEBOARD. The wide pine boards of this floor in a country kitchen gleam through several coats of polyurethane. The "poly" not only gives good protection from spills and hard wear, but also enhances the knots and natural shading of the wood.

◆ *SEE PAGE 95.*

NATIVE AMERICAN. Celebrated, multitalented hair stylist Kenneth Battelle, inspired by Navajo rugs, chose striking zigzags to dramatize the floor of his New York home.

◆ *SEE PAGE 91.*

DECKED OUT. The stairs in Barbara Plumb's vacation home were painted with sunny yellow deck paint. Deck paint gives a thick coating to stairs and floors, making them tough, durable, and washable.

THREE-POINT LANDING. In this stunning entrance gallery, artist Luis Molina painted a long runnerlike length of two-tone triangles. The design—Molina's own—is a sophisticated version of a traditional American pattern.

COMBED OUT. The technique called "combing" produces a two-tone exaggerated woodgrain effect. Designer Richard Neas used this method as a quick and easy way to add texture and interest to this floor. Neas used a "comb" of his own invention: a window washer's squeegee with teeth cut into its rubber blade. ◆ *SEE PAGE 92.*

GREEN ON GREEN. Richard Neas chose lettuce green as the base coat of this bedroom floor, and then sponged darker greens over it.

FLORA CLOTHS. For a client who loves gardens, designer Veva Crozer painted two floorcloths (above) for the front hallway. One—10 by 3 feet—has a leafy fern pattern; the other, a 4-by-6, in front of the door, is a flower design.

BRIGHT IDEAS. Painted carpets, or floorcloths, which were used as part of the decorative scheme of American homes for over two hundred years, are once again being designed and made. Veva Crozer based this one on a Kilim rug in her living room.
◆ *RECIPE, SEE PAGE 94.*

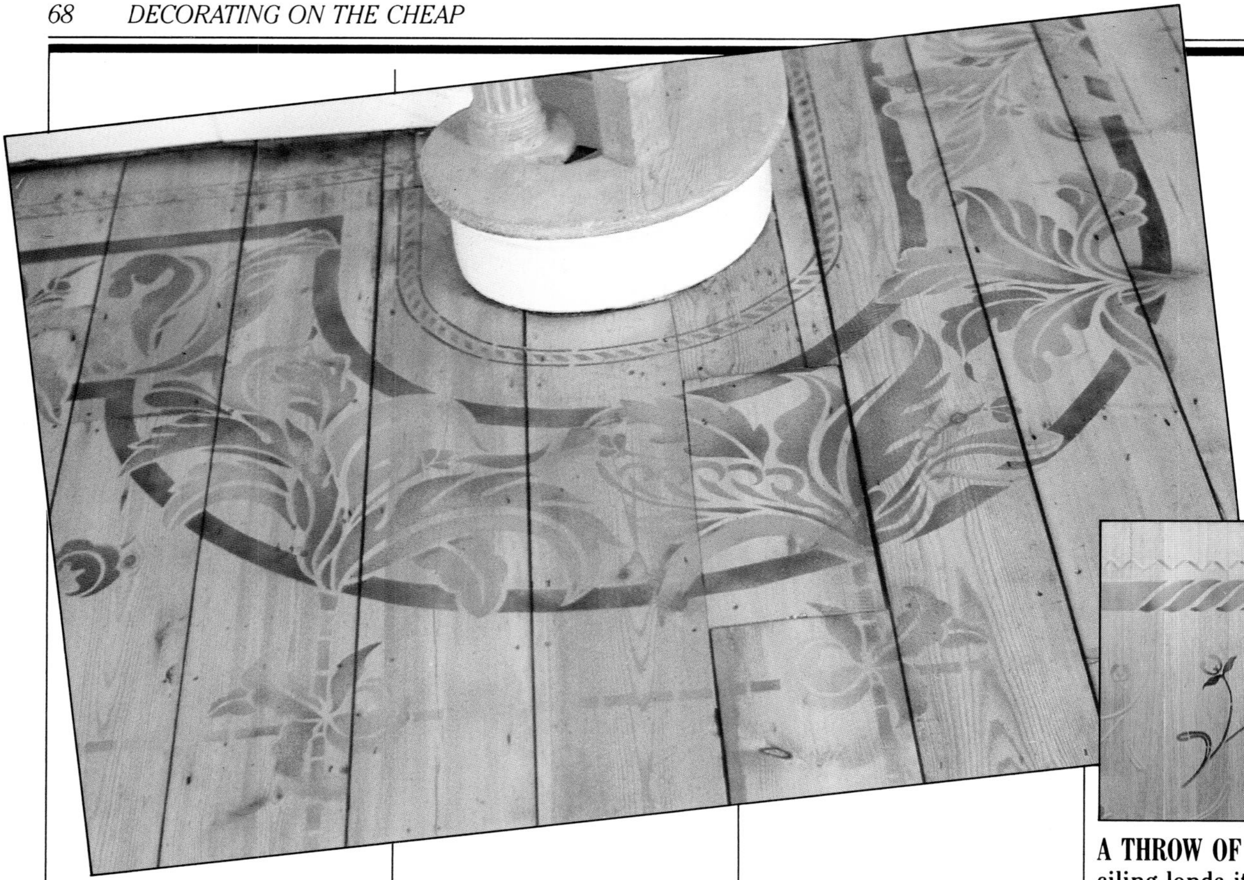

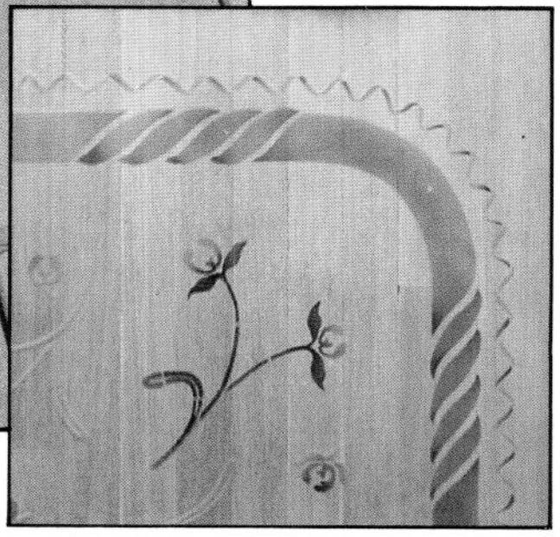

A THROW OF STEMS. Stenciling lends itself to the creation of light, airy designs. Above, we see one corner of a delicate monochromatic "area rug."

BORDER CONTROL. A lovely stenciled border, above, in a bold leafy motif follows the bottom of this stairway, giving character and delineation to the area. The most successful floor stencils stay close to the designs of more traditional types of floor coverings: fairly dark, subdued colors and regular, repetitive designs.

FAUX STONE. Richard Neas created the formality and elegance of a sandstone floor with a border of two marbleized effects. He plotted the design on graph paper, then applied it using cream and gray paint.

FURNITURE

Furniture—brand-new furniture, that is—can be a huge investment, as we all know. However, with a modicum of know-how and rather more time and patience, the most forlorn junkyard finds, hand-me-downs, and beat-up reproductions found in the attic can be recycled into pieces of considerable charm. Not only do you save money, but furniture of a certain age often has better basic construction and offers more individual panache and comfort than today's direct-from-the-factory items. Highly skilled and exacting restoration techniques can take years to master, but there are a number of imitative shortcuts—antiquing, marbleizing, faux gold leafing—or a simple coat of paint and varnish that can be done by anyone to breathe new life and freshness into second-hand furniture.

WELL-AGED. This pine cabinet, perfect for storage and displaying favorite objects, seems right at home in its early-American setting. Not as old as it looks, the mellowing effect of years was added by the magic of antiquing. ◆ *SEE PAGE 145.*

MATCHED SEATING. Paint alone can make a rather ordinary chair come to life. ◆ *SEE PAGE 145.* Bill Engel painted this one to coordinate with other elements in his multicolored apartment.

IMPROVISATIONAL IRIDESCENCE. The gleam on Bill Engel's bureau was achieved by spray-painting bright silver metal flakes mixed in clear lacquer (a finish often used on motorcycles). Accents were added with more pastel colors.

GOLD LEAFING. New York City artist Colleen Babington applied an overall coat of dark blue-green oil paint to this Victorian sheet music cabinet, then combined Dutch metal leaf (◆ *RECIPE, SEE PAGE 146*) with artists' oil paints to work out a tarot card-inspired design. Finally, the cabinet was given a coat of varnish.

LIGHTING

Since the day a century ago when Thomas Edison invented the light bulb, the possibilities for creating artificial lighting in our homes have multiplied and are now almost mind-boggling. This vast array might be broken down into three categories. Background lighting—diffuse illumination emanating most commonly from behind valances, above cornices, or from recessed fixtures in ceilings or floors. Task lighting—direct illumination for performing specific activities such as reading or cooking. Accent or decorative lighting—"focal points" of light that emphasize paintings, objects, or add a specific "touch" to a particular area. Accent or decorative lighting includes spots, wall washers, pinhole or framing projectors, uplights, and even tiny Christmas tree lights. The choices are many; high-cost systems can often be imitated with inexpensive substitutes.

STAR LIGHTS. Strips of Plugmold® were used by architect Richard Sygar to make theater dressing room-type lighting on either side of his bathroom mirror. The architect prefers the industrial look of these fixtures to the more finished look of similar store-bought vanity lights.
◆ *RECIPE, SEE PAGE 100.*

A HIP LIGHT. Deborah Berke and Denis Hector created this whimsical table lamp (right) by wiring a bulb inside a translucent girdle form. Looking like an oversized spool of thread, the table on which this amusing lamp reposes is made from a cable spool wrapped in fabric and bound in the middle by a rope.

SUSPENDED ILLUMINATION. Using electrical cord and clip-on outlet fittings available in any hardware store, architect Don Chapell came up with this ceiling lighting solution. The cord hangs by means of eye hooks and forms a series of triangles. White spot bulbs dominate the center; smaller-wattage red bulbs line the perimeter. The huge relief face was carved from Styrofoam, then spackled. It conceals a Murphy bed.

BLIND SPOTS. Designer Elizabeth Winchester demonstrates a high-minded use of Plugmold® with this hidden valance lighting in Richard Lamley's apartment. Shining downward, the bulbs reflect light off the metal louvered blinds at night to make a doubly dramatic effect. ◆ *SEE PAGE 101.*

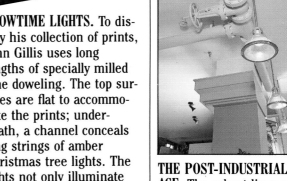

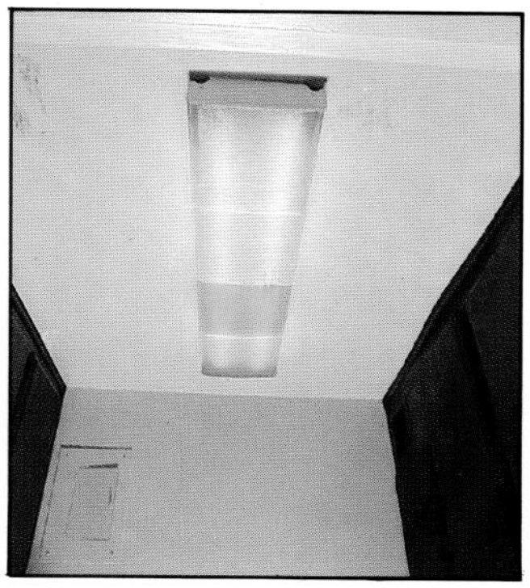

DRAMATIC IMPROVEMENT. Designer Charles Hughes softened the harsh light of an ordinary fluorescent ceiling fixture by lining it with pink and blue theatrical gels.

SHOWTIME LIGHTS. To display his collection of prints, John Gillis uses long lengths of specially milled pine doweling. The top surfaces are flat to accommodate the prints; underneath, a channel conceals long strings of amber Christmas tree lights. The lights not only illuminate the artwork, but also give the room a jaunty showboat look.

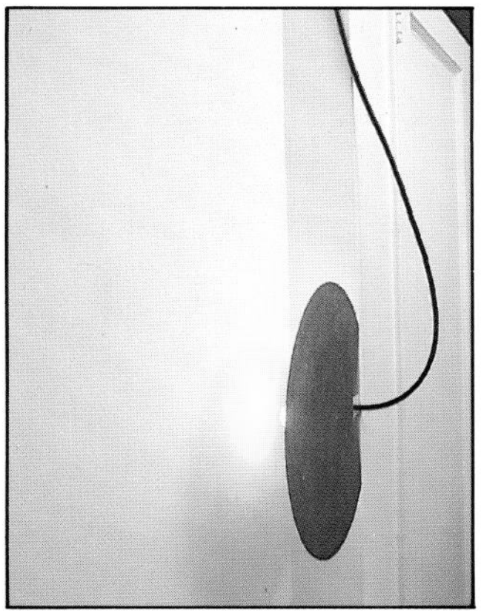

CUSTOM MADE. Architect Yann Weymouth constructed an unusual indirect corner light fixture from a disk of flat galvanized steel, cut and bent to order by a metal worker.

FLOATING. Louis Muller and William Murphy placed a low strip of Plugmold® behind a carpeted ramp in Peter Blaustein's apartment to light the long expanse of wall. ◆ *SEE PAGE 101.*

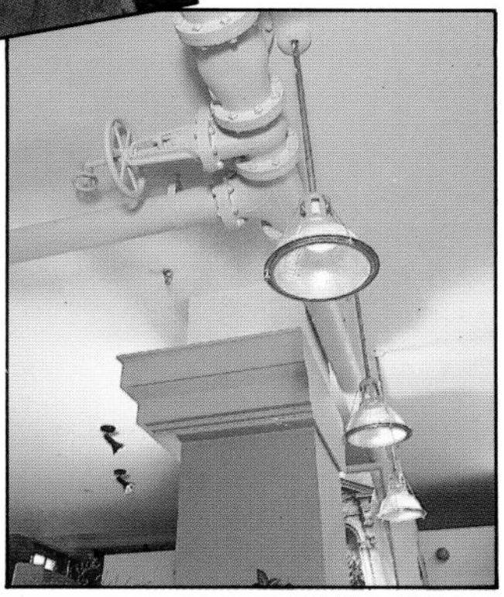

THE POST-INDUSTRIAL AGE. The robust lines of these heavy glass and metal ceiling lights are strong enough to hold their own against exposed plumbing and oversize, post-modern moldings.

POPULAR PAINT TECHNIQUES

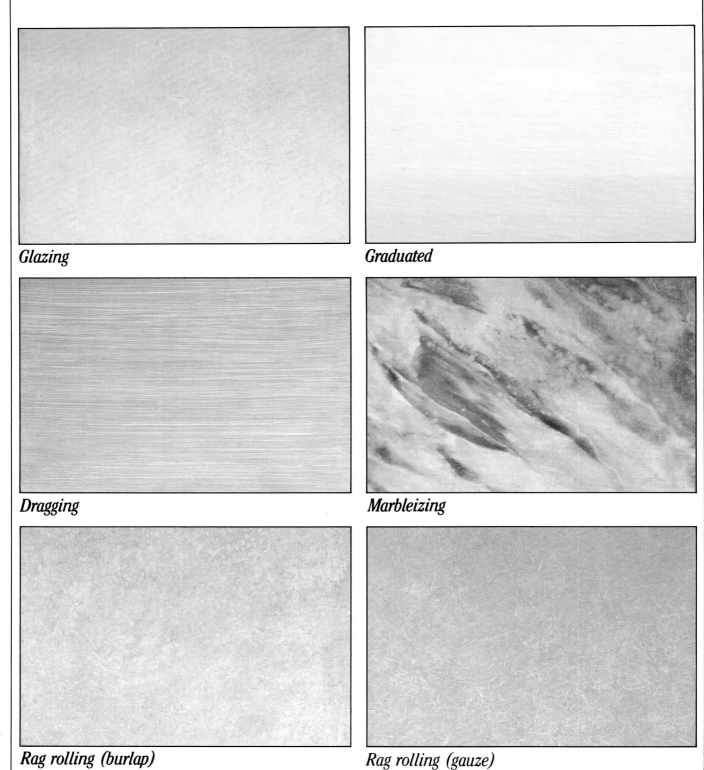

Glazing

Graduated

Dragging

Marbleizing

Rag rolling (burlap)

Rag rolling (gauze)

COVERING WALLS & CEILINGS

Besides creating a pleasant place in which to live, the aim in decorating a home should be to create an all-encompassing statement. Whether you plan to give a room a feeling of country comfort, contemporary high tech, casual eclecticism, or whatever the stamp of your personal style happens to be, your first and most important decision will be what to do with the framework: the walls, ceilings, windows, and floors.

The possibilities of wall and ceiling treatments may be engaging to ponder, but can put a big dent in your pocketbook. Luckily, there are many fresh and affordable ways to achieve good-looking—even glamorous—effects.

In modern decoration, ceilings often are treated as large, out-of-the-way areas that are difficult to reach and not important enough to merit significant creative attention. Until the end of the last century, ceilings frequently were the most lavish part of a room—sometimes richly painted, elaborately beamed or coffered, or laced with fanciful plaster reliefs, and all intricately corniced. A sophisticated ceiling still can make a major difference to a room and its feeling, and can be turned into a decorative feature. Painted a light color it will seem to add space and height. Painted a dark color it will lend a feeling of intimacy. Ceilings can be blended with the wall color to make a unified room, or separated from the walls by a painted stripe or two, a cornice of braid or molding, or a paper or stenciled border. If original moldings exist, they can be picked out in white or a paler color of the walls and ceilings, or in two colors if the moldings are deep enough and lend themselves to such treatment. Imaginative designs can be painted up the walls and over the ceilings, or just on the ceilings to suggest architectural details of a bygone grandeur. Sometimes a repeat of a floor treatment can look fetching, as can a muted version of a carpet or a tile design used elsewhere in the room.

Like carpenters and woodworkers (and doctors and chefs and coal miners), professional painters and paperhangers use a lingo all their own. If you familiarize yourself with a few terms, you will have an easier time at the paint or wallpaper store when asking questions and ordering supplies.

PAINT & WALL COVERING TERMS YOU SHOULD KNOW

ALKYDS. Synthetic resins that are used as a binder in most modern oil-base paint. They provide a hard, durable surface and have generally less odor than "old-fashioned" oil paints. Alkyd paint comes in flat, semigloss, or high-gloss finishes and can take many hours (overnight or longer) to dry completely. Thin and clean up with paint thinner, mineral spirits, or turpentine.

ARTISTS' ACRYLICS. A versatile type of paint that can be thinned with water to watercolor transparency, diluted with an acrylic medium for "transparency with body," or used straight from the tube for a more opaque finish. They are quick drying, so they are particularly good for stenciling. Both artists' acrylics and artists' oils come in a wide range of colors.

ARTISTS' OIL PAINTS. The fine paints artists generally use to paint on canvas. These fine paints are available in tubes of 1½ ounces and larger. They come in a wide variety of colors and can be used to tint any oil-base paint or glaze. Thinning and cleanup is with paint thinner, mineral spirits, or turpentine.

CANVAS LINING. Originally designed for use under brocades and tapestries, canvas lining is a low-grade artists' canvas with a hearty backing and a lot more versatility than lining paper. It is now used to cover bad walls when putting up a wall covering. Also it can be used as a wall covering by itself, which would require painting or varnishing.

COLOR RUN. The amount of rollage produced of a single-color combination at any one time. When the same combination is run again, there can be a slight variation in color from the previous run.

(continued on next page)

EPOXY ENAMELS AND EPOXY RESINS. Tough, hard, glossy, oil-base finishes that resist dirt, grit, and abrasion and are especially good for painting over metal, masonry, fiberglass, porcelain, and high-glaze ceramic tiles. Use for radiators, bathroom and kitchen sinks and tubs, and for pepping up old tiled walls. Surfaces to be painted must be clean and grease-free; they should also be given a primer coat. Two thin coats work better than one thick one, and 24 hours should be allowed between each coat. If you epoxy a basin or bath, wait at least three days before using to allow it to cure chemically.

FINISH. When describing the reflective quality of a painted or glazed surface, there are basically three finishes: flat (or matte), semigloss (or midsheen), and glossy (or high-gloss). A fourth finish—eggshell—is approximately halfway between flat and semigloss. It resembles the finish (not the color) of the shell of an egg.

JAPAN COLORS. Oil-base paints available from artists' suppliers, these come in a wide range of colors, are fast-drying, and have a matte finish. An alternative to acrylics for stenciling, except that they are quite expensive.

LATEX PAINT. Despite its name, this paint does not contain rubber. It is a water-base compound that uses a milk-like emulsion as a binder. Though latex does not provide as resilient a surface or as rich a finish as oil-base paint, it does have several advantages: it goes on easily, leaves fewer brush marks, and is usually almost odorless. Latex comes in flat or semigloss finishes, and thinning and cleanup is with water.

LINING PAPER. Lining paper is a thin white paper used over problem walls and under new wall coverings. Sold in paint and wall covering stores, it can be put up with paste in the same way one puts up unpasted wallpaper.

MATCHING. Hanging wall covering strips in such a way as to correlate the design from one strip to the next. The easiest to hang is a *random match,* where a pattern such as a vertical stripe or textured grasscloth looks right no matter how one panel or strip is placed in relation to another. In a *straight match,* the pattern of one strip must be "joined" with a portion of the pattern on the adjoining strip to complete the pattern. In a *drop match,* a portion of the pattern appears on each strip, as in the straight match; however, the pattern will not repeat at the same distance from the ceiling line across the various strips on the wall, but matches at the same horizontal point on alternate strips.

MINERAL SPIRITS. A general term for a variety of petroleum derivatives, of more or less low evaporation rate, used to thin varnish and oil paint.

PIGMENTED POLYURETHANE. Comes premixed in about ten bright colors. Good for any wood or metal surface—particularly bathrooms, kitchens, sash and trim, walls, porches, floors, and cabinets.

POLYURETHANE VARNISH. A clear, tough plastic varnish, polyurethane is noted for its resistance to abrasion, heat, acids, and solvents. Available in matte, semigloss, and high-gloss finishes, it is ideal for heavy-use interior wood surfaces such as floors, desks, bar and counter tops—even gymnasium floors. It also can give good protection to any painted surface. Polyurethane can be tinted, comes premixed, and is solvent in mineral spirits or turpentine.

PRIMING. The application of an undercoat (a primer), usually white, to a surface that is to be painted.

REPEAT. Distance from the center of one motif of a wall covering pattern to the center of the next.

SECONDS. A fabric with one pulled thread, or a slightly smeared or blotchy pattern. Seconds are usually not drastically damaged, but you should examine each roll carefully.

TINTING COLORS. Highly concentrated pigments that come in small tubes and are used to tint or change the color of paints and glazes. They are less expensive than artists' oil paints, but they come in a limited range of colors, most of them bright. They may, however, be combined to create more subtle hues. Some tinting colors are for oil paint only; others—universal tinting colors—can be used with any kind of paint.

VARNISH. Name given to any clear oil-base protective coating. Varnishes traditionally were painted on wood surfaces on top of stains. Made of resin and diluted with turpentine or mineral spirits, they may be tinted. All varnishes are available in flat, semigloss, high-gloss, and sometimes eggshell. Varnish is fine for furniture; polyurethane varnish is better for floors and walls. *See* Polyurethane varnish.

PAINTING WALLS & CEILINGS

Paint is a mixture of a base, a pigment, and a binder. The base is either water or oil, and gives the paint its covering quality. The pigment gives the paint its color (the more pigment any paint contains, the higher its price will be; price is also determined by the color itself—reds, for example, always tend to be the most expensive). The binder cements the pigment to both the base and the surface to which the paint is applied.

Of the three basic ways to cover a wall—with paint, paper, or fabric—paint is generally the cheapest, and also the most versatile. Even the simplest paint job can transform a room: from drab to lively, from cramped to spacious, or from big and cold to small and cozy. Clever painting can make a room seem grand and well cared for, however sparse the furnishings. Paint can emphasize good proportions or minimize bad ones; it can "lose" unwanted features, such as doors, pipes, and odd angles. By using paint you can raise a ceiling to airy heights. You can divide a space or, conversely, unite adjoining ones.

Most of us, at some point, have painted our walls, ceilings, and woodwork in a uniform finish of gloss, semigloss, or flat paint, with perhaps an occasional contrasting molding or supergraphic as an experimental touch. But until recently, widespread knowledge of decorative painting finishes has been sketchy and limited. Now, with the increasingly sophisticated range of types and colors of paint available, dozens of paint techniques—some old, many new—are being used by decorators and many of them can be learned and mastered quite easily. Subtle techniques such as glazing, graduated painting, lacquering, and stenciling all can be done with paint.

GLAZES & GLAZING

Glazing lends itself to myriad effects. The decorative finishes to follow—dragging, stippling, rag rolling—are various handlings of a glaze. By way of definition, a glaze is a transparent film—usually tinted—applied on top of an opaque base. A glaze adds richness, highlights, and depth to a wall that might otherwise be quite ordinary looking. And glazing has a practical, money-saving aspect as well. Since a glaze alters the color of the base coat, if you ever paint your walls and the color comes out "wrong," a glaze is much easier and cheaper than a whole new paint job—and you'll get a richer-looking room in the bargain.

If a glaze is a hue in the family of the base coat, the resulting color will be a delicately modified and deepened tone within the same family. On the other hand, if the glaze and the base coat are in different color groups, the resulting color will be an entirely new one, with the additional richness of translucence. You will find that any glazing technique will look best with colors that are similar in intensity, or with a darker color over a lighter one. A Sienna brown glaze over a deep green base, for instance, will produce a lovely terra cotta; dark gray over Pompeii red will look like Morocco leather; dark green over a medium green will turn your walls jade.

Though it is possible to mix your own glaze, it's a lot easier (and not much more expensive) to buy ready-made commercial glaze. Ask for "glazing liquid" at your local paint store, and explain that you'll be using it to glaze your walls. Good paint stores usually carry McCloskey's Glaze Coat and/or Pratt & Lambert's Lyt-All Glazing Liquid. Lyt-All Glazing Liquid comes in half-pints, quarts, and gallons. The half-pint covers about 60 square feet, the quart around 250 square feet, and the gallon approximately 1,000 square feet. However, if you measure the length and height of the walls you'll be glazing, someone in your paint store will be able to determine exactly how much you'll need. Generally, you'll need less glaze than paint to cover your walls as you'll be applying a much thinner coat. Professional painters sometimes thin the glazing liquid with mineral spirits or paint thinner. So if you find it's too thick (it looks something like cream of chicken soup) add some mineral spirits until you get the consistency you need. But probably you'll be able to use the glazing liquid in its straight-from-the-can consistency.

The finishes that follow must be applied to a base coat of semigloss or eggshell finish oil-base paint that will be tough and nonabsorbent. Latex-base paint will *not* do as they are too absorbent. You will probably have to paint the walls twice to achieve a good even base coat. At the same time that you paint your walls, you should also prepare a surface on which you can try out your glaze for color and consistency; a large piece of drywall or scrap lumber is suitable. This test surface should receive the same base coat as your walls. One word of warning: Some blue paints are inclined to turn green when mixed or combined with glaze. Experiment on primed pieces of board first and leave, if possible, for a week or so.

After you've glazed your walls, you may also want to give them a coat of polyurethane varnish. This will not only add protection, but also will tend to darken the finish a bit, giving it an "antiqued" look. The amount it will darken the finish will depend on how clear the polyurethane is and how many coats of it you apply—the more you put on the darker it will get. You can find at your paint store almost clear polyurethane, and since it comes in flat, semigloss, and high-gloss finishes, you can determine the amount of sheen your walls will have. Apply the polyurethane with a smooth roller. Brush it out with a large brush or cheap foam paint pad to get rid of small bubbles left by the roller; if you don't, the bubbles will harden and dry and the surface will look pocked and pitted. ◇

TINTING A GLAZE

The easiest way to tint a glaze is to have your paint store mix it for you—the same way you would have them mix a custom paint. If that's not possible, start out with a small amount of tinting medium and then build up the amount of color—experimenting along the way—until you get the shade you want.

Squeeze a blob of tinting color or artists' oil paint into an old saucepan and stir in several tablespoons of turpentine or mineral spirits; mix thoroughly until very smooth. Add about one cup of unthinned glaze to the pan and mix thoroughly. Test this mixture on a small area of wall or on a board prepared with your base coat. If you want to add more color (or change the color slightly) mix a bit more tint with some turpentine in another old pan or throwaway aluminum pie tin. Add this to the glaze; test this new color. Continue on in this manner until you get the shade you want. Never add the tinting colors or artists' oils to the glaze straight from the tube, as they will be difficult to homogenize.

PREPARING WALLS & CEILINGS

Before any painting begins, walls and ceilings should always be in good condition, or else your new and glamorous effects will be sadly short-lived. If there are major problems, such as long, deep fissures, pieces of plaster sagging ominously, or mysterious stains, you are probably going to have to enlist the services of a plasterer or a plumber in order to get things back into shape. Even if the rooms are in reasonably decent condition to begin with, there is still a bit of work to do. Walls should be scraped well to remove any loose paint or plaster (hardware and paint stores sell scrapers for this purpose), then all cracks and other uneven spots should be plastered over. When the plaster is dry, everything—including edges where large chunks of old paint may have come off in the scraping process—should be sanded smooth. Finally, wash the surface down—particularly if you're dealing with rooms that have not been painted in several years—with a solution of warm water and a bit of household ammonia.

BASIC GLAZING

The simplest form of glazing is applying a uniform coat of tinted glaze over an opaque base coat. Be sure your base coat is completely dry before applying the glaze. You should cover the floor with drop cloths, and protect baseboards with newspaper secured by masking tape. Glazing is not really difficult (particularly if you use a roller). The only "technique" is to apply the glaze evenly and confidently; it is mainly a matter of keeping the glaze at a workable consistency and handling it quickly to avoid drips or clumps. You will find that once the glaze is on the wall, it tends to dry quite fast.

MATERIALS

Ready-made commercial glaze.

Tinting colors or artists' oils.

5″ paintbrush or wide roller, short- or long-napped, depending on the texture you want.

METHOD

1. Ask your paint store to mix your glaze, or do it yourself by using universal tinting colors, artists' oils, or tinting colors to get the shade you want (see box, page 75). Use the tints sparingly and slowly to build the color, as described.

2. Test the glaze for color and consistency. Your test panel should be vertical and placed in the same room that is to be glazed; colors can change dramatically depending on the angle of the light.

3. Once you've got a workable color and consistency, start brushing or rolling the glaze on the wall. You should try to work quickly, keeping an even coat of glaze on all parts of the wall. Remember, if you do make a complete botch of it, it's possible to remove glaze with mineral spirits. It's a messy job to remove, but it's possible.

4. Allow to dry completely, up to several days if necessary. ◇

Wide curtains highlight glazed and stenciled walls.

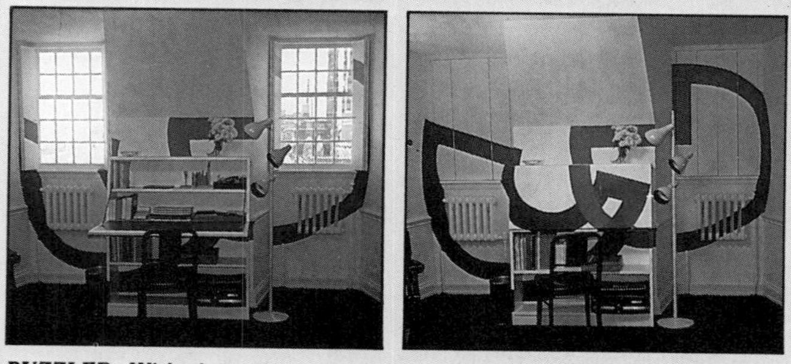

***PUZZLED.** With shutters open and desk panel down, the dramatic effect of the abstract wall design is not evident. With panels closed, the bold lines of the graphic come together like a jigsaw puzzle.*

DRAGGING

Dragging, a technique that lends an expansive appearance to wall surfaces, makes rooms appear larger, and disguises faults, is achieved by applying a glaze of transparent color over an undercoat and then by "dragging" the glaze—or brushing it down—with a wide, dry brush. The glaze is usually a darker hue of the undercoat. The resulting softly textured look of fine, irregular vertical striations gives a rich, distinguished effect.

Professional painters use expensive (about $25) "floggers"—brushes specially designed for dragging. They are expensive because they're handmade from top quality bristles that have carefully selected split ends. For a one-time user, however, the expense doesn't make sense. A standard 5″ paintbrush will work very well, although you'll have to work more quickly since each of your "drags" will cover less area. Or, you could try working with an old-fashioned straw broom (you may want to cut off some of the handle). You won't get a "fine-grained" look, but brooms certainly create their own distinctive striations, and they enable you to work much more speedily.

Graining tools may also be used, but they give a more insistent effect. The graining tool sold commercially for this purpose is a 3″ wooden triangle with either a fine-, medium-, or wide-tooth comb. Graining combs will create even, uniformly spaced lines and are reasonably priced. You can actually use *any* toothed object—an Afro pick, a dog comb—although if you're going to use one of these sharp-edged tools, you'll have to be very careful not to scratch and streak your freshly painted undercoat. Another option is a window washer's rubber squeegie with teeth cut into it, but with this you will really be "combing" your walls.

Since glaze dries quite quickly, dragging is definitely a two-person operation. One person (the "glazer") lays down the glaze; the other person (the "dragger") follows along and does the dragging.

MATERIALS

Ready-made commercial glaze.

Tinting colors or artists' oils.

5″ paintbrush or rough roller (for glazing).

Wide brush or other tool (for dragging).

METHOD

1. Tint your glaze. Test the glaze to make sure it's the right consistency and color.

2. Begin the glazing-and-dragging operation in a corner, so you will have a good vertical line to follow and no match-up or overlap problems.

3. The glazer should brush or roll a thin film of glaze on the wall from top to bottom in vertical bands about 18″ wide. The glaze should be smooth and even. As soon as the glazer finishes a band, the dragger should quickly drag a dry brush—or whatever tool has been chosen—down through the glaze with light steady pressure from ceiling to baseboard, aiming for a consistent effect. The dragger is actually taking some glaze off the wall in long strokes so that the base coat will show through. If the dragger has trouble going the full length from ceiling to baseboard in one long stroke, he or she should drag down as far as possible, then drag up from the bottom, joining the two strokes carefully and delicately; the height of these meeting points should be staggered to avoid a discernible "seam" around the room.

4. The dragger must often wipe his brush, comb, or whatever with a rag. If the dragging tool is gummy with accumulated glaze, it will put more glaze back on the wall than it will remove.

5. The glazer's timing is important. If he applies bands of glaze that are too thin, the glaze will dry too quickly to be properly dragged. If he puts on too much, it will run back together after the dragger has done his work. The glazer must also not allow one band to dry before starting on the adjacent one. When wet glaze overlaps dry glaze, a double-strength color results and gives a blotchy look. ◇

HOW TO CALCULATE PAINT QUANTITIES

To work out the amount of paint needed to cover a specified area, multiply the number of feet around the room by the height from the baseboard to the ceiling. You can calculate that one gallon of any sort of paint will give a base coat over 60 square yards. If you are covering new plaster, you may need a gallon for every 40 square yards. It's better to overestimate than under, since it's difficult to match colors exactly a second time.

STIPPLING

A less difficult, but equally decorative paint technique is stippling. Stippled walls are traditionally described as having an "orange peel" texture. Looking as soft as chamois, stippled walls are dappled with flecks of color, without emphatic "definition." A stippled finish gives depth to a wall, mood to a room.

The mottled effect that is the hallmark of stippling can be achieved by removing some of the glaze with any number of tools. A professional stippling brush is expensive; for cheap alternatives, try a janitor's broom, an oversize scrub brush, even a shoe brush. You want your brush to have a broad blunt cut. Using such a brush will produce an effect of speckles of the base coat showing through the glaze. Another option is crumpled-up rags or wax paper. When the glaze builds up on one hunk of it, throw it away and take another crumpled handful. You can also use a roller or large sponge, which will give a softer, muted look.

MATERIALS

Ready-made commercial glaze.

Tinting colors or artists' oils.

5″ paintbrush or roller (for the glazer).

A stippling brush (or other tool).

METHOD

1. Tint glaze if necessary. Test glaze.

2. The glazer brushes or rolls on the glaze in a thin film over a narrow vertical strip from ceiling to baseboard. The stippler follows to texture the glaze while it's still wet.

3. Except for wax paper or rags, which you can throw away, you must not let glaze build up on whatever tool you use. Keep wiping accumulated glaze from brush, roller, sponge, or whatever, or your texture will be lost. Stippling with a brush is slow and exhausting because stippling requires *dabbing* the wall rather than brushing the glaze off, as you would in dragging. If you do use a brush, keep in mind that the larger the brush is, the easier the task will be. Using rags is faster than working with a brush. Have many on hand. Bunch up one clean rag at a time and dab it on the wall with quick, decisive wrist movements to remove flecks of glaze. Stippling with a roller is the easiest method. Use a long-napped roller and roll over the glaze evenly and lightly.

4. If clumps of glaze appear on your wall and start to dry, soften them with mineral spirits on a cloth.

5. Allow to dry thoroughly before applying a protective coat of polyurethane. ◇

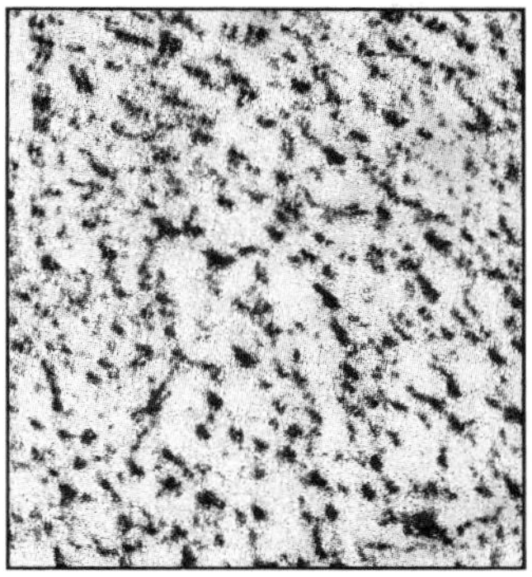

A stippled finish resembles the skin of citrus fruit.

***SUPER SUPERGRAPHICS.** Whole walls or details such as doors can be painted with designs (paintings in modern museums are good places to get ideas). These big graphics are excellent camouflage for problem walls or for simply pepping up otherwise plain spaces.*

RAG ROLLING

Rag rolling (also known as rag rubbing) is a rather raggedy version of rag stippling. It is much more free-flowing and irregular, and therefore easier—one person can do it alone. It's also good in a limited space because the "cloudy" effect creates an illusion of airiness and softness. Unlike the foregoing glazing techniques, which utilize dry implements, bunched-up rags that have been wetted in turpentine or mineral spirits are used.

Try rag rolling pastels such as pinky-lilac or mint green over a creamy white ground coat for a soft, elegant, and very 1930s look.

MATERIALS

Ready-made commercial glaze.

Tinting colors or artists' oils.

Roller or brush to apply the glaze.

Wads of lint-free rags, old sheets, net curtains, gauze, cheesecloth, or burlap. (Be sure you have enough. You should use only one kind of cloth for the job.)

METHOD

1. Tint and test glaze.

2. Starting in one corner of the room, brush the tinted glaze on a small area of wall.

3. While the glaze is still wet, in one hand bunch up a rag dampened with mineral spirits and dab and rub the glaze in a relaxed circular motion. Alternate the pressure and the direction of your rag to give the glaze an irregular but evenly distributed distressing. Aim for a look that's variegated in texture, yet uniform in its variegation.

4. Change rags as they stiffen. If the wet edges on the wall begin to dry, soften them with another wet rag.

VARIATION

Using paint as a "glaze" and literally rolling a twisted-up length of coarsely woven or nappy fabric down the walls of a room is messier than working with glazing compound, but it is a way to create a pattern with more definition, if that is what you are after. Roll up a 3′ foot square of fabric (denim or corduroy, for instance) and bind it at both ends and maybe in the middle with rubber bands. Soak the fabric roll in paint (a throw-away aluminum turkey roaster is ideal for holding the paint) then wring it out well. Starting at the ceiling line, roll the fabric down the wall like a soft rolling pin. Make side-by-side passes around the room, trying not to overlap. Each pass will have a slightly different pattern, depending upon how you manipulate the fabric roll and how the paint is distributed in it. Do not let paint run or get smudgy; try not to go over any area twice. Once down, let paint stay; wait till the wall is dry if you must attempt any touch-ups. If you want more patterning, try pouncing a sponge or tightly bunched-up piece of cheesecloth all over the wall using a different color paint. Be sure to protect the floor with drop cloths and your hands with rubber gloves. ◇

GRADUATED OR SHADOW PAINTING

As the name implies, this interesting effect combines various tones of a color on a wall. The darkest tone is usually at the bottom, flowing upward into progressively lighter shades. Before you begin the actual graduated painting, you should give the walls a first coat, and this should be a lighter shade than the lightest tone you want in the graduated effect. You can choose any color in the rainbow, of course, but to make these instructions easier to understand, we have chosen three shades of beige as an example.

MATERIALS

Pale ivory semigloss or flat oil-base paint.

White semigloss or flat oil-base paint.

Raw umber tinting color or artists' oil paint or (for a deeper tone) premixed, dark coffee-color paint.

Three inexpensive, disposable buckets.

Three paintbrushes.

Stippling brush, or substitute.

METHOD

1. Paint walls with a first coat of pale ivory. Allow to dry thoroughly.

2. Pour half the white paint into one of the buckets, half into another. Add raw umber tinting color or coffee-color paint to one of the buckets, stirring, until you get a shade of café au lait for the darkest, bottom section of the walls.

3. Add a small amount of the tinting color or paint to the other bucket until you get a light beige.

4. Pour equal amounts of these two shades into the third bucket, thus creating a middle tan color. If the lighter shades are too light for your taste, add more umber.

5. Brush the lightest shade onto the top third of one wall. By doing one wall at a time, the paint will remain wet enough to work with.

6. Change brushes and apply the middle shade, slightly overlapping the first. Using a stippling brush, gently blend the two sections together, eliminating all brush marks and any suggestion of a demarcation line.

7. Continue the middle section until you are about two-thirds of the way down the wall. Then with the third brush, apply the bottom, darkest tone, once again blending the two shades, eliminating any "seam."

8. Repeat painting and blending operation on other walls of the room, making sure all bands of color line up. ◇

Another style of graduated painting suggests mountain ranges and adds depth to these walls.

LACQUERING

The ancient skill of fine lacquering developed into a high art form in the Far East—first in China and then in Japan—where exquisite lacquered furniture and other household pieces were (and still are) produced. The process is complex and time-consuming, involving as many as 40 coats of lacquer—each buffed and burnished before the next layer is applied—producing a smooth, polished surface.

True lacquer derived from the lac tree in the Orient is a kind of varnish, usually containing pigment, that dries to a hard surface.

Today, in this country, real lacquer is difficult to obtain and very expensive. It is possible to have your walls professionally lacquered, but it will cost a great deal of money. The good news is that there are a number of ways to produce a convincing facsimile using readily available—and relatively cheap—materials and a bit of elbow grease. You will need to start with fairly smooth walls, but they don't have to be as absolutely and immaculately smooth as if you were using real lacquer.

The simplest method is to apply a couple of coats of clear thinned-down polyurethane varnish over two or three coats of oil-base flat or eggshell paint. Varnish can be used over a less-than-glass-smooth wall, because it actually fills in cracks and other blemishes. You can use either semigloss or high-gloss polyurethane, depending on how reflective you want your walls to be. The second method involves using tinted poly. The third method demands an added step, but is an elaboration of the first two: A series of tinted glazes are applied over a base coat and then polyurethaned for protection and increased depth. This last method, which creates a mesmerizing pearlized effect, is time-consuming, but you'll find the results gratifying.

In preparation for any of these methods, thoroughly clean and vacuum your room before you start working. Nothing spoils a lacquered effect more than pieces of dust or hairs trapped in the finish.

MATERIALS

Flat or eggshell oil-base paint.

Polyurethane varnish, semigloss or gloss, depending on the finish you want.

Mineral spirits.

A wide, clean brush of the best quality you can afford.

METHOD

1. Paint walls with an undercoat of the oil-base paint.

2. When dry, apply a second and possibly third coat of the same paint. Wipe the walls with a damp cloth or a tack cloth to make sure they are absolutely clean.

3. Thin your polyurethane, three parts poly to one part mineral spirits.

4. Apply a coat of clear varnish starting from the top and quickly working your way down. Don't try to spread it out as you would paint; try not to go back over the same area twice. Thinned polyurethane becomes tacky very quickly, so any reworking with your brush will leave telltale marks. One coat may give you the look you want if you know what you're doing and you do it well. If you do leave any marks on the surface, the answer is a second coat. The trick is that the varnish has to be as smooth as possible. Make sure the first coat is completely dry before applying the second. This whole process can take up to two days.

VARIATION

The effect achieved by using a tinted varnish is similar to what you get with clear varnish, but with added richness. To tint the varnish, first dilute a dollop of tinting color or artists' oils with paint thinner or mineral spirits. Then mix this liquid into a quantity of varnish. Finally, add this to your full container of varnish. Throughout this process, stir thoroughly. Then thin with one part mineral spirits to three parts varnish. You can tint the varnish the same color as the base coat, or a different color. (It doesn't add as much depth if it's not a different color.) Use the technique described above to apply the varnish. Again, you may want to apply a second coat to cover mistakes.

VARIATION

To achieve a beautiful pearlized effect with great depth, cover the base coat with three or four coats of tinted glaze (see page 75), and then varnish when completely dry. You can produce an interesting glow by tinting the glaze with different shades of the same color, putting the darkest shade first and getting progressively lighter, building up coat after coat of glazes, and finally one or two of varnish. It's important to make sure each coat is dry before applying the next. If you're looking for even walls with no texture, apply the glaze coats with a smooth foam roller. Otherwise use a brush. This is a time-consuming process (up to two weeks), but you'll be pleased with the end result. ◇

COLOR COORDINATED. *By painting such architectural elements as doors and steps to his sleeping loft in carefully chosen bright colors, Bill Engel turned his entryway into a geometric composition.*

VEVA CROZER'S STENCILING

Stenciling is an old craft found in a multitude of cultures and traditions, probably because it's based on the repetition of a simple design. The resurgence in popularity of stenciling reflects the current enthusiasm for the handmade, and it is a surefire way to personalize homes in an era of standardized mass production. Whatever time you devote to the art, you'll find the results original, colorful, and gratifying for many years to come. For walls, ceilings, and floors, stenciling offers a decorating solution at a fraction of the cost of wallpaper and other wall coverings. Veva Crozer, who teaches stenciling to beginners, gives her own well-tested recipe. It's worth noting here that this method uses only one stencil for all the colors. Many professional stencilers use different stencils for different colors, but it's easier to forgo all the complications involved with using many stencils.

When learning to stencil, the important thing is not to be concerned that each stencil turn out absolutely perfectly. The real appeal of stenciling is its handmade look. If your paint smears a little, don't worry about it—it will keep your walls from looking manufactured.

MATERIALS

Crayons.

Acetate sheets.

X-Acto knife and No. 16 or No. 11 blades.

Pencil.

Paper.

Artists' acrylic paints, 2-ounce tubes in as many colors as you need.

Masking tape.

Sponges, cut into small pieces.

Colorful stenciled creatures of the sea swim about in this bathroom.

Small, round artists' brush for details and touch-up.

Paper plates or cups for paint palettes.

Polyurethane varnish, optional.

METHOD

1. Ready-made stencils are available, but it's easy and fun to try your own. Begin by choosing a design. Designs can come from almost anywhere: books, magazines, quilts, fabrics, or wallpaper designs (which can be traced from wallpaper books borrowed from your paint store). If you're just beginning stenciling, keep your design simple, as you'll need to adapt it for the stencil. If, for example, you choose a daisy, you'll first want to consider the size of it. If you're uneasy about adjusting the exact size of the design freehand onto your tracing paper, take your design to a photocopier, have it reduced or blown up to the size you'd like your stencil, put the tracing paper on top of it, and trace. In tracing, isolate the parts of the design for cutouts. For example, with a flower you'll isolate the petals, the center, the stem, and the leaves. Outline each of them so that they fit together but don't touch: there should be a gap or a "bridge" between each of the parts. Your next step will be to color the parts of the flower on the tracing paper with crayons. Tracing paper is cheap, so try a few different practice color variations if you like.

2. Next, place a sheet of acetate over your design, secure it with masking tape, and trace your design onto the acetate. To simplify accurate and consistent placement of your design, use a large enough piece of acetate so that the space between your design and the top edge of the acetate is the same width as the distance you want your design to be from ceiling or baseboard. You will then be able to butt the acetate to the ceiling (or baseboard) and use that as your guide around the room.

3. Use the X-Acto knife to cut out the pattern. To make a smooth edge, don't lift the point of the blade. Instead turn the design as you cut. When you finish cutting, the stencil is ready for use.

4. Mix paints in paper cups or on plates to the colors you want. Artists' acrylics come only in concentrated colors, so if you want more muted or faded tones, this is the time to mix them to get your desired shades. Don't thin the paint, leave it thick. You want to be sure it doesn't run under the edges of the stencil.

5. Tape the stencil to the wall with masking tape. (If you want to remove some of the masking tape's stickiness to prevent it from pulling off the wall paint, first stick it on your forearm a few times.)

6. Dip one little piece of sponge into one color of paint. Remove the excess paint from it by pouncing—vigorously dabbing the sponge up and down—on a clean portion of a plate. Dab the paint on the wall through the proper openings of the stencil. With experience, you'll find the different effects that can be obtained with a very light up and down motion. Do one color at a time. For a small opening, work with a small sponge.

7. When you've filled in all the cutout areas (you may wish to leave the thin areas, such as the stem of a daisy, for a round artists' brush), untape the acetate and carefully lift it straight up.

8. Using a small artists' brush, add the details and touch up small errors. As you'll discover, using this kind of brush makes a crisper, more solid color. Brushes are more time consuming, but better for controlling tricky, thin areas.

FOR REAL BEGINNERS ONLY: VEVA CROZER'S CHEATER'S STENCILING

This is as obvious as the nose on your face, and for beginners it's sometimes easier and helps build confidence. Make your stencils following the method suggested. Then take a No. 3 pencil and lightly draw outlines of all the cutout areas on the surface to be stenciled. Don't paint through the stencil; just remove the stencil and paint directly on the wall in the outlined areas with small brushes. You may want to keep your original tracing paper handy so you can keep track of which colors go where.

9. Repeat the pattern. There are several ways to do this. Practiced stencilers usually go by eye, either by starting at one end of the wall, and working toward the other end; or by working their way in from both ends toward the middle; by paying some attention to the spacing, things usually seem to come out even. However, if the casual approach isn't for you, move your stencil over or down, depending on which way your pattern is going, and then mark the outline of the previous pattern on the acetate with a pencil. Use the mark to gauge and measure each repeat.

10. A coat of polyurethane varnish will be your last step, if you wish. It will make your wall completely washable (a good idea if children are around) and preserve your stenciling longer. Apply with a smooth roller. ◇

PAPERING WALLS & CEILINGS

Wallpapers and wall coverings, long the most taboo form of decoration for designers, have made a remarkable comeback, and the choice today is staggering, encompassing a wide range of materials, patterns, thicknesses, textures, and prices. Walk into any wall covering store and you'll find plain old-fashioned, machine-made wallpaper, hand-screened and hand-blocked decorators' wallpapers, photo murals, metallic wall coverings (foils and Mylars), vinyl, cork, Ultrasuede, velveteen flocks, and lots of textile wall coverings to brighten up dull, featureless rooms, adding interest where there are few other details. Textured wall coverings of any sort will do especially well where there are uneven, rough, or cracked walls. The particular advantage of thick papers and fabrics is that they can hide minor defects and blemishes. If you have a general knowledge of what's available these days, you will be better prepared to get good buys at sales and at discount houses, and you might also learn how to use less expensive wall coverings to imitate the look of expensive ones or those available only to decorators. You will also, of course, cut costs by being a do-it-yourselfer.

The factors that determine the price of a wall covering are 1) the manufacturing process, whether the covering was machine-made, hand-screened, hand-blocked, or hand-painted, and the number of colors involved in the design—the more colors used, the more expensive the product; 2) the value of the material used for the actual wall covering—imported textured fabrics will be more expensive, for example, than thin, domestic, machine-made paper; 3) the type of backing (if there is one) used. For example, prepasted wallpaper, which comes with a dry glue on the back, will be slightly more expensive than the unpasted variety.

HOW TO PUT UP WALLPAPER

When setting out to buy a wallpaper, the first thing to do is to settle on what kind of design you want. Go to a well-stocked wallpaper store, and spend a few hours leafing through wall covering books, always keeping in mind the space you'll be decorating. Vertical stripes will give an appearance of greater height to a room. Small patterns will be best for small rooms; large patterns for large rooms. A boldly patterned paper will dominate a room, detracting from the furniture and accessories (or, on the other hand, make less-than-wonderful pieces less conspicuous).

If your walls are in bad condition, scrape off all old loose paint and plaster, fill all cracks with spackle, and then put up a liner. For any wall covering, it's important to have a smooth surface so that as much of the backing as possible is in contact with the wall. A lumpy finish won't hold the material well, and there is a risk of peeling.

MATERIALS

Wallpaper.

Large, shallow container of water.

Premixed wallpaper paste.

Plumb line and chalk.

Smoothing brush.

Seam roller.

Mat knife.

METHOD

1. Measure and cut one panel of your wallpaper, allowing for 2″ of trim at the bottom and the top. Keep in mind the matching of the design.

2. To make sure your paper is perfectly straight, use a plumb line. Generally, the first strip is hung at about the center of a wall, so drive a tack into the wall at that spot about 2″ from the ceiling. The bob of your plumb line should be around 2″ from the floor. When the bob stops swaying, make a mark on the wall just above the baseboard. Coat the line well with chalk, then hold it on the mark and pull it out at center. Release it with a snap to make a vertical mark on the wall. The first strip of paper should align with this snapped line. The plumb line need not be used for subsequent panels; they will be butted against each other and will all be as straight up and down as the first.

3. If your paper is prepasted, activate the glue on the back by loosely rolling the length of wall covering as though you're going to put it in a tube, then submerge it in water for 20 to 60 seconds depending on the length of the strip and how heavy the paste is. Some people prefer to brush water onto prepasted paper, as the submersion process makes the rolls very wet and unwieldy. With unpasted paper, place the panel on the floor or a table, pattern side down, and

(continued on next page)

apply your premixed paste thoroughly to all areas except for a 2″ border at the top (for trimming). Make sure the paste is thin and even or you'll get lumps, and it will go unevenly on the wall. It's easier to handle your pasted panel if you "book" it: This simply means bringing the two ends together, pasted surfaces face to face and meeting in the middle without overlapping. This way you can handle the paper without touching any paste. Carry the panel to the wall for hanging.

4. Unfold the top half of the panel and place it in position on the wall, using the chalk line as a guide; be sure to allow for the 2″ trim area at the top. Panel may be moved around on the wall until it is straight. Holding the paper at the top with one hand, smooth out wrinkles with your other hand; then unfold the bottom section of the panel and continue holding and smoothing.

5. Follow the same procedure for the second strip, making sure the pattern matches. Once each panel is up, smooth the entire panel with your smoothing brush, starting from the center and moving out toward the edges. Blisters or raised paper should be gently brushed out. Smooth the seams with your seam roller.

6. Continue with this procedure all around the room. Try not to let a seam fall in a corner; it will be hard to seal and the panels will be prone to peeling.

7. Since some wallpapers may tend to shrink a bit as they dry, save the trimming job till last. Trim panels at ceiling line, along baseboard, and around doors and windows with a single-edge razor blade, using a metal ruler as a guide. ◇

SEAMLESS PAPER

Used by photographers when an absolutely plain background is necessary for a photo setup, seamless paper can change the color on your walls in a flash. Available in professional photographers' supply stores, seamless paper comes in 50 or more colors, depending on the manufacturer. A 9′ × 36′ roll costs $20 or so, depending on the quality of the paper. Seamless photographers' paper can be hung from spring-loaded tension rods or from rods attached to the wall or ceiling with special brackets (both hanging systems also available from photo supply houses). The bottom of the paper, to hang straight, must be weighted with a heavy wooden dowel or a section of ½″ plumbers' pipe.

Seamless paper might be hung out from the wall to create an instant storage space behind it. See pages 30–31.

IMITATING & DRESSING UP WALLPAPER

DO-IT-YOURSELF HAND-BLOCKED WALLPAPER

The most expensive wallpaper ($100 a roll), available only to the trade, is that which has been hand-screened. Many of these would be impossible to imitate (those that have a sophisticated repeat pattern), but others aren't. Some lining paper ($5 a roll), which is made to go under wallpaper, looks a good deal like the plain background to an expensive paper, so why not use lining paper as your wallpaper, and paint it yourself? That's essentially what designer Angelo Donghia did for the paper illustrated here. Spend some time choosing special colors and try something easy and modern: Donghia's random dots, drips, and splotches, for instance, or perhaps a grid. You could even try a Rollerwall® (see box at right) on lining paper. To try handpainting your own paper, put it up and *then* paint it. Once your paint has dried, give it a coat of matte polyurethane to protect it from fading.

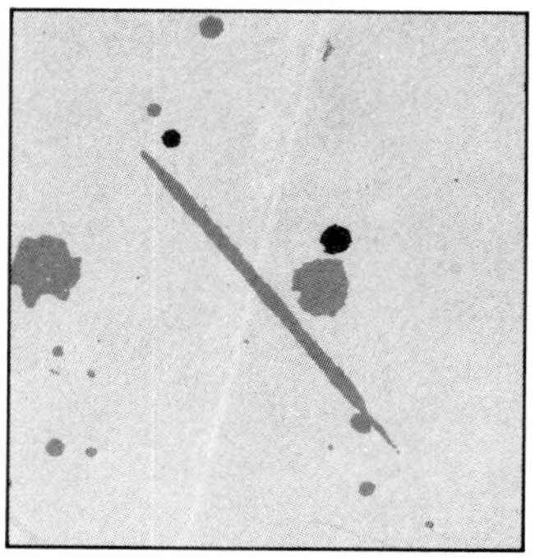

Angelo Donghia's abstract spatter-and-drip wallpaper.

ANTIQUING CHEAP WALLPAPER

A much more mellow effect can be achieved by putting up a cheap, thin wallpaper and then applying a coat of matte varnish—or glaze—on it. You could also experiment by distressing the still-wet finish.

HELP FOR CON-TACT PAPER

For heavy-moisture, hard-use areas such as kitchens and bathrooms, washable wall coverings are needed, and vinyl or vinyl-coated papers are perfect. They can also be expensive. A good alternative is Con-tact, the thin, plastic-like paper with the pressure-sensitive adhesive. It is easy to put on and is relatively cheap. However, Con-tact does have several drawbacks: It has a tendency to curl and peel off in a relatively short time; and unless the surface you are applying it to is as smooth as glass, it will be lumpy and bubbly looking. One way to

CAN'T DECIDE BETWEEN PAINT AND WALLPAPER?

Try Rollerwall®, a nifty way to give your walls the luxurious look of patterned wallpaper for the low cost of paint. No muss, no fuss, no paste, no cutting, no plumb line, no seams. Each pass with the two-part roller system serves as a guide for the next pass. The paint rolls from a regular roller onto another one that is embossed with a raised design and then onto the wall. It's a mini-lithography press! Write for a brochure (P.O. Box 757, Silver Spring, Md. 20901) and choose from over 50 patterns for your very own handheld designer's roller.

offset this is to choose a relatively "busy" pattern (and there are some quite attractive designs available) and then add a hard, protective surface with a coat or two of polyurethane.

LESS IS LESS (MONEY)

Another idea is to use fairly expensive wall covering, but use less of it. Many older buildings have borders or "framings" of decorative molding on the walls. Consider covering just the enclosed area of one wall with paper and then painting the rest of the wall with a color that matches or complements the wall covering. If your walls do not have this decorative detailing, you can buy wooden molding at a lumberyard (it comes in many shapes), miter the corners, and nail it up. Or else use the new cellular plastic molding available at lumberyards—it is cheap, lightweight, and easy to handle and install.

PAPER BORDERS

With wallpaper borders you can create instant "trompe l'oeil" architectural features and other interesting effects that quickly dress up a room at the ceiling line (or on the ceiling), at chair rail height, along baseboards, or around windows, doorways, or built-in cabinetry. The trouble with these wallpaper borders is that they tend to be very expensive (anywhere from $2 to $6 a yard); they cost much more, in fact, for the amount of material you get, than wallpaper. A way around this is to find a wallpaper that has a linear design that would look good or appropriate cut into long strips. With papers such as this you can make your own borders with nothing more than a straight-edge and a mat knife or a sharp pair of scissors. There are papers that have side-by-side vertical repeat patterns of floral motifs, for instance, that might look good as a border. Or stripes, meant to be hung vertically, might be used. Search through the sample books at your wallpaper store to see what you can find.

WASTEPAPER AS WALLPAPER

Another trick is to recycle "trash" paper. Anything will do: foreign-language newspapers, magazine photos, playbills, or even music scores (for the ceiling of a music room, perhaps). You could create a montage of family and friends with a sampling of 8½″ × 11″ color Xeroxes made from slides. (This can be done at a copying shop.) Once the wall or ceiling has been papered, it will need at least one coat of polyurethane or shellac. (Shellac is more amber than polyurethane and will render a more antiqued effect.)

FAUX GRASSCLOTH

If you like the textured look of grasscloth, which is made by weaving Chinese reeds and is *very* expensive (up to $145 a roll), buy a plain vinyl grasscloth (approximately $22 a roll), and once it's up paint it the color of your choice.

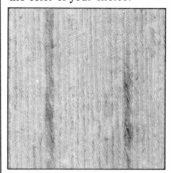

A coat of paint helps the look of vinyl grasscloth.

FAUX TUSSAH

Tussah silk weave runs about $140 a roll. To imitate its soft luxurious look, try buying the thickest grade of muslin or canvas lining (a low grade of artists' canvas originally designed to go under brocades and tapestries) or nice Haitian cotton. Put it up, prime, and then paint or glaze.

ORDERING WALLPAPER

All you really have to know about ordering wall covering is which paper or other material you want (and can afford), and the size of your room. Any reputable dealer will advise you of the correct amount to order. Most American coverings come in standard rolls of 27″ by 5 yards (about 30 square feet). French and English coverings come in rolls that are 20½″ by 5½ yards untrimmed (25 square feet). Order by the square foot to avoid confusion about widths and lengths. Order at least three weeks in advance and order generously; better to have too much than too little. The following chart will give you an approximate idea of how much wallpaper you will need.

Size of Room	Number of Single Rolls Needed for Height of Room*		
	7′	8′–9′	10′–12′
6′ × 10′	7	8	11
6′ × 12′	8	9	12
8′ × 12′	8	10	14
8′ × 14′	9	11	15
9′ × 12′	9	11	15
9′ × 14′	10	12	16
9′ × 16′	11	13	18
10′ × 14′	10	12	16
10′ × 16′	11	13	18
12′ × 16′	12	14	19
12′ × 18′	12	15	20
14′ × 18′	13	16	22
16′ × 18′	14	17	23
16′ × 20′	15	18	24

*Deduct one roll for every two doors or windows.

COVERING WALLS WITH FABRICS

STAPLING FABRIC

Having a professional decorator "fabric" your walls is always an expensive undertaking. But the look of fabric on walls creates its own warmth and suggestion of luxury and is an especially good cover-up for problem walls. It *can* be done for comparatively little if you do it yourself.

The absolute easiest way to put fabric on your walls is to staple it. A serviceable staple gun costs less than $20 and can be purchased in the hardware store. You can use any fabric, but you're best off with one that has a tight, close, weave so it won't sag or buckle. In cottons, you'd be best off with denim, seersucker, broadcloth, shaker cloth, or 2-ply chambray (which is sturdy without looking heavy). Linens are good if they have a little polyester or cotton in them to make them sturdier and less likely to wrinkle. Raw silk and moiré are elegant, but more expensive. Plain burlap is less expensive than the paper-backed burlaps you'll find in a wall covering store, and can be bought already dyed and primed. Generally speaking, you'll also be better off to select a sturdier fabric, but you can adapt thinner fabrics such as calicos, cheesecloths, and muslins if you're willing to prepare them with an underliner. (It's cheaper to use an underliner made of polyester than one of 100 percent cotton designed for curtains.)

Basically, what you will be doing is simply stapling the fabric to the wall with staples about every 3″ along the tops and bottoms of each length of fabric. "Seaming" the panels can be done in a number of ways. For the most polished look, sew them. The most rudimentary way of joining adjacent panels is to overlap them and staple. Gluing butted or overlapped panels can cause discoloration and almost invariably will harden a fabric so that it loses its softness. However, there's a way to use glue that can look almost as good as sewing.

Staple the edge of the fabric down the wall, then lay a bead of glue down the face of the fabric about ½″ in from the edge. Line up the edge of your next panel with the stapled and glued panel already on the wall. With the "good" side of the fabric facing the wall, press the fabric into the glue and then staple it in place just a little beyond the glue line. Fold back the newly attached panel and continue stapling as you did for the first panel.

Always begin stapling the panels at the top, smoothing the fabric—not stretching—as you go along until you get to the corner. If you're using staples down the side, this is the time to do it. Then staple the bottom as you did the top. As you work along the bottom of each panel, give your fabric gentle tugs to make it taut.

Note: If you are using an underliner (for thin fabric), cut the underliner panels the same size as the covering fabric. If they are not the same size, the seams of the underliner will show through.

The staples along the ceiling can be hidden with decorative trim. Choose from assorted braids, eyelets, grosgrain ribbon, velvet ribbon, or even strips of wooden or gilded or silvered picture molding. You might even want to make "molding" out of remnants of the fabric itself. If you use bed sheets, for example, and you want the look of coordinated "molding," choose sheets that have doubled-sided decorative panels at the top, then staple up the sheets so that the bottom of those panels is at the ceiling line, leaving the panel as a "flap." The panels will fold down and become instant "molding." You can let them hang loosely or, for a more tailored look, staple them at the corners. ◇

SOARING. Kites come in an endless array of designs and make inexpensive decoration for walls.

SHIRRING WALLS WITH FABRIC

For a room that envelops you in plush comfort, lightweight fabrics such as sheeting cotton, cotton polyester, and tight-weave muslin or cheesecloth can be shirred on rods or dowels mounted at the ceiling and just above the baseboard. If there are doors in the wall, the rod must be attached above it; if there are windows, rods must be mounted above and below them. You will need generous amounts of fabric—about three times the wall's width. Hem the fabric to accommodate the rod or dowel and gather the fabric along the rod. You could use shirring tape, but it's much simpler to allow the fabric to gather itself naturally. ◇

Simple shirring will make any room elegant, with or without the tented ceiling.

PLEATED FABRIC

To give your walls the tailored yet sculptural look of knife pleats, you don't have to have any sewing skills whatsoever—all you need is the fabric, a plumb line, a staple gun, and a ladder. Pleated walls look best in a small room, such as a study or den, or on one wall of a larger space—a long corridor, perhaps. This is a terrific way to cover a wall that is in really bad shape. But don't plan to hang shelves or pictures on the walls you choose for this treatment.

The fabric should be fairly sturdy and definitely not at all transparent. If there is a pattern, it should be a small, overall design.

To figure out how much fabric you will need, you must first decide how far apart you want your pleats and how wide they will be. If pleats are 2″ wide and the space between them is 9″, fabric that is 54″ wide will make five pleats per width. Space between pleats can be any width, but 8″ to 10″ is average and economical, in terms of "wasted" yardage. The following instructions are for 2″ pleats that are 9″ apart.

First, cut a length of fabric the height of your wall. Fold and press 1″ of material (back sides together) along the right long edge of the material. Invisibly staple up and down the fold in the far right corner of the room. Using a plumb line, neatly staple the fabric to the wall up and down a line that is 10″ to the left of the corner. Next, fold the fabric back on itself (fronts together) and, again using the plumb line, staple through the two thicknesses of fabric along a line that is 1″ to the right of the fold. Again fold the fabric back to the left, and you have made your first pleat. Move the plumb line 10″ to the left and start the process again.

When you get to the left edge of the first length of material, staple it all along its length. The edge should fall 45″ from the corner where you began. Fold and press 1″ along the right edge of a second length of fabric and staple it in place 1″ to the right of the edge of the material already on the wall. Continue on in this way until the entire wall is covered.

You might want to consider pressing and folding under an inch or so of each length of fabric at the top and bottom as you work. This will require a bit more dexterity and more stapling, but it will give a nice smooth line and will eliminate the need for trimming.

To save fabric (and some work) you might want to nail or stick lengths of molding to your wall at chair rail height, or maybe a bit higher, and then just use the pleated fabric on the upper portion of the wall. It's a good look. ◇

***STORED DECOR.** Keeping utilitarian possessions and work supplies out in the open instead of hiding them away in a closet can be a good idea. Here Bruce Bierman's colorful rolls of fabric become an effective wall covering in the dining room. See page 46.*

WILLIAM MACHADO'S LINEN PANELS

To impart a feeling of quiet orderliness, William Machado devised a way of "paneling" a room with linen-covered ½″ A/C plywood. All the panels are identical, and though most of them simply hang against the wall, some act as hinged doors. This spare, modern-looking treatment is a particularly good idea if your walls are not in mint condition. The panels, padded as they are with cotton, also absorb a lot of sound.

Linen panels add texture and warmth to a room. See page 16.

Since plywood comes in 8′ sheets, there may be a space left between the top of the panels and the ceiling. In William Machado's room this was acceptable because of the structural detailing, but you might want to put up molding or in some other way fill up the space.

Since you will want all your panels to be the same width, measure your walls and figure out how they will divide most efficiently—keeping in mind, of course, that plywood comes in 4′ widths. If any of your panels will be doors, you will have to take the width of the existing opening into account. If your panels are, say, 2′ wide and the doorway is 3′, you could use two panels, hinging one on each side so that they open like French doors.

First cover each panel with cotton batting, available from upholstery supply shops. Let about 1″ of batting overlap on all sides, and staple it onto the back in a looser version of the method for stretching linen described below. If any of your panels will be doors, wrap and loosely staple these panels completely with batting, for both sides will be covered in linen.

In much the same way that an artist stretches a canvas, the linen is stretched around the plywood and secured with staples. Cut a length of linen to a size that is about 4″ larger—in all directions—than the plywood. Loosely fit the linen around the wood, then staple it to the back of the board in the middle of the top edge beyond the batting. Turn the panel 180° and, stretching the linen so it is fairly tight, put in another staple on the back of the bottom. Turn the panel onto its side and staple. Again turn the panel 180° and, still pulling the material quite tight, secure once more. Return the panel to the original position and insert two more staples, each about 3″ on either side of the first; turn panel, repeat on bottom; then sides. Continue stretching and stapling until you have reached the corners. Make tight "hospital corners" and secure the folds in place with two or three staples.

To completely stretch linen on door panels, cover the back (the side not facing the main room) first, then carefully do the front side in the usual way, perhaps folding the raw edge of the fabric under before stapling, creating a narrow hem for a neater look. You might want to nail

(continued on next page)

molding over the staples and the edge of the fabric or the folded hem for an even more finished appearance.

With wood screws, mirror hangers, picture wire, and picture hooks, secure hanging panels to the wall, butting them together. For door panels, set hinges in panels and in walls or door frames. Nail or screw a flat loop of soft leather or canvas into the back of each panel to serve as pulls. ◇

MIRRORS

If shiny walls and other surfaces increase the apparent size of a room, cleverly used mirrors can double, triple, or quadruple it. Mirror panels are expensive, but it's often smart to scrimp on other things and spend money on mirrors.

- Used floor to ceiling and opposite or at right angles to a window, a mirror will double the light and the view. Used in recesses on either side of a fireplace it will look as if you can walk into a whole extra room.

- Narrow strips of mirror along baseboards, or as a "cornice" around a room, can greatly expand the space.

- Judiciously placed strips of mirror can look like slit windows in a wall.

- Mirrors sold for closet doors are often surprisingly cheap compared to custom-cut pieces, and—frames removed—they can be hung side by side or cut into strips.

- Glaziers often sell scraps of mirror at a fraction of the custom-cut price, or even great expanses of mirror they have on hand from a botched job. These usually have one or two uneven edges, but if you can cut glass you're in business.

COVERING CEILINGS

MIRROR TILES

An age-old design trick to expand space is to use mirrors, and a ceiling can be a terrific place for them. Hanging a large mirror safely on a horizontal surface is an enormous (and expensive) undertaking; happily there is a less expensive alternative: mirror tiles. Sold in hardware and housewares stores in packs of twelve, mirror tiles are easy to install yourself; and by picking up and reflecting light and images, they will add height and interest to any room. Architect Gerald Allen, for instance, created a checkerboard pattern of mirror tiles on a ceiling. Allen discovered that since his ceiling was old and bumpy, the squares of double-sided adhesive that came with the tiles did not adequately hold them in place, and so he substituted the type of mastic usually used to hold vinyl floor tiles in place. This material does not affect the silver backing of the mirrors and it is simple to use; a large amount is applied to the back of the tiles, and then the tiles are individually held in place until the mastic is dry enough to hold the mirror securely. Double-sided tape should work on a new, *absolutely* flat surface.

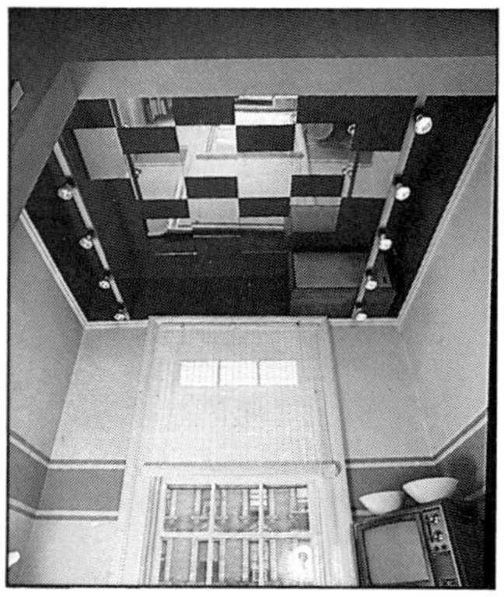

Mirrors always add interest, but on a ceiling they must be securely installed. *See page 43.*

You might want to consider other less-than-full-coverage configurations for hanging mirror tiles on your ceiling: strips running down or across the length or width of the room; a border of them around the edges; a solid square in the middle of the ceiling for a heightening effect. Tip: Mirror tiles generally look better on a dark ceiling. ◇

STAMPED TIN CEILING

Architect Tom McHugh wanted to conceal the unsightliness of some newly installed pipes in his bathroom and didn't want the sometimes severe look of a standard drywall ceiling. An old-fashioned, patterned, pressed-tin ceiling became the affordable answer. Tin ceilings in about 20 different patterns can be ordered by mail through AA-Abbingdon Ceiling Co. in New York City.

A tin ceiling adds period charm and is a good cover-up.

MATERIALS

Furring strips.

Roundhead or panhead wood screws, 1″ long, or 10-penny common nails.

Panels (2′ × 8′ each) of pressed tin.

METHOD

First, nail a framework of furring strips to the ceiling. The framework should be a 2′ × 8′ grid that corresponds to the size of tin panels. Screw or nail the panels to the furring strips about every 10″ to 12″. The edges of the tin panels have a "bump/groove" feature, so that sections can overlap without an obvious seam. If the room is irregularly shaped, it may be necessary to make cardboard templates of each irregularity around the ceiling's edge; then, using the templates, cut the tin to the proper size and shape with metal shears. Once the tin is all in place, gaps and irregularities around the edges can be covered by lengths of pressed tin cornice (also available from AA-Abbingdon) or strips of wood crown molding. Paint the ceiling with any oil-base paint or give it a coat or two of clear polyurethane.

VARIATION

Faux Tin. You can create the look of a vintage tin ceiling with the heavy embossed papers that are now on the market. These papers—trade named Classic Coverups—come in patterns that closely replicate old tin ceilings; they can be put up just like wallpaper and can be painted any color. Besides the authentic look, these papers are heavy enough to hide cracks, bumps, lumps, and other flaws. At your local paint or wallpaper store, or through Decor International Wallcovering, Inc., 37-39 Crescent St., Long Island City, N.Y. 11101. ◇

FIXING UP FLOORS

The question of what to do with floors deserves careful consideration, for almost more than any other design element, floors can add to—or detract from—a feeling of comfort and distinction in any interior. However good and interesting the wall and window treatments, however original or precious the furnishings, the effect can be totally ruined by shabby or uninspired floors.

When considering how to deal with your floors, the first decision you must make is whether to give them a transparent finish (stains, dyes, and so forth that let the grain of the wood show through) or an opaque painted surface that covers everything up. Each type of finish has its own uses and its own advantages and disadvantages. There are, as usual, various practical factors to keep in mind: the condition of the existing floor, the use of the room, the length of time you may be in residence, your budget, the look you would like to achieve and how it will fit in with the rest of the decoration you have in mind, and the amount of time and money you are willing or able to spend on maintenance.

Luckily, elderly stained and worn carpeting can be covered with rugs placed in strategic places, or if the stains and worn spots are not too bad you might try dyeing the whole carpet a dark color. Battered and stained tiles or linoleum can be painted and sealed, or, if this seems undesirable, the floor can be covered with squares of Masonite and then painted, stenciled, or marbleized. The same, of course, goes for wooden floors, except that most wood, if it is in halfway reasonable condition, can be sanded down (or not) and given a handsome new finish.

In any discussion of flooring and floor restoration, there are a number of specialized terms that are often used. A few of these follow. Other terms, many of which have to do with painting and finishing surfaces in other ways, are found in the sections dealing with woodworking and with furniture.

TERMS YOU SHOULD KNOW ABOUT FLOORS

BRING UP THE GRAIN. Water—or water-base compounds such as bleach—when applied to raw wood, will cause minute splinters to rise up, causing a rough, fuzzy surface that will have to be sanded. Also called raising the grain.

CASEIN PAINT. A cheap water-soluble paint that has milk as its base. Casein dries fast, is easy to apply, and thin translucent layers of it can quickly be built up to a hard (for a water-base paint) finish.

GRAIN OR GRAINING. The grain is made by lengthwise fibers, and wood is cut either along the grain or across it. Graining usually means the painted, simulation of the natural grain in wood.

GRAPH PAPER. Paper printed with a grid pattern; paper with squares ranging from 1/10″ up to ½″ is made. See-through graph tracing paper is also available from artists' supply houses.

HARDWOOD. Wood that comes from deciduous trees—oak, walnut, cherry, birch, poplar, and maple. Technically a misnomer; most hardwood really is quite hard and dense, but a few types are actually softer than softwood (q.v.).

PARQUET. Hardwood flooring (about ¼″ thick) laid in mosaic-like patterns. Inlaid or plated parquet consists of a veneer of decorative hardwood glued in patterns to squares of softwood backing. These squares are then laid on a wood subfloor.

POUNCE. To pounce is to use a paint technique in which an almost dry paintbrush is lightly tapped on a surface to create a stippled or lightly shaded effect.

SOFTWOOD. Wood that comes from coniferous trees—pine, larch, spruce, cedar, redwood, and hemlock. A bit of a misnomer, because a few softwoods are actually quite hard. *See also* Hardwood.

FINISHING FLOORS

If somewhere under the stains, scuffs, gouges, old finishes, and years of waxy build-up, there lurks a floor of very nice wood, you may well want to go to the trouble of sanding (also known as scraping) it down to the raw wood and then applying a transparent or semitransparent finish that will show off the natural pattern of the grain.

The following section deals with things you can do to give your floors this kind of face-lift: staining, bleaching, lightening, polishing, polyurethaning. Even if you think your floors are hopeless, they can almost certainly be improved quite dramatically with any one of these comparatively easy techniques.

SANDING FLOORS

Before you start in on most floor finishing projects you will probably have to go through some basic preparations, which almost always means sanding the surface. You can, of course, have this done professionally, but doing the job yourself isn't all that difficult, and can save a lot of money.

You will need to rent a drum sander (so called because it works by a belt of sandpaper revolving around a drum) and a handheld disk sander—also called a rotary sander or edger—for finishing.

A drum sander is a large machine that looks somewhat like an upright vacuum; a rotary or disk sander is smaller and looks a little like R2-D2. A rotary sander uses a circular disk of sandpaper that spins in a horizontal plane. Be sure, before you start, that no nail heads are sticking out of the floor. Such protrusions will rip the sandpaper and could seriously damage the sander drum.

Be forewarned that even though both sanders have dust bags, sanding your floors will create an extraordinary amount of flying dust. You will want to move everything portable out of harm's way, and if you're sanding in a room with closets, you should seal them with masking tape before starting the job. Buy some dust masks and goggles from the hardware store and use them to protect your face and eyes. And remember, sanding a floor is hard work; you should allow at least one full day for the job.

Natural wood floors give rooms an uncluttered look.

For working on standard strip flooring, you need two grades of sandpaper—nos. 1 and 3—unless you are sanding a floor that is in *really* bad shape, in which case you will need a third, coarser grade. A drum sander is a powerful thing, and it's important to make sure it's always unplugged when changing the paper or fiddling with it in any way. Ask the salesman for a detailed explanation of how and when to change the paper. This isn't complicated, but it's easier to understand when you actually see the machine itself.

Start with your coarsest grade of paper and begin at one end of the room, keeping in mind that you will be sanding *with* the grain of the wood. (If you are working on a parquet floor, use medium-grade sandpaper and sand diagonally across the room.) Tilt the machine back toward you so the drum is off the floor; turn it on. Slowly lower the sander and as soon as it makes contact with the floor, allow it to start pulling you forward. Using a drum sander is like walking a headstrong dog. Your job is to let it pull you, but not as fast as it would like. Always keep the machine moving, or the sander will eat down into the floor and you will end up with an uneven surface. When you've finished one pass down the room, tilt the machine so that the drum is once again raised, and drag it back across the room to where you started. Position it so that the drum overlaps the strip you've just sanded by about three inches, lower the machine, and you're off again. Repeat this process of overlapping strips—changing sandpaper whenever necessary—until you've gone over the entire floor.

When you have covered as much of the floor as possible, switch to the rotary sander and, using the coarse grade of sandpaper, go around the room and work on the edges and other parts unreachable by the drum sander. While it is less formidable than the larger machine, the rotary sander should also be kept on the move so it doesn't eat down into the floor in any one spot. After you finish with the edges, there will probably still be corners and other out-of-the-way spots that you will have to scrape and/or sand by hand.

Damp-mop your floor before the next go-round; this will raise the grain. Now change to your finer grade of sandpaper. This time, start at the other end of the room, so that you sand across the floor in the opposite direction—but still *with* the grain. Repeat the operation with the rotary sander, this time with finer sandpaper.

Sweep and vacuum up all the dust and debris, then mop the floor with a solution of one part vinegar to four parts water. Allow this to dry completely.

If you don't intend to stain, bleach, or paint your floor, you should apply shellac, varnish, or the protective finish of your choice.◇

STAINING

Stains modify the color of a wood floor, while at the same time clarifying and highlighting the grain pattern. Stains are available in oil-, water-, and alcohol-base mediums, each of which gives a slightly different finish and which are applied in different ways.

Pigmented oil stains are mixed with turpentine or mineral spirits and will generally deliver the most even, lustrous finish. They dry relatively slowly. Dye stains come in powdered form; some are soluble in water and some in alcohol. Water-base stains—thin watery solutions—go on easily and soak into the wood quickly, but they tend to dry in splotches. Alcohol-base stains—also very thin—dry almost instantly, thus their application can be a bit tricky; if you accidentally get a second coat on an already dry section, for instance, the color will build up on the overlapped section and you will end up with an uneven look.

The difference between oil stains and water- or alcohol-base dyes is that the oil-base stains seep into the wood rather slowly and you have a fair amount of control; water and alcohol dyes do their work almost instantly, and you have little or no time to "play" with the depth of tone. In fact, with oil stains you *must* wipe off the excess (if you leave an oil stain on for too long it will harden into a gummy, paint-like mess); with a water or alcohol base there is very little excess to remove.

The more coats of any kind of stain or dye you apply, the deeper the tone will be. This is the way to deepen the color. Remember that the final protective coat you put on your floor will darken the color even more.

Any given stain will look different on different kinds of wood, so you should always try out your stain on either the same kind of wood as your floor, or, better yet, an obscure, hidden corner of the floor itself.

Stain dyes are available in wide array of colors—scarlet, peacock blue, bright green. But if you can't find a color you want, you can mix two or three powders together—or you can even use fabric dye. If you use fabric dye, use less water than the manufacturer recommends for fabric-strength dye. How durable your actual stain is isn't really all that important, because you will always want to cover it with a protective coating of polyurethane (see page 95).

Stains and dyes can be purchased in any hardware store; often you will find charts of the effects you get, depending on the type of wood you are staining. One good mail order source for stains and dyes is W. D. Lockwood & Co., 450 Greenwich St., New York, N.Y. 10013. Their catalog has dozens of intriguing colors to choose from.

The recipes that follow are for raw floors that have been newly sanded. If your floor does not need sanding, at least give it a good scrub and a final wash with mineral spirits or a mixture of two parts water to one part cider vinegar.

MATERIALS

Stain or dye, premixed or powdered.

Clean rags.

Sponge.

4″ brush.

Mineral spirits, denatured alcohol, water, depending on your medium.

Polyurethane.

OIL STAIN METHOD

1. Apply the stain with a rag or brush, rubbing across as well as with the grain. If the room you are working in is small, you may be able to do the whole thing all at once. If the room is large, work on one approximately 10′ × 10′ area at a time. Let the stain set for about 10 minutes; then wipe off the excess with a clean dry rag.

2. If the resulting color is too light, let the floor dry overnight (putting a new coat of stain over a wet one is like putting on two coats of paint at once—the two coats will combine into one), then repeat step 1. Two applications will generally be sufficient to do the job.

3. Again let the floor dry overnight, then apply two or three coats of polyurethane.

WATER OR ALCOHOL STAIN METHOD

1. If you are using powdered dye stain, mix according to package directions. Be sure you make enough; it's difficult to get the same color twice.

2. Apply the stain or dye with a sponge or rag to one small area at a time, rubbing across the grain. Work quickly, trying to put down an even amount of stain all over the floor, not overlapping or going over an already dry area.

Apply a lighter color than you actually want and use a second coat to increase the depth of tone. As pointed out above, with water and alcohol stains, you are not going to be able to control the tone (as you would with oil stains) by wiping up whatever does not soak in. Try for a thin first coat, then strengthen and deepen, if necessary, with a second thin coat after the first has dried. Since water-base stains will raise the grain of the wood a bit, you may want to sand the floor lightly—followed by vacuuming and wiping clean—after the first coat is down.

3. When you have achieved the color you want, let your floor dry overnight before applying up to three coats of polyurethane.◇

STAINED PATTERNS

Treating pigmented oil stain somewhat as if it were paint—using different shades to create patterns—is a bit time consuming, but the effort can be well worth it. Alternating two or three wood stains on individual boards of a standard or parquet floor can be very interesting. Or, using two or three different geometric shapes and two or more different shades of stain, you can make your own fake parquet. You will have to score the shapes lightly to control the stain and keep it from spreading to areas where you don't want it.

BLEACHING FLOORS

Bleaching looks just as it sounds: Some of the natural color of the wood is actually removed, resulting in a clean, light, airy look. A floor that has simply been bleached and polyurethaned can look quite spectacular indeed.

Ordinary household bleach will often give the desired result; scrub it in well and let it work for 10 or 15 minutes, then rinse it off. If, after the floor is dry, it does not look as light as you would like, repeat the process until the desired stage is reached. Then rinse the floor with water and a mop. No matter how well you rinse, some residue of the bleach will remain, so the surface will have to be neutralized somehow. The easiest way to do this is with a half and half solution of vinegar and water. Rinse the floor one final time with clear water.

All the bleaching and neutralizing with water-base solutions will raise the grain in the wood, so the floor should be lightly sanded after the final rinse, then vacuumed and wiped clean before applying two coats (at least) of polyurethane.

A light floor will brighten the whole room.

If you want a *really* blond floor, you might try a professional or industrial-strength bleach. Follow package directions carefully; this substance can be very caustic. The same rinsing and neutralizing steps indicated above should be followed for professional bleach.

Remember: Always wear rubber gloves when using any kind of bleach, and be sure the room is well ventilated.◇

LIGHTENING

A technique called lightening gives floors a somewhat more finished look than bleaching does. Basically, it is just painting the floor and then wiping the paint off.

Working with one relatively small, manageable area at a time (say nine square feet), brush flat white oil-base paint onto the floor. You might want to make the paint a bit less stark by tinting it slightly with an earth-color artists' oil color or universal tinting color, or use an ivory or creamy-white paint.

After a few minutes, wipe off most of the paint with a clean dry rag, working against the grain. The idea is to leave a slight film of paint over the entire surface, with small nooks and crevices in the wood filled with thicker dabs and slivers of paint. The overall effect is an "antiqued" look. This technique is especially effective on soft wood such as pine.

Allow the floor to dry overnight, and then polyurethane.◇

PAINTING FLOORS

If your floors are in such poor condition that they cannot be revived by sanding, sealing, staining, dyeing, or lightening, they might still be rescued by paint, which can cover a multitude of pits and potholes. You may want to keep things simple and just apply a coat or two of floor or deck paint. But with a bit of effort and a minimum of artistic ability, you can create hundreds of interesting effects: stenciled patterns (either an overall carpetlike design or a border around the room), dramatic supergraphics, variations on wall-type glazes, or any number of trompe l'oeil effects.

Whatever painted treatment you decide upon, the surface should be finished off with several coats of polyurethane; for longer wear, give your floor a coat of polyurethane every year or so. Painted floors can stand up to a surprising amount of wear, if cared for properly. The good thing about using this protective coating is that there's no need to work in expensive enamels; you can use almost any paint for your decorative effects.

An asymmetrically painted checkerboard floor defines a sitting space in Mark Hulla's loft.

PATTERNS IN CASEIN

The striking thing about the floors designed by hair stylist Kenneth Battelle, and painted in several rooms of his own home, is that they have the soft, distressed look of a finish from a former time, combined with bold contemporary patterns. He used water-base latex paint for the "background" and painted the design itself with casein paint—a fast drying, easy-to-work-with medium. The other noteworthy thing about his technique is that it involves scoring the edges of the various design elements. This scoring not only provides clean visual breaks, but it also makes it easy to achieve sharp, well-defined edges. This is a useful idea for many types of floor painting, but hard edges are almost mandatory in a geometric pattern of this kind.

The floor was first sanded and then given a base coat of light-colored water-base paint. After working out the design on graph paper, a grid was laid out on the floor and the design transferred to the floor itself (see How To Use a Grid, page 96). Using an awl and a long metal ruler, the lines of the design were etched into the wood. This might make a bit of a mess and may require a light sanding of some of the grooves; before any further paint is applied, the floor should be vacuumed so that all wood shavings are removed from the etched lines.

Using one color at a time, work out the design using the casein paint; casein colors are strong, so use a light coat at first, feeling your way. To strengthen or deepen a color, just give it another coat.

Next, using both coarse- and fine-grade steel wool, rub in a "random" way to impart a distressed, antiqued effect.

A casein and latex floor designed by Kenneth Battelle.

When you are satisfied with the look, vacuum the floor and then apply at least two coats of polyurethane varnish—flat or semigloss will probably look best—and when the floor is completely dry, finish things off with two or three coats of liquid wax.◇

OVERSIZE "TILES"

Richard Neas, a New York City-based designer who has built a strong reputation for his painted-floor ideas, came up with this floor, using several shades of green to create "tiles" that have a mottled effect. While Neas chose green, any color could be used.

After sanding, the floor is given a base coat of oil paint in a very light tone of whatever color you choose for your final main color (if your overall color will be brown, base coat should be light beige; if overall color is dark gray, base should be pale gray; and so forth).

Decide on what size you want your squares to be and when the base coat is dry, lightly lay out a grid pattern on the floor (Neas set his grid on a diagonal; see How To Use a Grid, page 96) with soft lead pencil or a stick of charcoal.

Now carefully put down a grid of 1″-wide masking tape over the lines of the grid. The strips of tape should be as straight as possible and pressed down well so paint won't seep under them when the darker coat of paint is applied.

Choose three or four different shades of oil-base paint in the color you've chosen and put a bit of each into different containers. With a large sponge, swab the paint onto the squares in an irregular pattern, letting the whorls and eddies of the various shades overlap and swirl around one another for a marbleized effect. You may want to pounce some of the darker tones over lighter ones (and vice versa) here and there. Treat each square separately—that is, rather than working on the whole floor at once, think of each square as an individual "canvas."

When you have achieved the look you want, allow the floor to dry thoroughly. Then carefully remove the strips of masking tape and wipe off whatever remains of the lines underneath. Give your floor at least two coats of polyurethane and a coat or two of liquid wax.◇

A diagonal grid pattern on a floor makes a room look larger.

COMBED SQUARES

Another good idea from Richard Neas is what he calls his combed floor. It is a tile pattern—a distinctive double stripe separates the "tiles"—that employs a technique similar to dragging glaze on a wall (see page 76). The difference here is that the striations are more pronounced and in definite patterns. As his "comb," Neas uses a window washer's squeegie that he notched with teeth. Again, Neas used two shades of green, but any color or colors could be used (far-out, fantasy effects can be achieved with wildly contrasting colors).

First the floor is given an overall base coat or undercoat of oil-base paint. When this is dry, mark off a grid on the floor of fairly large squares (Neas's are 27″ square) using a long metal ruler and a soft pencil. To make guide lines for the double stripe, measure carefully and pencil two more lines parallel to the first, ½″ on either side of it. You should end up with a grid of three parallel lines, ½″ apart. (You might want to settle for a single stripe between "tiles," in which case you will just need a regular single-line grid.)

Run long lengths of 1″-wide masking tape along the outer set of lines, leaving a 1″-wide space between the tapes. Press the tape firmly to the floor.

Now, using a mat knife or razor blade, cut teeth into your squeegie. The gaps should be about ⅛″ to ¼″ wide, leaving teeth of about the same width. You might want to try various widths and configurations cut into throw-away "combs" made from cardboard. They might not hold up very long, but they will enable you to experiment until you get the effect you

The striations were combed into the paint with a rubber squeegie.

like; then you can notch the squeegie itself.

Starting in one corner of the room, pour a cup or two of the darker color paint onto one of the squares and immediately begin shoving the paint around. (Semigloss oil-base paint will probably work best. You might want to thin the paint a bit, but you'll have to experiment to see which consistency works best. The paint should not run together after combing, but it shouldn't be so thick that the striations become exaggerated ridges.) Depending upon how you move the squeegie, striations will automatically be formed, in straight lines, long sweeping curves, undulating waves, nervous squiggles, or any number of other patterns as the teeth scrape away the viscous paint, revealing the undercoat beneath. You can create an infinite number of patterns—you may want your floor to look like an aerial photograph of contour plowing, or you may want it to be simple straight striations in an alternating design resembling parquet. Whatever you decide upon, adjacent squares should have patterns that move in different directions.

One of the good things about painting floors this way is that you have time to "re-comb" any part of the work that you don't like. Again, work on one square at a time, treating each square as a separate "picture." If you need more paint to finish one square, simply pour out more paint. Likewise, if you have too much paint, just squeegie the excess over onto the next square.

Squeegie the narrow space between the masking tape—as well as the small squares that are formed at the corners—with short, crosswise strokes to create a ladderlike pattern.

When you are happy with your efforts, allow the floor to dry and then carefully pull up the masking tape. You can leave these strips as is, for a well-defined, hard-edge look. Or you can do as Richard Neas did and mottle the strips with a little dark green paint on a sponge.

After everything is totally dry, give the floor two or three coats of polyurethane.◇

QUICK FIX

Floors dehydrate with age and inattention, and in many older houses and apartments, nice floors—parquetry, interesting wood, patterns of various kinds—lie hidden beneath years of neglect. These floors sometimes need only a little work to look beautiful, not a total reconditioning job. If you have floors like this, try giving them a good scrubbing and a coat or two of paste wax, then buff to a high shine. Paste wax is not a very durable finish, but it is quick, easy, and cheap—worth a try, at least.

MARBLEIZED FLOORS

Marbleizing a floor will add instant, somewhat formal splendor to almost any space, be it a small bathroom, a narrow corridor, or a large living room. If the marbleizing is done in pale colors, it will substantially increase the feeling of light and space in a room; really dark colors create instant drama.

There are as many ways to imitate marble finishes as there are varieties of marble, with their different colors and veining patterns. A really accurate simulation requires a good deal of research, patience, and practice. However, there are some methods that provide dramatic results and yet are comparatively easy to master. The following will provide some general guidelines.

Apart from looking at a photograph or at an actual piece of marble (or a piece of marbleized wood), try to remember that what you are after is an overall cloudy effect, with drifts of color moving across the surface; then more definite (darker or lighter or both) veins streaking across in a variety of patterns, depending upon the type of marble you are trying to imitate.

After priming your surface, lay down an undercoat of your basic color, using eggshell or semigloss oil-base paint. Allow floor to dry thoroughly.

Brush on a glaze (read about glazes, pages 75–76), tinted a darker color than your undercoat, in an irregular random pattern. Some patches of glaze should be in broad, raggedy bands, or drifts.

Before this glaze dries completely, dab the entire surface with a rag or sponge dipped in turpentine or mineral spirits. This will soften the edges of the glaze, and if some of the glaze is removed here and there, will produce a desirable mottled effect.

Glazing compound or thinned oil paint can be used for marbleizing. See page 52.

Note: For this and for the veining described below, you might want to work with a very thinned-down oil-base paint as your glaze. It will probably dry more slowly, and therefore be easier to use.

Next, using a small brush or a feather and two stronger tones of glaze—either in your basic color, or different colors altogether, depending on the effect you want—run nervous, narrow veins across the cloudy background. Depending upon the type of marble you are trying to duplicate, these may run in the same general direction as your larger, broad drifts of color, in the opposite direction, or both. When your veining looks acceptable, dab at the veins with your turpentine-dampened rag or sponge to again blur the glaze somewhat. If your marbleizing still looks too "harsh" or well-defined, drag a wide paintbrush—either dry or dampened with turpentine—across the whole thing.

Finally, again using a small brush or feather and the strong colors you used for the veining, quiver in a few short contrasting veins here and there, alongside and/or over the now-smudgy veins. Don't overdo this.

When all is thoroughly dry, give your floor a few coats of semigloss polyurethane varnish. Semigloss comes closest to the look of real marble.◇

FOUR TIPS ON MARBLEIZING FLOORS

While perhaps the best advice one could give a first-time marbleizer is to find a piece of marble to copy, then buy some paint and fearlessly plunge in and give it a go (one quickly learns from trial and error; the floor, after all, can always be repainted), here are a few suggestions that might help.

- When doing a floor, even in a relatively small room it is a good idea to lay down a grid pattern (see page 96) and do your marbleizing square by square. It is much easier to work on one small area at a time, and your finished work will look more like real marble. Change the direction of your banding and veining from square to square.
- Stick to the more common marble colors—beiges, off-whites, grays, gray-greens. Although real marble comes in many, many colors, the rarer and more unusual types will be difficult to make look real.
- Try to have an actual piece of marble in mind while you work. Or find a color photograph of an actual piece of marble or a photograph of something that has been marbleized. You probably won't be able to copy it exactly, but you will get the general idea.
- Working on precut Masonite squares (as suggested on page 95 for stenciling a floor) has several advantages: When glued or nailed down, they will look like actual squares of marble. It's a way to hide a bad floor. The spaces between floor boards will not be a distraction as they might be if your marbleizing is done directly on the floor. If you botch up one or two squares, they can easily be given another base coat and you can start over.

VEVA CROZER'S FLOORCLOTHS

Hand-painted and heavily varnished floorcloths were popular in 18th- and 19th-century England and America as an alternative to expensive carpets and tiles. While not really a technique of applying paint directly on the floor, a floorcloth is a good cheap way to cover a floor and in recent years they've had a wonderful renaissance. Floorcloths are still inexpensive, but with modern fast-drying paints and polyurethanes, they are much easier to produce than they were a century ago.

Floorcloths lend themselves to a staggering array of designs, from simple checkerboards to complicated Indian rug patterns, from antique quilt designs to neo-Art Deco shapes, from borrowings from Greek vases to simple high-tech grids. A world of choices is at your feet.

Most designs—and by all means, don't forget about stencils for floorcloths—will probably work out best if you take the trouble to put the design down first on graph paper an then transfer it to a grid on the cloth itself (see How To Use a Grid, page 96).

Use the finished cloth only on a smooth, hard-surface floor. Avoid the temptation to use a pad underneath; this would cause the brittle surface to crack when it is walked on. If your floorcloth has a tendency to slide around, keep it in one place with double-sided carpet tape.

Here is how to go about the quite easy task of creating a floorcloth as outlined by designer Veva Crozer. Even if you don't consider yourself the least bit artistic and you are not interested in tackling complex designs, keep in mind that one of these floorcloths painted in a single

With a little care, floorcloths will last for years. See page 67.

color, perhaps with a wide, contrasting border, can look stunning.

Your floorcloth will look better for longer if you stick to medium to dark colors. Pastels will look fine at first, but any floorcloth develops cracks over time and they show up less on the darker tones.

MATERIALS

Umprimed or primed (a lot more expensive) artists' canvas; available at artists' supply stores. Buy enough to allow for a 1½″ edging.

Cheap, white water-base paint, if you are using unprimed canvas.

Water-base interior paint for the main or background coat in whatever color you choose.

Large paintbrush or cheap sponge brushes in a variety of sizes.

Pencil.

Ruler.

Masking tape (optional).

Tubes of acrylic artists' paints in colors you choose for the design.

Small paintbrush.

Polyurethane.

White glue.

METHOD

1. Decide on the size and shape you want your design to be, then cut the canvas so that it is 1½″ wider than your design all around.

2. Lay out the canvas on a clean floor. If the canvas is unprimed, give it a coat of white water-base paint. Allow it to dry thoroughly. It may need a second prime coat for good coverage.

3. Pencil a crisp line 1½″ in from the edge of the canvas on all sides. This border will later be turned under to make a finished edging.

4. Cover the canvas with your main background coat right up to the penciled line. You might want to put masking tape along the line for a cleaner edge, but it's really not necessary. Depending upon the color and the quality of the paint, you might need a second or even a third coat—perhaps preceded by a light sanding. If your design has no main background color but has several large color areas instead (either as background or the total design), follow the same procedure. That is, keep the design within the border and give second and third coats as necessary.

5. When the background paint is dry, lightly chalk down your grid (if you are using one) and then the outlines of your design.

6. Mix your acrylic paint and begin painting (or cut stencils and begin stenciling). Tips: It is usually a good idea to start with the predominant color. Make sure you've mixed enough paint—matching is difficult.

7. Allow the work to dry thoroughly, using care not to mar the surface in any way, and then give your design two or three coats of polyurethane in the finish of your choice. Flat or semigloss will look less like linoleum than will high gloss.

8. When the polyurethane is dry, turn the canvas over and carefully fold under the 1½″ borders. Snip off a triangular piece of canvas from each corner, which will allow the folded-under canvas to miter itself and lie flat. Lay a heavy bead of glue in the fold, then brush out the glue to the edges. Press the border down, holding it in place with canned goods or other weights until completely dry and ready to use.

9. Touch up the edges if the paint cracks slightly. It is a good idea to give your floorcloth a light coat of liquid wax. You may want to apply a coat of polyurethane every year or so depending on the amount of wear your floorcloth gets.◇

This floorcloth was custom-made to fit the angled L shape of the kitchen.

STENCILING FOR FLOORS

The method for stenciling floors is basically the same as for walls (see page 80), but here are a few special tips.

• If your floor is in good shape, of a fairly decent wood with an attractive grain, you may want to use the grain pattern as a background for your stencil. If so, sand the floor, give it a coat of stain or dye, and then stencil. If your floor is less-than-wonderful or if you don't want to go to the trouble of sanding, you can give the floor a couple of coats of paint (oil-base) and then stencil on this background.

• In choosing a design, it is a good idea to stick with simplified versions of the symmetrical designs often found on traditional floor coverings—tiles and carpets, for instance.

• Consider adapting a design—simplifying and enlarging it, perhaps—or choosing colors already used in the room in curtains, upholstery, and so forth.

• As with walls, borders are a good way to use stencil designs on floors. They are also less work than an overall whole-floor job, and frequently look better. Simple, bold designs look good as borders: circles, triangles, arrow, and so forth, perhaps boxed in with stenciled lines or stripes.

• Since it is in the nature of stencils to be somewhat smudgy, which may not always look as good on a floor as it does on a wall, you may want to score the edges of the design with an awl through the stencil before doing the actual painting. This will help control the paint and also sharply delineate the design.

• For a square stencil pattern that covers the whole floor, decide on the size of your design and how much space you want between elements, then work out a grid pattern on your floor with squares the same size as your stencil; this will allow you to use the stencil itself as a guide.

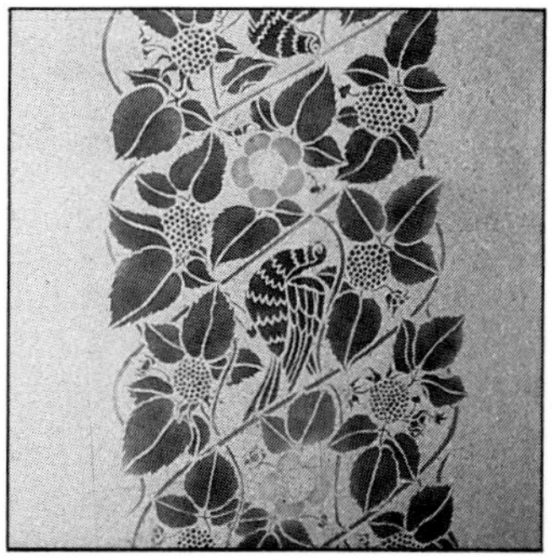

A stencil suitable for a floor in a large room. See also page 68.

• For an overall pattern, consider using *two* designs, alternating them either in checkerboard fashion or in "stripes." Also remember that with overall designs, big, bold shapes generally look best when spaced quite far apart; more complicated "feathery" designs look better when closer together.

• You will definitely want to give your stencil pattern a protective coating of varnish; you can therefore stencil with the same fast-drying acrylics that you use on walls.

• If your floor is in very bad condition, you might want to think about "tiling" with squares of stenciled Masonite. Have your lumberyard cut the Masonite into squares (any size—even as large as 2′ or 3′), then prime, paint, stencil, and varnish the "tiles" before gluing (or perhaps nailing) them down. Before laying the squares, it's a good idea to dampen the backs to prevent edges from curling and buckling.

PRACTICAL POLYURETHANE

While a polyurethane finish is like a varnish—indeed, the term "polyurethane varnish" is often used—the coating provided by "poly" is harder, more durable, and more water-resistant than regular varnish. Polyurethane can be used as a finish all by itself, or as a protective coating over almost anything else—stains, dyes, most types of paint, and even wallpaper. While this protection is useful, and often necessary, beware that polyurethane always tends to darken any surface.

If you are using polyurethane as a finish on a newly sanded floor, your first coat should be a sealer; for this, use a very thinned-down (half and half) solution of polyurethane and mineral spirits. When this is dry apply at least two more coats of straight poly. Allow each coat to dry for at least 24 hours, even though it may be dry to the touch before that. After a couple of days, apply two coats of paste wax, buffing each with an electric floor polisher (rentable at hardware stores).

"Poly" brings out the natural beauty of a floor. See page 66.

On large surfaces such as floors, by far the quickest way of applying polyurethane is by roller, however rollers tend to leave air bubbles, so you should go over the still-wet surface with a dry brush to get out these bubbles.

Polyurethane comes in matte, semigloss, and high gloss finishes, and should always be used in well ventilated areas.

HOW TO USE A GRID

A grid makes it easy to align a black and white floor.

Except for totally random "accidental"-type work (marbleizing, for instance), most decorations that you put on large surfaces such as floors will need a bit of planning. The best way to ensure that the elements of your design will be properly placed and proportioned is to use graph paper and a full-size grid on the floor itself.

Carefully measure your floor and then decide what size unit will be most useful for you to work with (you may want to tailor your design to fit the dimensions of your floor; the more intricate the design, the more squares you will want in your grid). Measure squares of this size both up and down the floor, then count off the same number of squares in both directions on the graph paper to make an exact scale model of the floor.

Work out your design on the graph paper (if you want to *trace* a pattern or a picture, use graph tracing paper) and then transfer it, square by square, with chalk, charcoal, or soft lead pencil, to the floor. A grid on the floor is also handy, if not essential, for checkerboard and other "tile" patterns, as well as for stenciling that will cover the entire floor.

A diagonal grid pattern for checkerboards, stencils, and so forth, will always create the illusion of a larger room, and it's easy to do. First lay out a regular grid, then—perhaps using different color chalk to avoid confusion—draw or snap lines diagonally across the floor, using opposite corners of the squares as a guide. Carefully wipe away or erase the lines of the first grid and the diagonal one is ready to use.

UTILIZING LIGHT

Lighting is—or should be—one of the most important and dramatic elements in decorating. It can alter shapes and colors, emphasize details, enhance textures, disguise faults. It can generally make everything look better—better furnished, better finished, better designed. But, versatile as it can be, lighting has always been one of the most confusing of the decorating elements, and this has never been more true than today, with the welter of fixtures, fittings, and bulbs available. Most people are aware that there are many new concepts of lighting that they should somehow be taking advantage of, but they are often bewildered by the choices and beleaguered by the prices. And even if one is fairly knowledgeable about what is obtainable in today's market, it is extremely difficult to know how a particular light or lighting system will work when it finally is in place in your home (see box, page 100).

Perhaps it is easier to understand light and use it to its best advantage if you recall what Douglas Baker and I said in our book, *Lighting Your Home: A Practical Guide.* Think about light in three distinct categories—general or background, local or task, and accent or decorative. To be well lighted—as opposed to *brightly* lighted, which people all too often seem to think is the meaning of the term—every room in your house should have some lighting of the first two types, and rooms that are used a lot should have all three types.

General or background lighting is a low level of illumination for a particular area; it is really a sort of foundation on which to build other lighting. General lighting is usually provided by ceiling or wall fixtures, concealed lights behind baffles or valances, or by floor or table lamps.

Local or task lighting is for work or other specific activity. In living areas it is most often supplied by table, desk, or floor lamps. In kitchens and work rooms, fluorescent or incandescent strips and/or spots are usual for this purpose. In bathrooms, a strip of bulbs just above or at the sides of a mirror might do the job, as could downlights over baths and basins.

Accent or decorative lighting is used to emphasize specific details such as paintings or sculpture—or else used simply as decoration. More than either of the other types, accent lighting can instantly change the mood or look of a room. For this lighting you can use various types of spots, projectors, uplights, downlights, or even strings of Christmas tree lights concealed behind narrow baffles.

There is one aspect of lighting that is not confusing in the least: price. All types of store-bought lamps, lights, and fixtures are expensive and—with the exception of uplights, floor lamps, and table lamps—generally cost a good deal to install. Happily, anyone who is imaginative and somewhat handy can save a considerable amount of money by improvising their own fixtures. In this section you will find good ideas for doing just that. I am not talking about major rewiring here, because this should always be done by a professional, never attempted by an amateur.

The following is a list of some terms that I hope will make these projects easier and less threatening.

LIGHTING TERMS YOU SHOULD KNOW

BAFFLE. Specifically, something that obstructs. In lighting, a baffle is usually a narrow panel behind which light bulbs or tubes are concealed in order to direct light in a particular direction or to create indirect lighting.

BAKELITE. A type of lightweight plastic.

BALLAST. A small electrical device that stabilizes the current in fluorescent tubes and other lamps that operate on vapor or gas.

CANOPY. In electricity, the caplike cover that fits over and conceals wires and other hardware in a ceiling light fixture.

DOWNLIGHT. Any light that casts its light down.

KEYLESS SOCKET. In this sense, keyless means lacking a switch. Keyless sockets come in various styles and materials, each for specific applications, but all have a female receptor, usually threaded, that holds a light bulb and in which the bulb makes contact with a power source.

PANHEAD SCREW. A screw with a flattened head used in metal work.

RACEWAY. In contracting or electrical work, a raceway is a covered metal channel that houses and protects electrical wires.

TWO-CONDUCTOR WIRE. The type of wire commonly seen around the home as extension cord, lamp cord, and so forth. The two conductors—themselves actually two separate "wires" made up of many thin twisted strands—are separated by a crease or seam.

UPLIGHT. Any light fixture that shines light up. Also used as another word for the descriptively named can light. These fixtures are usually found on the floor (and sometimes on a table) shining up on walls and/or ceilings.

VALANCE. A narrow panel used in window decoration to conceal the top of curtains or draperies that is also sometimes used as a baffle (q.v.) for lighting.

JUG OR BOTTLE TABLE LAMP

By using a kit available at hardware, housewares, or well-stocked dime stores, you can make a simple, inexpensive lamp out of a jug or bottle (or any other object that has a small opening at the top and is heavy enough to support a socket and a shade).

These kits come in various styles, but they basically consist of a bulb socket, a plastic or cork fitting, and a cord and plug. The cord sometimes comes out of the side of the socket (as in the diagram); sometimes it drops out of the bottom of the plastic or cork fitting. The latter configuration allows you to make a lamp with the cord going *through* the jug or bottle. Some kits come with a harp (the two-wire hoop with a threaded portion on top for holding the shade); sometimes you must buy the harp separately.

Installing the kit is seldom more complicated than simply pushing the cork or plastic down inside the neck of the vessel, screwing in a bulb, mounting an appropriate shade, plugging the cord into an outlet, and turning it on.

However, if you buy the kind of kit that has the cord coming out of the bottom of the socket, you will have to drill a hole in the bottom of the jug or bottle. A power drill and a special drill bit will be necessary for this drilling—a tungsten carbide-tipped bit for masonry, a special glass-drilling bit for bottles. Drilling glass must be done very carefully, for bottle glass is often poor quality and may splinter. Always wear safety goggles when drilling glass or masonry.

The accompanying diagram shows this kind of kit installed in a bottle. ◇

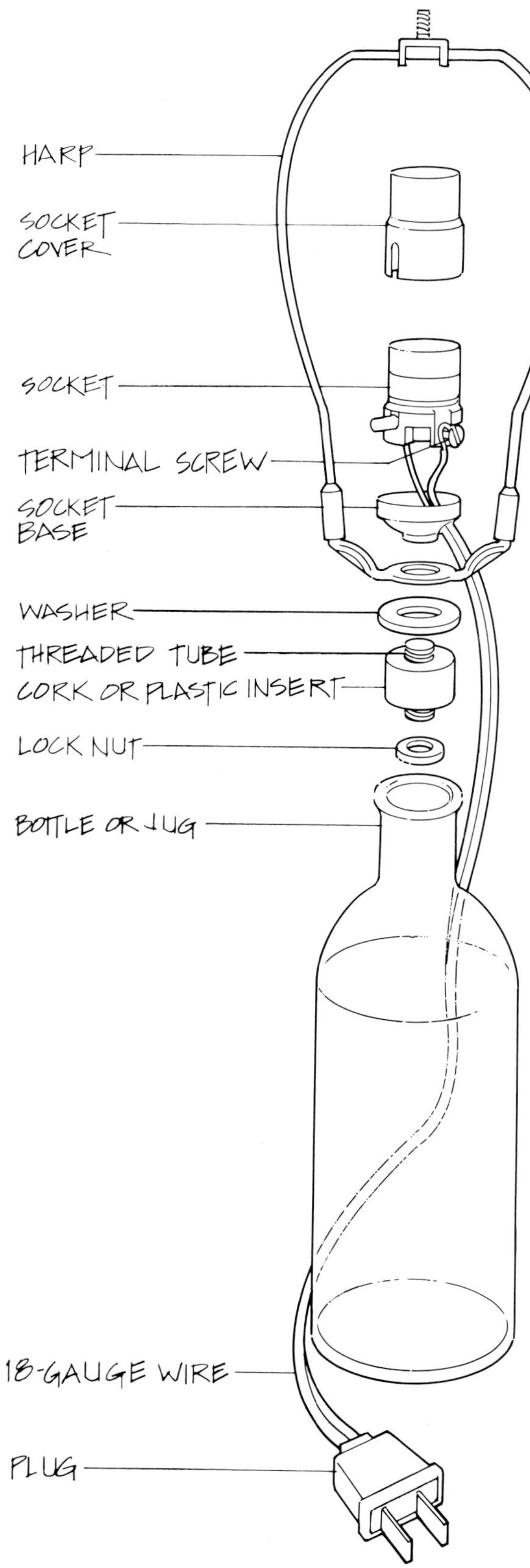

A DRAIN TILE UPLIGHT

Uplights, or can lights, are used for their instant, subtle, indirect light without any of the hassle of recessing, rewiring, and refinishing walls and ceilings. Shining up through the leaves of a large plant, or reflecting off softly glowing walls, uplights add immediate theatricality to a room. While there are many different styles available in stores, a very serviceable and attractive uplight can be made out of a clay drain tile (found at builders' supply outlets or well-stocked lumberyards). Actually, a light such as this could be made out of virtually any plastic, metal, ceramic, or pottery object that has a fairly wide opening at the top.

MATERIALS

A clay drain tile about 12″ long, with at least a 3½″ *inside* diameter.

About ½ a foot square of wood, plywood, or Masonite, not more than ¼″ thick.

Lamp-type keyless socket.

18-gauge two-conductor wire.

Length of ⅜″ threaded tubing, or nipple, about 1½″ long, with washers and two lock nuts. (Note: The commonly used threaded tubing is called "⅛" IPS, but is actually ⅜″ in diameter. That size threads into the bottom of most standard sockets.)

Epoxy adhesive.

On-line on-off switch.

Standard two-prong plug.

40-watt standard bulb or 30-watt spot.

ASSEMBLY

1. Carefully measure the inside diameter of the drain tile, then cut the ¼″-thick wood into a disk that fits snugly inside. Drill a 7⁄16″ hole in the center of the disk.

2. Wire the socket (see page 106), passing the wire out through the center hole in the socket base and through the ½″-long threaded tubing, or nipple.

3. Thread the nipple into the base of the socket. Screw one lock nut onto the nipple all the way up against the base.

4. For added reflection, paint the inside of the tile white, leaving a 4″-wide unpainted area at the bottom.

5. When the paint is dry, drill a ¼″ hole in the tile near the bottom, using the masonry bit.

6. Fit the disk inside the tile about 3″ up from the bottom, then mix the epoxy adhesive according to package directions and cement the disk in place. Place the tile on its side while the epoxy is setting.

7. Insert the socket from the top of the pipe, threading the wire through the hole in the disk. Seat the ⅜″ nipple in the hole in the disk. From the bottom of the pipe, fasten the socket in place with another lock nut tightened onto the nipple. The socket should stand upright and centered in the upper portion of the pipe.

8. Thread the wire out through the ¼″ hole, then add an on-line switch at a convenient location along the cord. Usually, installing an on-line switch necessitates cutting and removing a ½″ section from one of the two conductors of the wire, then taking the switch apart, placing the wires where indicated on the inside of the switch, then screwing the two halves back together.

9. Install a plug to end of cord, screw in a bulb, and your light is ready to use.

VARIATION

A common everyday clay flowerpot can be used to make a good uplight using much the same techniques as above. The advantage of a flowerpot is that most of them already have a hole in the bottom. Use a pot that is fairly deep and not too big around. You might be able to use a store-bought, prewired bottle lamp kit (see facing page) and forgo the wooden disk, if you epoxy-glue the cork or plastic fitting right into the hole in the bottom. You would, of course, have to cut the plug off to get the cord through the hole, then rewire it. ◇

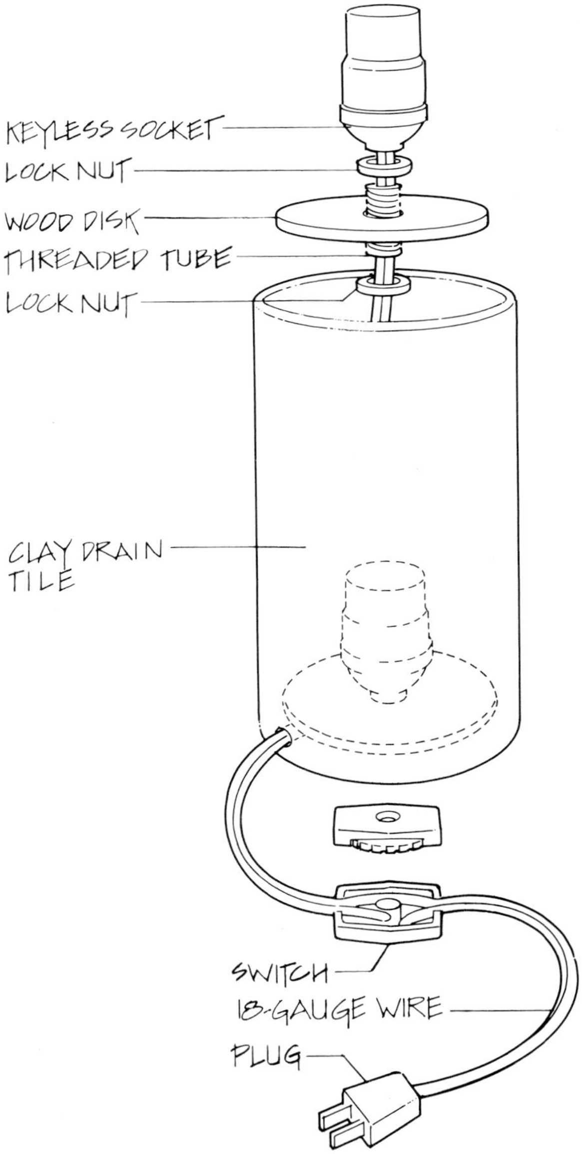

MIRROR LIGHTS

A strip of small globe lights along the sides or across a dressing table or bathroom mirror not only has a jazzy look, but also provides good light for close work. Bonnie August's bedroom and Richard Sygar's bathroom feature this kind of lighting made with Plugmold® 2100, a type of electrical raceway. This raceway, which comes unwired, has special sockets that clip right onto the U-shaped base; the cover is scored every few inches so that it can easily be split into sections that snap onto the base in the spaces between sockets.

MATERIALS

Length of Plugmold 2100.

End fittings and mounting hardware.

Spray paint.

White porcelain Plugmold keyless sockets.

18-gauge two-conductor wire, long enough to wire sockets in molding and then reach an outlet.

On-line on-off switch.

Spherical frosted 25-watt bulbs.

ASSEMBLY

1. Spray-paint the base, cover, and other hardware in the color of your choice. It will probably take at least two coats to get a good hard finish.

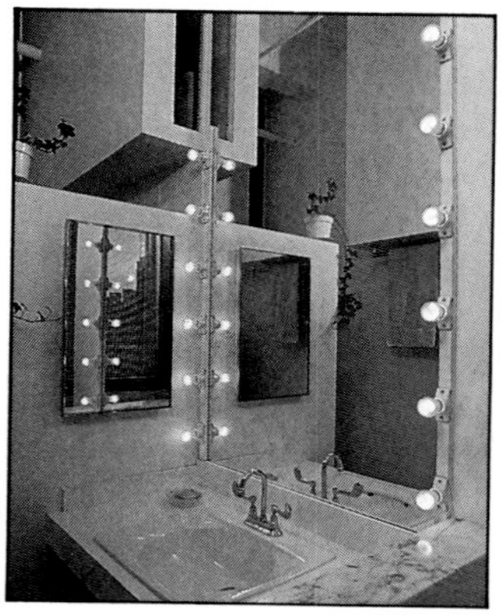

Many configurations are possible with this type of homemade strip lighting. See page 70.

2. Position the Plugmold 2100 at the sides of the mirror or across it (or in whatever configuration you wish) for mounting, using the predrilled mounting holes. If the molding will be flat against the wall, 2″ screws will usually be long enough; if the Plugmold 2100 crosses in front of the mirror, it will have to be held out from the wall by spacer blocks, and longer screws will have to be used. If it is impossible to find a stud, it may be necessary to use plastic anchors, molly bolts, or toggle bolts to mount the Plugmold 2100.

The reflection from bulbs close to a mirror almost doubles the light. See page 59.

3. With the cover off, snap the keyless sockets onto the base, spaced 3″ apart.

4. To wire the sockets, split apart enough of the wire to run the length of the Plugmold raceway. Then strip insulation as needed to wrap wire once around each positive terminal screw. Repeat with the other wire for the negative side.

5. Snap apart the cover into 3″-long pieces. Clip the cover pieces to the base between the socket fixtures.

6. Snap on the end caps, one of which should have an opening for the wire to pass through. Attach on-line switch at some convenient location. Extend the wire to an outlet, perhaps attaching it to baseboard, cornice, or ceiling with clips or electricians' staples. Install plug to end of wire.

7. Twist bulbs into sockets. Plug fixture into outlet. ◇

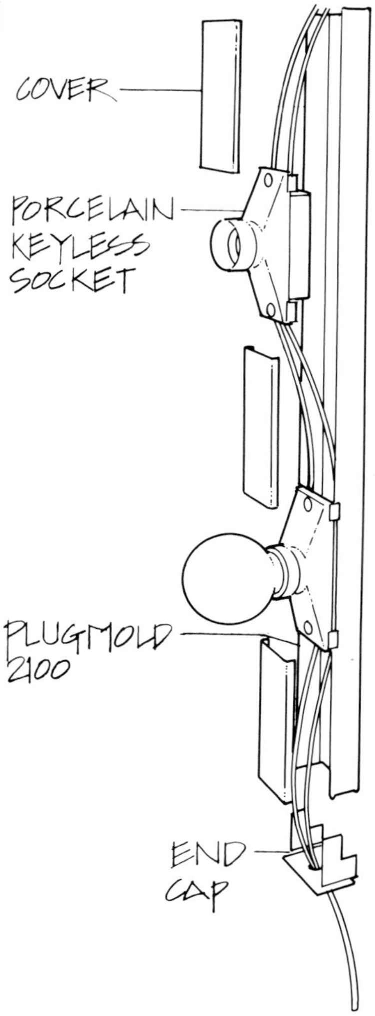

DISCOVERING WHAT WORKS BEST

It can be very expensive to go out and buy a fixture that you think will provide you with the sort of light you want and then discover it does not work; you cannot borrow fittings on approval. Yet to make lighting work for you, you have to be able to decide on the direction, kind, and placement of light that will suit your way of life, room, and possessions. But how do you experiment?

A most useful piece of equipment to invest in is a lamp with a bell-shaped metal hood and a swiveling spring clamp, available inexpensively in any hardware store, that will be useful as a work lamp for testing the quality, quantity, and direction of light best suited to different situations. You can clamp it to the leg of a chair, the edge of a door or table, or a brick or piece of wood on the floor, and experiment with it to determine what sort of light looks best where, where it should come from and at what angle, and what different kinds and wattages of bulbs will work best for your particular needs and tastes. Besides ordinary bulbs you could invest in a 100-watt spot bulb. You could make your experiments even more successful by buying an inexpensive on-line dimmer switch for your work lamp.

SUSPENDED TRACK LIGHTING

Commercial track lighting is versatile, contemporary looking, and has many advantages. It can be mounted on walls and ceilings of almost any material and in a wide variety of configurations: down or across the middle of a ceiling; along one, two, three, or all four sides of a ceiling; even down a wall. Its lamps can be variously positioned and aimed in all directions—they can be used to wash walls with light, pick out specific objects or areas, or for general room light. And should you move, you can take it with you.

It is, alas, expensive.

However, by using Plugmold 2000—prewired electrical raceway with regularly spaced outlets—you can put together a very reasonable (in look, function, and price) facsimile of "real" track lighting. Plugmold 2000 comes in 1′, 3′, 5′, and 6′ lengths, with outlets every 6″ or more. These instructions are for suspended track, but if you have a relatively low ceiling you can mount this molding directly into the ceiling.

MATERIALS

Lengths of Plugmold 2000, according to your needs.

One bulb plug (that turns a plug-in outlet into a screw-in socket) per light.

Spray paint.

Small-gauge chain or copper, brass, or stainless steel wire.

Screw eyes.

Plastic anchors, molly bolts, or toggle bolts, if necessary.

18-gauge two-conductor wire.

Plugmold 2000 hardware (end caps, cover clips).

On-line on-off switch or dimmer.

50- to 75-watt spot bulbs.

ASSEMBLY

1. Spray-paint the Plugmold 2000, if necessary.

2. Connect wires of two or more lengths of Plugmold if you are using more than one; shield the joint with a cover clip after wire is installed.

3. Attach end caps, one of which should be an entrance fitting with an opening that will allow wires to pass through.

4. Splice the 18-gauge wire to the Plugmold wires. Install on-line switch or dimmer at convenient location on the cord.

5. To suspend track, knock out sets of two adjoining mounting screw holes on the back of the Plugmold strip at 2′ to 3′ intervals. Thread wire or chain down and up through the holes. Attach screw eyes to ceiling the same distance apart as the holes in Plugmold 2000, using plastic anchors, toggle bolts, or molly bolts if necessary. Attach wire or chain to screw eyes so that your track hangs at the proper level.

6. Twist bulbs into bulb plugs, plug in the cord, and turn on your track.

VARIATION

This kind of lighting can also be made to work in many other situations besides ceiling or wall track: as a line of light beaming down from a baffle up near the ceiling; over a work area in a kitchen; as a different kind of vanity strip lighting; or, as it is found in the living room of Peter Blaustein, glowing up from the floor between the wall and a built-in ramp. ◇

An original use of Plugmold strips. See pages 25 and 71.

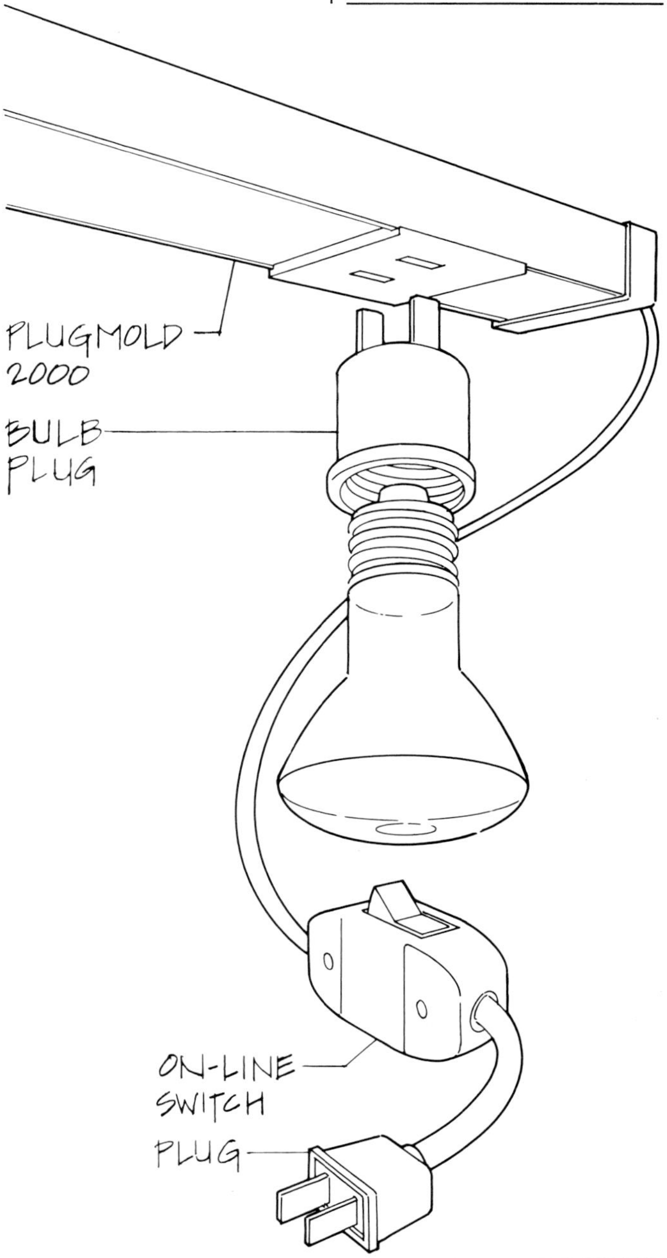

INDUSTRIAL BATHROOM LIGHTING

Normal-size vanity fixtures look fine with most mirrors, but an oversize mirror may call for something more substantial looking. Bill Engel used lengths of deep U-shaped raceway (available at electrical supply houses) and heavy-duty porcelain keyless sockets with screw-on caps to make the light fixtures on either side of the large mirror in the bathroom of his parents' home. The lengths of the fixtures and the number of lights may be varied to suit a specific situation, but here is one way to do it.

MATERIALS

Two 36″ lengths of raceway that is at least as deep as the bottom part of the porcelain fixtures.

10 white, flush-mounted, 110-volt a.c. keyless sockets, with screw-on caps.

14-gauge two-conductor wire, long enough to wire sockets in each molding box and then reach an outlet.

End caps and other hardware, if used.

On-line on-off switch or rotary dimmers.

10 frosted, spherical 25-watt bulbs.

ASSEMBLY

1. Snap off the top pieces (lid) of the raceway. Drill five equidistant pilot holes down the length of each lid. On these centers, cut or punch out larger holes (probably 1¼″ or 1½″, depending on the brand and size of the socket) with a circle cutter or chassis punch.

2. Have the lids, bases, end caps, and other hardware spray-painted in the color of your choice by an auto body shop, or spray-paint it yourself.

3. Position the raceway boxes on the wall next to the mirror for mounting. Most come with predrilled mounting holes every 2″, 8″, or 11″. If possible, position each box over a wall stud and mount them with panhead screws long enough to reach through the plaster and lath and into the wall stud—typically, a 2″ screw is long enough. If a stud is inaccessible or cannot be located, it may be necessary to wall-mount the raceway with screws in plastic anchors, molly bolts, or toggle bolts.

4. Fit porcelain sockets through holes in lids, screw on caps to secure sockets to lids. For each box, split at least 3′ of the wire in two. Connect all the positive terminal screws in one box to one wire, stripping the insulation as needed to wrap the wire once around each screw. Repeat with the other wire for the negative side.

5. When boxes are wired, snap the raceway lids and end caps back into place on the wall-mounted boxes. If end caps do not have predrilled or scored knock-out openings, drill a ¼″ hole in whichever caps are closest to existing outlets. Thread wires through the openings. Attach on-line switches or dimmers at convenient locations. Play out wires to an outlet or outlets, perhaps attaching wire to baseboard, cornice, or ceiling with clips or electricians' staples. Install male plugs to ends of wires.

6. Twist bulbs into sockets. Plug in fixtures. ◇

Oversize fixtures for an oversize mirror. *See page 48.*

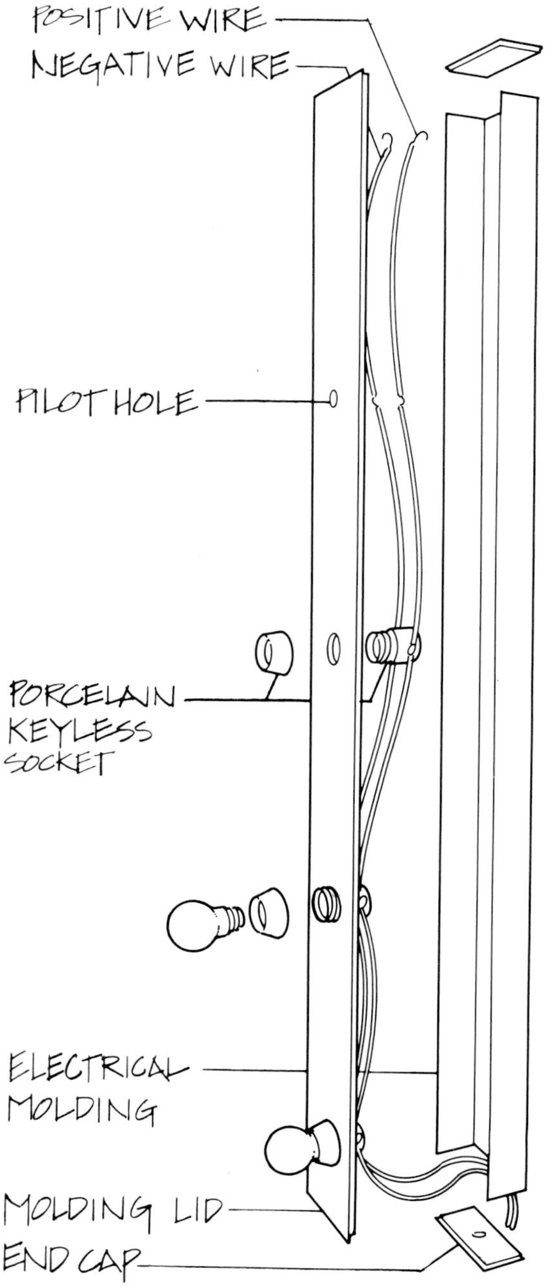

COILCORD CHANDELIER

The design of this attractive ceiling fixture was made possible by the introduction to the consumer of a corkscrew-type product called coilcord. Long a feature of telephone equipment and industrial applications where tidy power cords are essential, the spiral wire is now available in 110-volt a.c. in assorted colors. The chandelier effect is achieved here by draping the coilcord as it suspends five clustered lights housed in industrial shades.

MATERIALS

Five decorative hooks that can be mounted into a plaster or drywall ceiling.

Five lengths of white coilcord.

Five lamp-type keyless sockets, preferably Bakelite.

Five lightweight, factory-type shades, preferably aluminum.

Five medium-watt frosted incandescent bulbs.

One wall-mount rotary dimmer switch, if necessary.

ASSEMBLY

1. On the ceiling, measure and mark a circle around a ceiling light box (if one does not already exist where you want it, you will have to call upon the services of an electrician). This circle will determine the location of the decorative hooks and the lamps below them, so the circle's size should be determined by the size and type of table to be illuminated. (In the Frazers' dining room, the circle has a radius of about 14″.)

2. Mark locations for hooks at five equidistant points around the circle (every 72°, that is). Mount the hooks in the ceiling; you may have to use plastic anchors, molly bolts, or toggle bolts if the plaster is weak.

3. Wire all the coilcords to the keyless sockets, then thread the cords through the center holes in the shades. The lightweight shades can simply rest on the sockets.

4. Drape each coilcord over its ceiling hook; this will hold things in place while completing your chandelier. Slip the cords through the canopy (the shallow canister that hides the wiring of the ceiling box) and splice the cords' conductor wires to the two wires in the ceiling box. Probably the best way to do this is to twist the positive wires and negative wires of all five coilcords into two large leads and then secure them to the main positive and negative wire with two large wire nuts. Replace the canopy over the completed wiring. Twist in the bulbs.

5. Adjust the coilcords up or down on their hooks to achieve the proper level. Install the rotary dimmer if the present wall switch is a standard type. ◇

MICHAEL DUNNE

These lights can be adjusted up or down by moving the coilcord on the ceiling hooks. *See page 62.*

FLUORESCENCE

Fluorescent lighting has long been used in the home: Kitchens, bathrooms, basements, and other places generally considered as work spaces have traditionally been lighted by its somewhat harsh glow. If they were found in other areas of the home at all, it was as indirect lighting behind baffles or valances, or diffused with translucent plastic panels, often in ceilings. But recently, home decorators have discovered the *colored* fluorescent.

Whether throwing an aurora of strong orange up onto a wall from behind a sofa or casting a cool green wash over a room from a bare bulb propped in a corner, the venerable fluorescent tube has found a new niche in home decorating.

Fluorescent tubes "light" because the inner wall of the glass tube is coated with phosphors that glow when an electric charge is passed through gas in the tube, so a fluorescent requires completely different hardware from an incandescent bulb. It must be mounted on a platform or box that has special female receptors and it also must have a kind of transformer called a ballast as well as a small cylindrical starter. Fluorescents are more expensive to install than incandescents, but they give off far more light per watt of electricity, and the bulbs last a lot longer.

A WOK-LID LIGHT FIXTURE

The lid of a wok can be turned into a functional light for over a dining table. The lid's bowllike shape is reminiscent of the popular industrial shade; it is lightweight and, with the handle removed, has a hole already drilled in exactly the spot you want it.

MATERIALS

An aluminum wok lid in whatever diameter will fit your needs.

Length of ½″ copper plumbing pipe, as long as needed. (You can substitute thin-wall conduit; it's cheaper, but harder to work since the bends must be made with a tubing bender.)

18-gauge two-conductor wire, as long as needed.

Conduit hangers, with mounting screws.

Lamp-type keyless socket with a ½″ diameter threaded opening at the bottom.

On-line on-off switch or dimmer.

Standard, two-prong plug.

50-watt mirror-dome reflector bulb.

ASSEMBLY

1. Enlarge, if necessary, the hole in the wok lid so that the ½″ pipe will just fit into it.

2. Rough up the surface of the lid with emery paper, then spray-paint it the color of your choice. (Leave the inside unpainted or paint it white to increase the amount of light that will be reflected.)

3. Have a plumber or plumbing supplier cut a 1″-long thread on the outside of the copper pipe.

This wok has moved from the kitchen to the dining room. See page 12.

4. Feed the wire through the pipe. There should be enough wire at the fixture end to attach the socket; enough at the other end to reach an outlet.

5. Carefully measure the distance from the point in the air where the lamp will hang, up to the ceiling, across the ceiling and down the wall. Bend the copper pipe to fit. This installation will probably look best if the pipe ends more or less directly above a wall outlet. The pipe should end about half or three-quarters of the way down the wall so that the on-off or dimmer switch can be placed in a convenient spot.

6. Secure the tubing to the ceiling and wall with three or more hangers as needed. If the ceiling is of dubious strength, mount the hanger screws in plastic anchors, molly bolts, or toggle bolts.

7. Slip the wok lid onto the threaded end of the tubing and secure it in place with ½″ lock nuts or conduit connector. Strip the wires and attach them to the socket (see page 106) then thread the socket onto the end of the tubing.

8. Install the on-line switch or dimmer at a convenient place on the wire and a male plug at the end. Twist in the bulb and you're on. ◇

A VERSATILE PRODUCT

Plugmold Systems are manufactured by The Wiremold Company, a maker of a broad line of electrical distribution products generally used in commercial applications. Plugmold Systems are multiple-outlet raceways made in a variety of styles. Most types are prewired and several are a boon to home-lighting innovators. Available from electrical suppliers.

Plugmold 2000.

OVERHAULING A STANDING LAMP

As with many undertakings, the actual task is much less daunting than it may seem at first. How to restore and rewire standing lamps is one such project. The good thing about knowing how to do it is that old, nonworking standing lamps are not only useful and often very decorative, but they are common objects to be found at the back of the attic and inexpensive items in second-hand shops.

Cast or fabricated-metal floor lamps can often be refinished and rewired with a minimum of difficulty. If the metal has a plated finish, it cannot be stripped, but it *can* be painted another color. First rough up the entire surface with No. 120-180 emery paper (to provide "tooth" for the paint), then with a tack cloth wipe it free from dust. Cover any openings and switch (if it seems to be working) with paper and masking tape, and spray-paint the lamp.

If a metal lamp has a painted finish, it can be stripped with ordinary paint remover, then given a final clean-up with fine emery paper (No. 220 or finer) or steel wool. Do not use any abrasive until you know the type and condition of the metal that lies under the paint; it would be a shame to scratch irrevocably the surface of an otherwise-fine brass or pewter lamp. If what lies beneath the paint is an undistinguished steel or bronze metal finish, the brushed-metal look achieved by careful scouring with steel wool could be an asset. First, completely strip the lamp of any and all former paint, then scour it all over with medium steel wool, then fine steel wool. For a glossy final finish over the burnished metal, apply a spray enamel, such as Krylon.

Austin Chinn found and restored this 1930s torchere. *See page 41.*

If there is any doubt at all about the condition of the old electrical socket, cord, switch, or plug, replace them. First, determine what type of socket was originally installed (metal or porcelain, one-way or three-way) and how the socket is mounted. The replacement you purchase should be similar if not identical for ease of installation. If the switch arrangement cannot be duplicated, install an on-line switch on a new lamp cord (18-gauge two-conductor wire).

Before pulling all the old wires out of the lamp, figure out how they are routed through the body of the lamp. If openings are small or other difficulties with threading the wire through the lamp seem likely, it may be a good idea to tape the old and new wires together securely by butting their ends together and then wrapping them tightly with masking tape or friction tape. The new wire will be threaded through automatically when you pull out the old one. ◇

DESIGNERS' TRICKS WITH BULBS

Once you begin to realize that you can play around with light and use it to make changes in a room—to pep it up or calm it down, say, or make more subtle differences—you will find it useful to understand the uses to which different colors of bulbs can be put.

- Pink bulbs will warm up any lamp and make its light much more flattering. Use pink in white or blue rooms and in table lamps.
- Blue and green bulbs will calm down light, make it much cooler. Use in hot weather, in rooms you want to make feel cool and shadowy.
- Cool white fluorescent tubes used behind shutters, baffles, or valances at the sides of or above windows will give an impression of sunlight filtering through. Use them in generally dark and gloomy rooms during the day, not by night when this kind of light is too harsh.
- Warm white fluorescents offer good light for kitchens; their light enhances food much more than the cool white varieties.
- Colored filters or gels come in all sorts of colors and can be fitted over the tops of bulbs to totally change the mood and feeling of a room. Red will make it warm and glowing; green, dark and mysterious; blue, ghostly.
- To make rooms seem much larger, flood the walls with light from bright bulbs that are either recessed or put on track about 18″ to 2′ out from the wall. Place uplights in corners so that the harsh outlines of a room become diffused.

WIRING A SOCKET

Knowing how to connect a wire to a socket is a handy thing to learn—and a real money-saver. Not only can you replace sockets in lamps if and when they wear out, but you can make a number of different kinds of lamps with easy-to-come-by parts. Wiring a socket is really quite simple; as the old saying goes, it's easy when you know how.

MATERIALS

Lamp-type socket.

Length of two-conductor wire.

Wire stripper, wire-cutting pliers, or knife.

Screwdriver.

METHOD

1. With a screwdriver, carefully pry off the bottom cover (base) of the socket. Then lift off the cover. Thread a length of 18-gauge two-conductor wire through the hole in this base.

2. With a knife or sharp fingernail, split the end of the wire, pulling it apart until you have two single wires about 1½″ long. Then with a stripper, a knife, or a lightly closed pair of wire-cutting pliers, strip about ¾″ of insulation. Do this gently. It's easy to chomp through both the plastic insulation *and* the fragile wires within. The idea is to cut through only the plastic insulation, then pull it off.

3. When the two lengths of multi-strand wire are exposed, twist each length individually between thumb and forefinger to roll and compress the strands into single stiff wires—that way, it is much easier to manage.

4. Locate the two terminal attachment points of the socket. Usually these are two ¼″ flathead metal screws, and often they're different colors or metals. With a screwdriver, back these terminal screws out about three complete turns. Do not unscrew them completely—the idea is to gain enough clearance to wrap one wire around the threaded part of the screw, then tighten the screw back down.

5. Wrap one of the stiffened wires around one of the screws in a clockwise direction. Otherwise, the strands in the wire will separate as the screw is tightened down. Attach the other wire around the other terminal screw in the same way. Check carefully to see that no part—not a single strand—of one wire is touching the other.

6. Carefully fit the cover back down over the socket, then snap the base in place again.◇

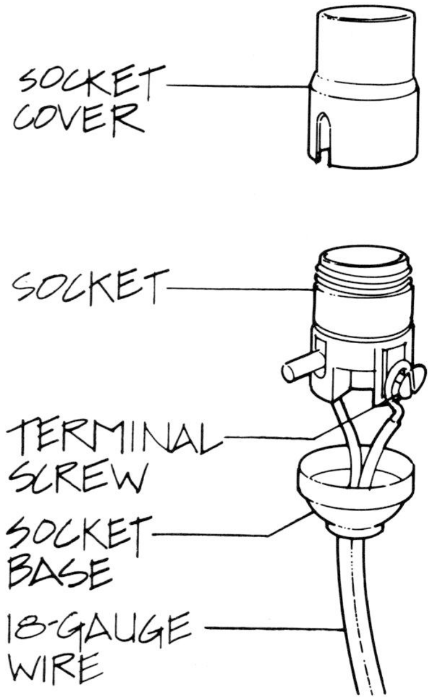

DIMMER SWITCHES

Dimmers are almost essential to any flexible or subtle lighting scheme, since they give a variety of illumination levels at the turn of a knob. They also save energy, bulb life, and operating costs. There are inexpensive dimmers that can be installed in place of the usual wall switch, as well as units that control several circuits from one point. There are also table lamp and floor lamp dimmers that will work with uplights. Dimmers with special ballasts can be operated with fluorescent tubes.

BUILDING THE BASICS

While the price of wood tends to cause a psychological condition that might best be termed "lumberyard shock," the fact remains that one of the best ways to save money on basic home furnishing items is to build them yourself. Besides saving money, there are other bonuses from do-it-yourself carpentry projects. For one thing, with a store-bought item you might have to compromise in terms of size and shape, whereas you can custom-make your own projects to whatever specifications your needs call for. Also, the quality will be much better than what you would buy in a store for the same amount of money.

Some of the projects suggested here call for precise cuts that can be made at home only with a fairly elaborate workshop setup. However, they can all be made at a lumberyard. If you do plan to have cuts such as these done by a lumber man, it is a good idea to find one you can trust. This will give you greater assurance that the sizes and cuts you ask for are what you will receive, and that you are getting the type and quality of wood you asked for. This is also a good source of advice about short-cuts and possible lower-cost substitutes—a good lumberyard can be a big help.

Whether you pay a lumber man to make all the major cuts or you do everything yourself, throughout these projects keep in mind the old cabinetmaker's adage: Measure five times, cut once. It's another way of saying "slow but steady wins the race," and it is nowhere more applicable than in the field of carpentry. Following this advice can save you a lot of time and frustration—and money.

The field of carpentry and woodworking—as with all specialized fields of endeavor—has its own jargon and its own idiosyncracies. Thus, at least a knodding acquaintance with some of these terms and peculiarities will help the novice feel more at home around the lumberyard and the hardware store. While the following won't make you an expert, it will give you the basic information needed to build carpentry projects presented here.

WOODWORKING TERMS YOU SHOULD KNOW

ANCHORS. Tubular fastening devices made of a variety of malleable materials; for use in solid walls. A hole is drilled and the anchor is inserted into the hole. When a screw or bolt is tightened into the hole, the anchor expands inside the hole and holds tight. (*See* Lead anchor, Plastic anchor.)

BACKSAW. A short handsaw with many teeth used for making smooth, straight cuts. A backsaw has a reinforced spine and is often used with a miter box.

BAFFLE. An upright structural member similar to a joist, that is used for reinforcing large flat surfaces.

BEVEL. To saw, plane, or file panels or boards at an angle so that two surfaces meet smoothly.

BOLT. A fastening device that usually has threads and a nut. Often used with a washer to increase strength. (*See* Carriage bolt, Molly bolt, Stove bolt, Toggle bolt.)

BUTT JOINT. A simple joint where the end of one board meets the side or face of a second board.

CARRIAGE BOLT. A coarse-threaded bolt with a round head and a faceted shank that bites into the wood as the bolt is tightened.

CEMENT-COATED BOX NAIL. *See* Nail, cement-coated box.

CHAMFER STRIP. A narrow, triangular strip of wood used to add strength and adhesive surface to a joint.

CHIPBOARD. A woodlike sheet of building material formed of compressed chips, sawdust, and adhesive. It is inexpensive, dense, stable, but it is also heavy and does not hold nails and screws well. It comes in $4' \times 8'$ sheets, and is also known as particleboard.

CIRCULAR SAW. An electric saw with a round blade used for making straight cuts on all types of wood. Circular saws can be table-mounted or hand-held.

CLEAT. A narrow strip of wood applied to a vertical surface for the purpose of supporting a horizontal surface, such as a shelf, counter, or table.

COMMON NAIL. *See* Nail, common.

CONTACT CEMENT. A strong adhesive for porous and nonporous surfaces, used for applying plastic laminate. It holds instantly, after being applied to both surfaces and allowed to dry. Smelly and flammable, it should be used only in a well-ventilated area.

CONTINUOUS HINGE. A long, thin hinge like the ones characteristically seen on pianos and other applications where the door or lid being hinged is fairly heavy and the weight must be distributed along a long, thin surface.

COUNTERSINK. To drill a conical hole (with a countersink drill bit) for the purpose of recessing a flathead wood screw below the surface.

CROSSCUT SAW. A saw used to cut across the grain and to cut very exact lengths. The wood is held in one place and the blade is drawn across the wood on its track.

DADO. A U-shaped groove, or trough, cut into the face of a piece of wood across the grain. It is often used as part of a dado joint, where the end of one board fits into a dado cut in another board.

DRILL STOP. A small adjustable device that controls drilling depth. Fits on drill or drill bit; many varieties.

DRYWALL. Sheetrock, gypsum board, and drywall are all names for the solid wall material often used instead of plaster. It comes in various thicknesses (⅝″ is standard for walls) and sheet sizes (4′ × 8′ is most common, but 4′ × 6′ and 4′ × 10′ are available).

DRYWALL TAPE. Paper tape that is used over joint compound to conceal seams in drywall.

EDGEMATE TAPE. A tape used to edge shelving or to give wooden edges a veneer. It comes in 8′ strips and in ¾″ and 1¼″ thicknesses. It is applied by heating the glue on one side with an iron and then ironing it on to shelving.

FILLERS. Two types of fillers are commonly used on wood: wood dough and spackle. The former is usually a compound of sawdust plus an adhesive, the latter is a fine-textured vinyl compound. Wood dough should be used to fill nail or screw holes where the final finish will be transparent—e.g., varnish. Spackle should be used where its white color will not show—e.g., under paint.

FINISHED LUMBER. The ready-cut (into widths and thicknesses, that is) wood that you buy at the lumberyard. It is the material used for beams, shelves, braces, and is usually priced by the linear foot. Most finished lumber is pine, and it comes in three grades: construction, common, and clear. Construction grade pine is unfinished raw board, also called "undressed" wood, and is used for very rough applications when looks and quality of the surface are no considerations whatsoever. Common pine is graded by number—1, 2, 3, 4, and 5—and the higher the number, the lower the quality (more knots, more pitch). Clear pine is graded by letter—A, B, C, and D—A being the best quality. For structural work that will never be seen, buying top-grade finished lumber is simply a waste of money. Note: It may pay to shop around; some lumberyards sell clear B pine that is far better than what other places pass off as clear A.

FINISHING NAIL. *See* Nail, finishing.

FORSTNER BIT. A drill bit with a round cutting head, used to drill shallow, flat-bottom depressions in wood. It should be gently tapped into the surface before starting to drill to ensure its being properly positioned.

FURRING STRIPS. Narrow (usually 1″ × 2″), rough-sawn strips of wood placed perpendicularly across beams to provide a surface for attaching drywall or other material.

GLUE BLOCK. A small strip or block of wood attached to the inside of a joint to provide added strength.

GROUT. Cement-like adhesive compound usually used between ceramic tiles.

HACKSAW. A small handsaw with interchangeable fine-toothed blades, used for making straight cuts in metal.

HOMOSOTE. A gray fiber-composition material with a soft, absorbent surface. It is somewhat like very heavy cardboard. Comes in ½″-thick, 4′ × 8′ panels. Good for sound deadening; more expensive than drywall, but easier to work with.

JIG. A jig is a template or pattern that assures accurate placement of a series of holes, notches, curves, or other such elements that must be repeated identically. (For how to make and use one type of jig, see pages 123–124.)

JIGSAW. A general name for a table-mounted or handheld saw with a narrow vertical blade made for cutting curves, shapes, and tight corners.

JOINT COMPOUND. A substance used between drywall panels. Drywall tape is applied over it to make a solid seam.

BUYING LUMBER

When buying lumber and planning a woodworking project you must remember that the *actual* dimensions are not the same as the *nominal* ones. The nominal dimensions are the size to which the lumber was rough sawn while green. The actual dimensions are what the lumber turns out to be after it has been dried and planed smooth. Therefore, what everyone calls a "two by four" is really about 1½″ × 3½″. (Actual sizes vary slightly from batch to batch.)

STANDARD LUMBER SIZES

Nominal dimensions	Actual dimensions
1″ × 2″	¾″ × 1½″
1″ × 3″	¾″ × 2½″
1″ × 4″	¾″ × 3½″
1″ × 5″	¾″ × 4½″
1″ × 6″	¾″ × 5½″
1″ × 8″	¾″ × 7¼″
1″ × 10″	¾″ × 9¼″
1″ × 12″	¾″ × 11¼″
2″ × 2″	1½″ × 1½″
2″ × 3″	1½″ × 2½″
2″ × 4″	1½″ × 3½″
2″ × 6″	1½″ × 5½″
2″ × 8″	1½″ × 7¼″
2″ × 10″	1½″ × 9¼″
2″ × 12″	1½″ × 11¼″
4″ × 4″	3½″ × 3½″
4″ × 6″	3½″ × 5½″
6″ × 6″	5½″ × 5½″

JOIST. A structural beam used to support a horizontal surface.

LAMINATE ROUTER. A bit to be used in a router that makes flush or beveled trim cuts on plastic laminates.

LAMINATE TRIMMER. A hand tool for making finish trim cuts—straight, curved, or beveled—on plastic laminates.

LATH. A thin, narrow strip of rough-sawn softwood, used as a support for stucco or plaster, to form latticework, as a trim, and for other purposes. *See also* Window screen lath.

LEAD ANCHOR. A soft metal anchor designed to receive and hold screws in masonry walls.

LUMBER. *See* Finished lumber.

MASONITE. A common brand name for a dense composition board made of compressed wood fibers. It generally has one very smooth surface and one roughly patterned surface, but it is also available with both sides smooth. It usually comes in ⅛″ or ¼″ thicknesses, and is sold in 4′ × 8′ sheets. It is not strong enough to span large areas unsupported, but it is a useful surface for backing or "flooring."

MITER. A joint in which two joining pieces of wood are cut to equal angles, usually 45°.

MITER BOX. A three-sided box with sides that have angled slots to facilitate making precise 45° and 90° cuts in a board, usually with a backsaw.

MOLLY BOLT. A type of fastening used on hollow walls. Inserted into a drilled hole or pounded into the wall, depending upon the type, the molly has a metal webbing that spreads as the head is tightened. The expanded webbing functions as a nut, holding the device in place.

NAIL, CEMENT-COATED BOX. Thin, strong nails that have a head. Actually coated with a resin that gives them extra holding power.

NAIL, COMMON. Heavy-duty nail used for construction and other jobs where strength is called for; common nails have heads and do not bend easily.

NAIL, FINISHING. Thin nails that do not have heads and, once in place, are less conspicuous than other types of nails. These nails can be set (q.v.) below the surface of the wood and the resulting small hole filled with wood dough or spackle for a completely smooth surface.

PARTICLEBOARD. *See* Chipboard.

PINE. *See* Finished lumber.

PIVOT HINGE. An inside-mounted cabinet hinge for flush or overlapping doors. This type of hinge pivots on a rivet.

PLASTIC ANCHOR. A solid-wall fastener that expands as it accepts an inserted screw.

PLASTIC LAMINATE. Thin plastic material with a hard-surface finish, available in many colors and textures and often used on counter tops. Popular brands include Formica and Micarta. (*See also* Laminate router and Laminate trimmer.)

PLYWOOD. A building material made of thin layers (plies) of wood glued together. It is strong, and is used to cover large areas. The grain of adjacent plies are at right angles for strength and to prevent warping. It is available in a wide variety of strengths, finishes (including veneers of fir, birch, and ash) and glue types to suit almost any job. Like clear pine, plywood is graded by letter, with A designating the best quality. Two letters are used for plywood grades (A/B, A/C, and so forth), the letters referring to the qualities of the "front" and "back" surfaces.

The disadvantage of plywood is that its edges are rough, with occasional gaps, that are prone to splintering. These plywood edges must be filled in with wood dough or spackle, or covered with lath, tape, or something else.

Like most building panels, plywood comes in 4′ × 8′ sheets, and is sold by the square foot in thicknesses of ¼″, ⅜″, ½″, ⅝″, ¾″.

RADIUS. A wood-finishing technique. To round off a 90° junction of two wood surfaces into a uniform curve.

ROUTER. An electric tool used for cutting tracks and grooves (dadoes, e.g.) into wood. An electric chisel.

SABER SAW. A handheld jigsaw that, fitted with the correct blade, cuts softwood up to 1½″ thick. It can cut irregular shapes and curves.

SET. A small steel spike used to drive the heads of finishing nails and brads below the wood's surface. Keep the set square to the nail and use a hammer, even when you're sinking only small brads. The word is also used as a verb—as in "to set nails."

SPACKLE. *See* Fillers.

STOVE BOLT. Named for original use in bolting together stoves, these general-utility bolts come with heads in a variety of shapes. The entire shank is coarsely threaded.

TABLE SAW. A stationary electrically powered circular saw, used for making a variety of straight, precise cuts in wood.

TOGGLE BOLT. A permanent, hollow-wall fastener with metal "wings" that expand after insertion to grip the wall from the opposite side.

WHITE GLUE. Water-resistant (but not waterproof), milk-base wood glue such as Elmer's, Sobo, or Franklin's Tight Bond.

WINDOW SCREEN LATH. Lath that has rounded top edges for a more finished look.

WOOD DOUGH. *See* Fillers.

PENNY SIZES OF NAILS

Because nails were once classified according to price, and they weren't very expensive, "penny" became the standard unit of measurement for all nails (3-penny nails, 10-penny nails, etc.). The term penny (it is abbreviated "d," because that is the British abbreviation of "pence") is still used, but now it indicates length, not price.

Penny Size	Length
2d	1″
3d	1¼″
4d	1½″
6d	2″
8d	2½″
10d	3″
12d	3¼″

SIMPLE BOXES

THE BASIC BOX

A chest is basically a box. So is a cabinet, a drawer, a platform bed, a bookcase, and even a refrigerator—remember the ice*box*? Make a sturdy box and you have something to sit on, to store gear in, to work on. Make a sturdy box and by varying its dimensions, its openings, and its surface treatments you make . . . furniture.

The five-sided box shown here is 18″ high, 24″ long, and 20″ wide.

MATERIALS

For all five surface panels (sides, ends, and top), use ½″ A/B plywood. (Note that two of these boxes can be made from a single 4′ × 8′ sheet of plywood.)

For the glue blocks, use 1″ × 1″ pine.

No. 8 flathead wood screws, 1″ long.

White glue.

Spackle or wood dough.

Paint or finish of your choice.

ASSEMBLY

All plywood cuts are best made with a table saw or circular saw. A neat final appearance in a plywood object is largely a matter of clean cuts and true, right-angle edges, which are difficult to achieve with a handsaw. It might be worth paying the lumberyard to cut these pieces, *if* you can be sure that they will make exact cuts.

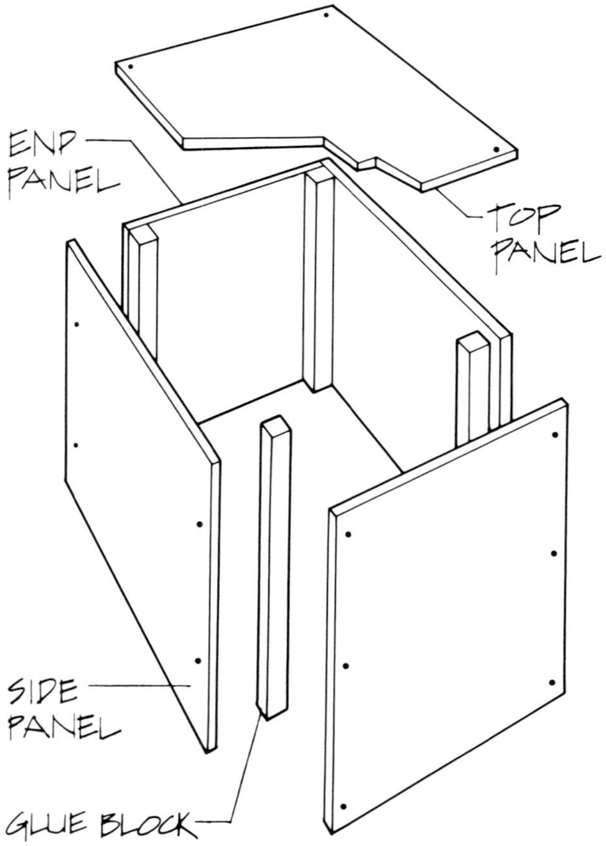

1. Cut two 17½″ × 24″ side panels, two 17½″ × 19″ end panels, and a 20″ × 24″ top panel. Cut four 17½″-long glue blocks.

2. Mark, countersink, and drill three evenly spaced 5⁄32″ holes ½″ in from each side edge of each end panel. Then mark, countersink, and drill two evenly spaced 5⁄32″ holes, ⅞″ in from each side edge of each side panel (positioned, as shown in the diagram, so that the screws will not interfere with the ones in the ends).

3. Fasten the four glue blocks to the end panels with glue and three screws each, making certain that the edges of the panels and glue blocks are flush.

4. Fasten the side panels into place with glue and two screws at each edge. The side panels should cover the side edges of the end panels.

5. Mark, countersink, and drill one 5⁄32″ hole in each corner of the top. These holes should be ⅞″ in from the side and end panels or 1 3⁄16″ in diagonally from each corner. Apply glue generously around underside perimeter of top, then fasten down with the glue and four screws.

6. Fill all screw holes, joints, and plywood edges with spackle or wood dough. Sand the box smooth. Paint or apply finish of your choice.◇

A cantilevered slab of glass atop a basic box makes a table for Charles Hughes. *See page 31.*

A MIRRORED BOX

Mirrors achieve a reflective finish on any furniture with a simple geometric shape. The Basic Box is ideal for this application, and a five-sided, open-bottom box of ½″ plywood serves as the foundation for this mirrored table. When completed, the table measures about 14⅜″ high, 29¾″ long, and 29¾″ wide.

MATERIALS

For the box, use ½″ A/B plywood.

For the glue blocks, use 1″ × 1″ pine.

Five mirrors ¼″ thick with polished edges—two 14⅛″ × 29¼″, two 14⅛″ × 29¾″, and one 29¾″ × 29¾″.

No. 8 flathead wood screws, 1″ long.

White glue.

Spackle.

Silicone rubber sealant.

ASSEMBLY

The dimensions above are calculated to accept ¼″-thick mirrors. However, before ordering the mirrors, it might be a good idea to build the box. Two different people building a box for the first time could each come up with working, functional projects, but ones with slightly varied dimensions—which would, of course, vary the sizes of the mirrors. Obviously, if you change the thickness of the mirrors or the size of the box, take this into consideration when ordering the mirrors.

1. Cut two 13⅝″ × 29¼″ side panels, two 13⅝″ × 28¼″ end panels, one 29¼″ × 29¼″ top, and four glue blocks 13⅝″ long.

2. Assemble the box with glue, glue blocks, and screws, following steps 2–5 of instructions for the Basic Box, page 110. The box should be 14⅛″ high, 29¼″ long, and 29¼″ wide.

3. Use penny-size dots of silicone rubber sealant to fasten the mirrors to the plywood surfaces. Place the dots—six to eight per side—within 2″ of the edges. This adhesive will adhere to clean plywood and—unlike contact cement—will permit adjusting the placement of the mirrors and will not destroy the mirror backing. ◇

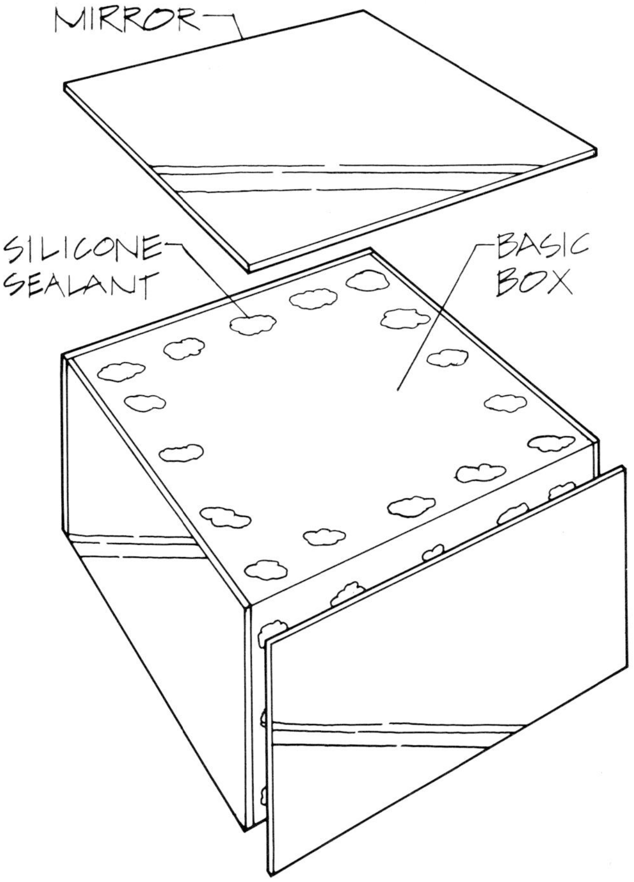

A mirrored box makes an interesting coffee table. See page 49.

BOX WITH A LID

With the addition of a hinged lid, the Basic Box becomes a base for a banquette, a storage chest, an occasional table, or a very low bench. If you wish, you can cover the unit with carpeting.

To construct this banquette base, build the Basic Box, but make it lower, deeper, and longer. The one described here measures 12″ high, 48″ long, and 36″ wide, and at those dimensions can be made of ¾″ plywood or chipboard. Turn the box upside down so that the solid top becomes the bottom, and add the hinged lid to what was the open bottom.

MATERIALS

For side and end panels, bottom, lid, and flanges, use ¾″ A/B plywood or chipboard.

For glue blocks, use 1″ × 1″ pine.

No. 8 flathead wood screws, 1″ long.

One continuous (piano) hinge 48″ long, with ¾″ leaves.

White glue.

Contact cement or staples.

Spackle or wood dough.

Paint, finish of your choice, or carpeting.

ASSEMBLY

The only tricky part of this project is hanging the hinge. A secret is to keep everything absolutely parallel—the hinge, the lid, and the flange. First, fasten the hinge to the lid, then to the flange.

1. Cut two 10½″ × 48″ side panels, two 10½″ × 34½″ end panels, and one 36″ × 48″ bottom. Cut four glue blocks 10½″ long.

2. Assemble the box with glue, glue blocks, and screws, following steps 2–5 of instruction for the Basic Box, page 110, taking into consideration the dimensions of the thicker plywood.

3. Cut two flanges 4″ × 48″. Mark, countersink, and drill seven 5⁄32″ holes in each flange, ⅜″ in from the edges and located as shown in the diagram. Fasten the flanges into place with glue and screws.

4. Cut the lid. It should be about 27¾″ × 48″ long; remember that it must accommodate the thickness of the hinge and the wraparound carpet (if you are using it). You should allow room for the hinge and ⅛″ clearance between the front edge of the lid and the front flange.

5. Position the hinge against the edge of the lid, with the hinge's pin loops just above the lid's top surface. With a pencil, mark four to six screw hole locations evenly spaced along the edge, then make small nail holes to help you start the screws. Snug screws down but do not tighten them. Repeat this mounting procedure with the other hinge leaf butted against the flange. It helps to have a second person hold and position the lid.

6. Check the hinge action for free swing. Make any adjustments necessary, then insert the remainder of the screws and tighten them all down.

7. Fill all screw holes, joints, and plywood edges with spackle or wood dough, then sand and paint or apply finish of your choice; or fasten carpet to the box and lid using contact cement or a staple gun.

Note: If perfection is less important than easy access, consider a modest overhang—make the lid 48½″ long to facilitate raising and lowering it. Or, if the box is not carpeted, you might install a brass, flush-mounted pull ring.◇

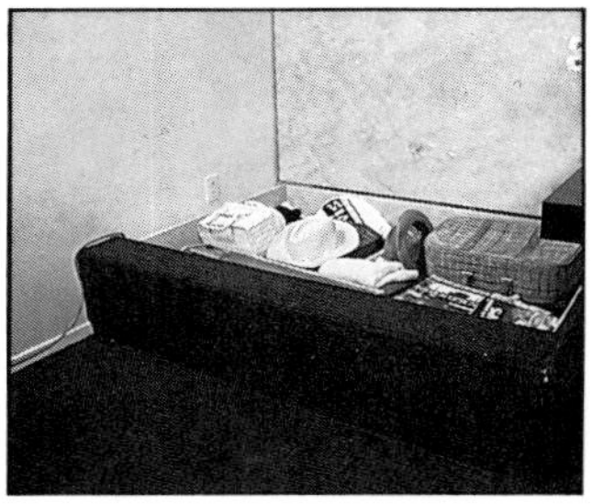

Storage boxes cum banquettes make for compact versatility in Jamie Roper's apartment. See page 11.

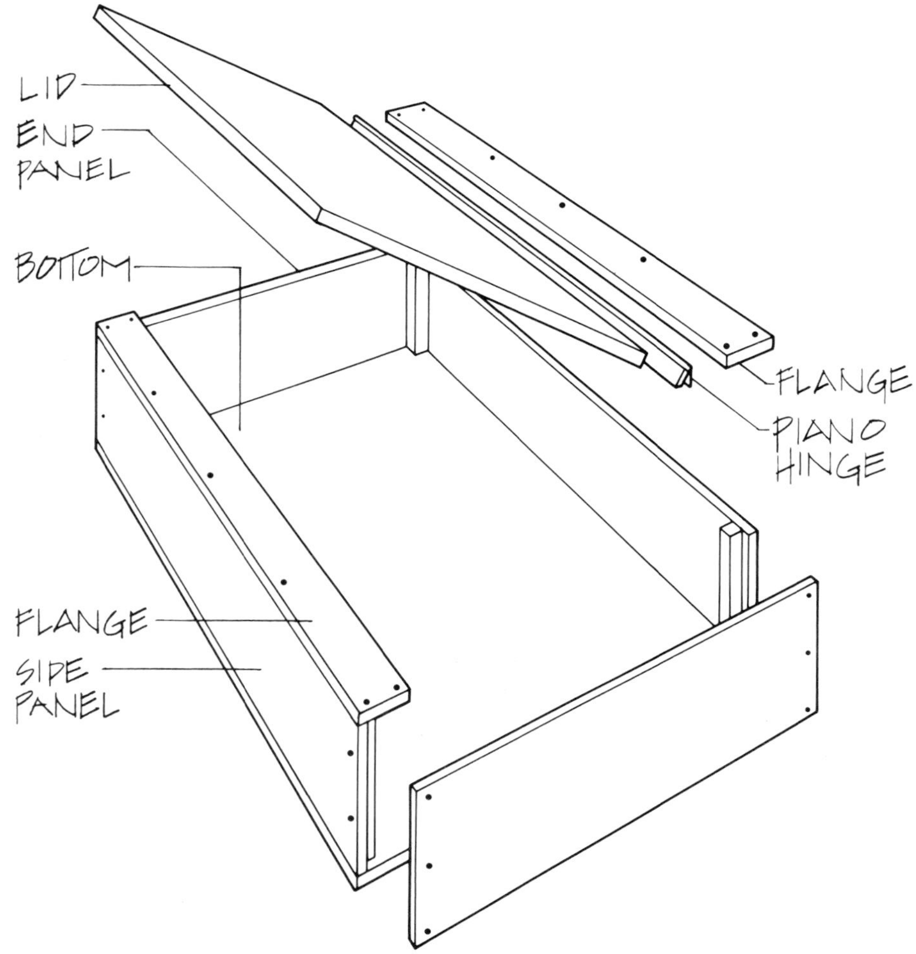

COFFEE TABLE WITH BOXY LEGS

The contemporary look of this square table is achieved through unadorned geometry plus the hard finish of matte white plastic laminate. It is really another Basic Box, resting on four smaller boxes. Plastic laminate can be difficult to work with even for experienced carpenters, so you might want to first practice applying a few small pieces to some scrap wood. The table without the laminate is 11¼″ high and 40″ square.

MATERIALS

For the top panel use ¾″ A/B plywood.

For the side panels and leg sidepieces, use ½″ A/B plywood.

For the glue blocks, use 1″ × 1″ pine.

No. 8 flathead wood screws, 1″ long.

White glue.

4-penny finishing nails.

Plastic laminate, such as Formica or Micarta.

Contact cement for attaching the plastic laminate, preferably water-base.

ASSEMBLY

1. Cut four pieces for the side panels 11¼″ × 39½″; four glue blocks 11¼″ long; and a top panel 40″ square.

2. Because the side panels of this table are butted together in succession, and the legs will be square, the thickness of the panels will have to be taken into consideration when sawing the panels. The left leg pieces should be 3½″ wide and the right ones 4″ wide. Therefore, mark off these dimensions on the bottom of each side panel and saw out a rectangular piece 5″ high and 36″ long. Assemble the box with glue, glue blocks, and screws following steps 2–4 of instructions for the Basic Box, page 110, except butt the sides together in succession.

3. Cut four boxy leg sidepieces 3½″ × 6″, and four 3″ × 6″. Cut twelve glue blocks 6″ long. Assemble four L-shaped units using one 3½″-wide leg sidepiece, one 3″-wide leg sidepiece, and one 6″ glue block per leg with glue and screws.

4. Using the eight remaining 6″-long glue blocks, attach the L-shaped pieces inside each corner of the table with glue and screws.

5. Apply glue generously around the underside perimeter of the top, then fasten the top down with the glue and 4-penny finishing nails. Set the nails.

6. Measure and, using a laminate cutter, cut plastic laminate pieces to match the top, sides, and legs of the table, allowing about ⅛″ overlap around all pieces—to be trimmed and to ensure even and straight edges.

7. Fasten plastic laminate to the smooth plywood surfaces with contact cement, carefully following the instructions on the container. A good tip: Once the cement is dry to the touch, one can more carefully position the pieces by placing a sheet of wax paper between the two cemented surfaces. When satisfied with the positioning, carefully pull the wax paper out. This adhesive offers the advantage—and disadvantage—of instant and absolute adhesion. No clamping is necessary, but also no adjustments are possible. (To allow for minor errors, cut pieces slightly oversize and then trim flush.) Work carefully. Once contact is made, you've completed the job—ready or not.

8. Carefully trim the laminate at each joint. Corner finishing is the most difficult part of the job to do neatly. This can be done easily with a power laminate-trimming router, with slightly more difficulty by hand with a laminate cutter (available for about $14), or painstakingly with a hand file.◇

A modern adaptation of the basic box table. *See page 32.*

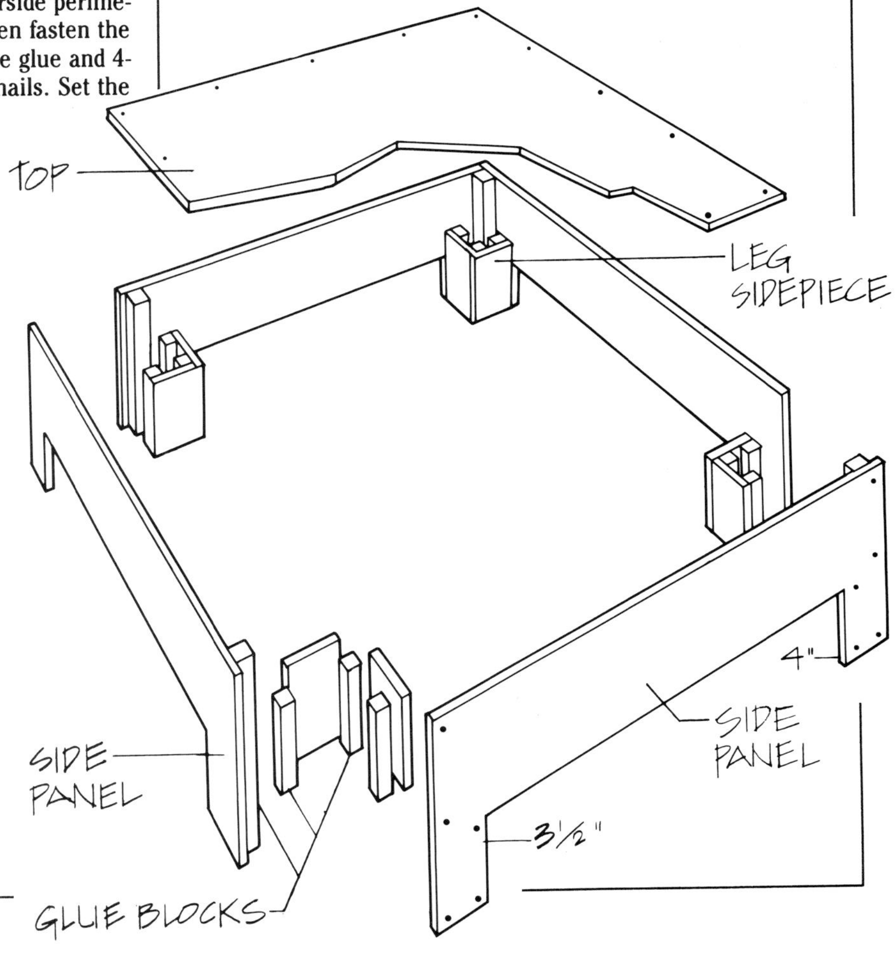

STORAGE BOX WITH DRAWERS

A box can perform triple duty as a low seating/sleeping/storage unit through the addition of two smaller boxes that nest inside it—commonly known as *drawers.* The elongated Basic Box here is 12″ high, 75″ long, and 38″ deep. It has five sides of ¾″ plywood for solidity; the sixth side is left open to accommodate the two large drawers. A center baffle divides the space and helps guide the drawers. The kick space along the front lets the drawers be opened without the use of pulls or other hardware. Each drawer is another basic box 7½″ high, about 34″ long, and 32″ deep, depending on the size of the glides and slides.

MATERIALS

For the five sides of the large box, as well as for the baffle and kickplate, use ¾″ A/B (or veneered) plywood.

For the drawer sides, backs, and bottoms, use ½″ A/B plywood.

For the drawer fronts, use ¾″ A/B (or veneered) plywood.

For all the glue blocks, use 1″ × 1″ pine.

For the chamfer strips in the drawers, use 1″ × 1″ pine or (for a smoother look) cove molding.

No. 8 flathead wood screws, 1″ long.

Steel drawer glides and slides.

White glue.

Edgemate tape, wood dough, or spackle.

Polyurethane varnish or finish of your choice.

ASSEMBLY

The large box and the two drawers are assembled in the same way as the Basic Box, page 110. The butt-jointed box-type drawers are the easiest of all types of drawers to assemble, but they tend to come apart under the stress of opening and closing unless they are very securely fastened with glue and screws. Therefore, drive screws every 3″ to 4″ along each joint and install the chamfer strips as shown. The drawers ride on store-bought steel glides and slides. Installing this hardware is the trickiest part of making drawers. Because the necessary clearances will vary among types and brands, it's a good idea to select and purchase the hardware *before* starting on the boxes themselves.

1. Cut two side panels for the large box 11¼″ × 37¼″, then cut 3″-square notches out of the bottom front corner of each.

2. Cut the remaining parts for the large box as follows: one back panel 11¼″ × 73½″; one bottom 36½″ × 73½″; one center baffle 7½″ × 36½″; one top 37¼″ × 75″; one kickplate 3″ × 73½″; and two glue blocks 7½″ long.

3. Assemble the large box; remember that the bottom and back panel fit between the sides. Fasten the sides and back together with glue blocks at the corners as indicated in the diagram. Secure the bottom by gluing and screwing through the sides and backs into the edges of the bottom; the bottom should be 3″ off the floor, its underside flush with the tops of the notches at the front. Secure the center baffle by gluing and screwing up through the bottom and in through the back. Position the kickplate so that it is flush with the sides of the notches; attach it by gluing and screwing down through the bottom and in through the side panels.

The drawers in Tom McHugh's unit pull out somewhat like a trundle bed. See page 38.

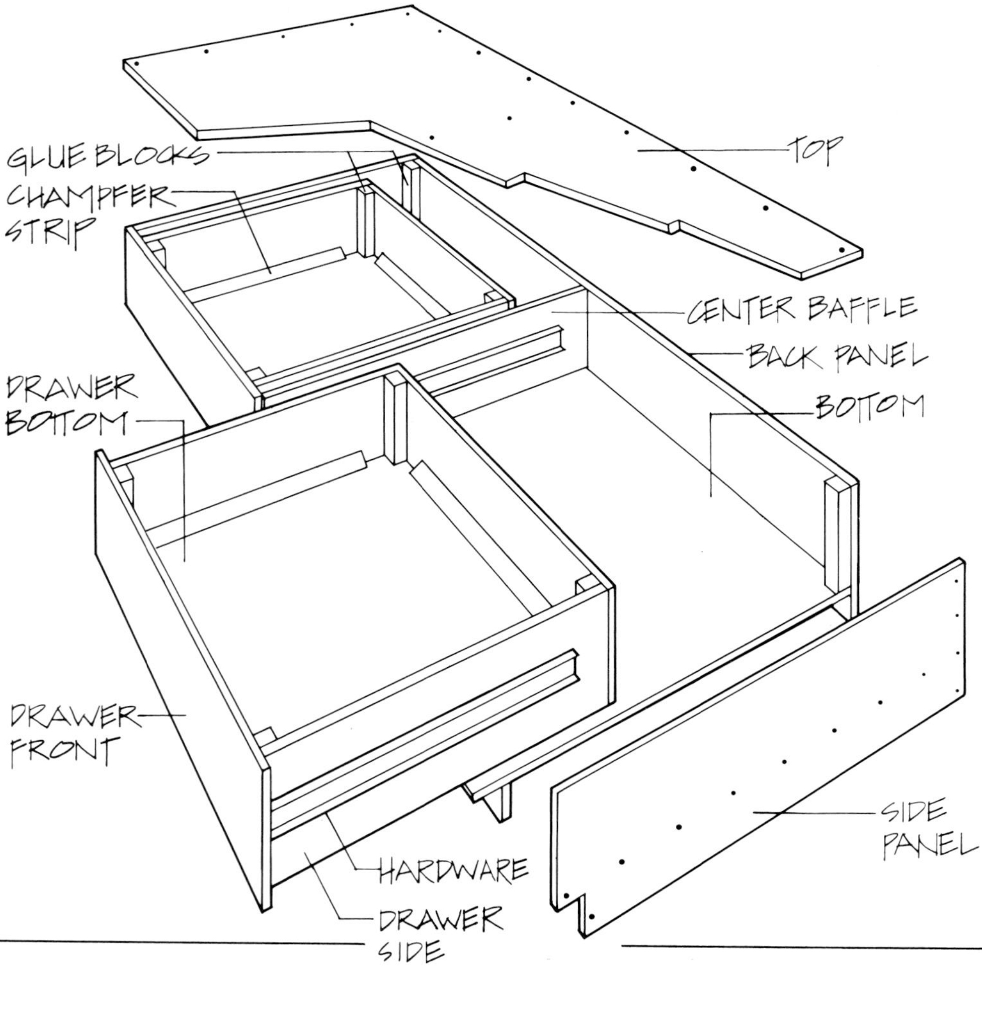

4. Measure the distance between the baffle and the sides of the large box and subtract the space the drawer hardware will take up to determine the width of the drawers. Cut two drawer backs to that length (about 7½″ × 34″); cut two drawer bottoms 1″ shorter than the backs (or about 33″ × 32″). Cut four drawer sides 7½″ × 32″; two drawer fronts 9″ × 37⅜″; eight glue blocks 7″ long, and eight chamfer strips 30″ long.

5. Assemble the two drawers, screwing on the drawer fronts through the glue blocks from the inside, making sure the screws go well into but not through the fronts. Glue and screw the chamfer strips inside the drawers along the joints where the drawer bottoms meet the drawer sides, backs, and fronts.

6. Install the drawer glides and slides. Follow the directions that come with the hardware, but be sure to carefully measure and mark the locations for the slides. It is essential to keep the glide and slide mounts exactly parallel. First mount the glides to the inside walls of the big box, then mount the slides to the outsides of the drawers. Most brands of drawer hardware have slotted screw holes to allow for fine adjustments before tightening down.

7. Glue and screw on the top of the big box by driving screws through the top into the edges of the sides, back, and center baffle. Fill all holes, then sand the box and drawers smooth. Cover exposed plywood edges with Edgemate tape and finish the piece with polyurethane varnish, or fill the edges with spackle or wood dough and paint or apply the finish of your choice.◇

PLATFORMS

THE BASIC PLATFORM

A platform can lend a certain staginess to an otherwise plain space. It can change the look and the feel of a room without dramatic loss of headroom. It can also serve as an acoustical barrier, and can double as floor *and* furniture, with spaces for sitting, sleeping, and storage.

A platform is really just another box, albeit a thin one. This platform is butt-jointed, glued and nailed together, and supported inside by joists. Plywood is the structural material of choice if the platform is to be covered with carpeting, but if a finished-floor look is desired, the top surface should be formed of 1″ × 4″ or 1″ × 6″ boards, or 1″ × 6″ tongue-and-groove siding.

If a platform is to be permanent (that is, custom-fitted to a specific space), it can be built in any size. And if it's permanent, consider putting electrical outlets along the sides or adding access doors and drawers for storage. If a platform is not a permanent installation, it should be built in modules of a size that can be moved easily and that will fit through your doorways.

The directions that follow are for constructing a five-sided platform module, 12″ high, 36″ wide, and 60″ long. The dimensions can, of course, be varied to fit your needs and spaces.

Peter Blaustein's platform improves his view of the New York City skyline. See page 25.

MATERIALS

For the side panels, end panels, joists, and top, use ¾″ A/D plywood.

6-penny finishing nails.

White glue.

Carpet, stain, or finish of your choice.

(continued on next page)

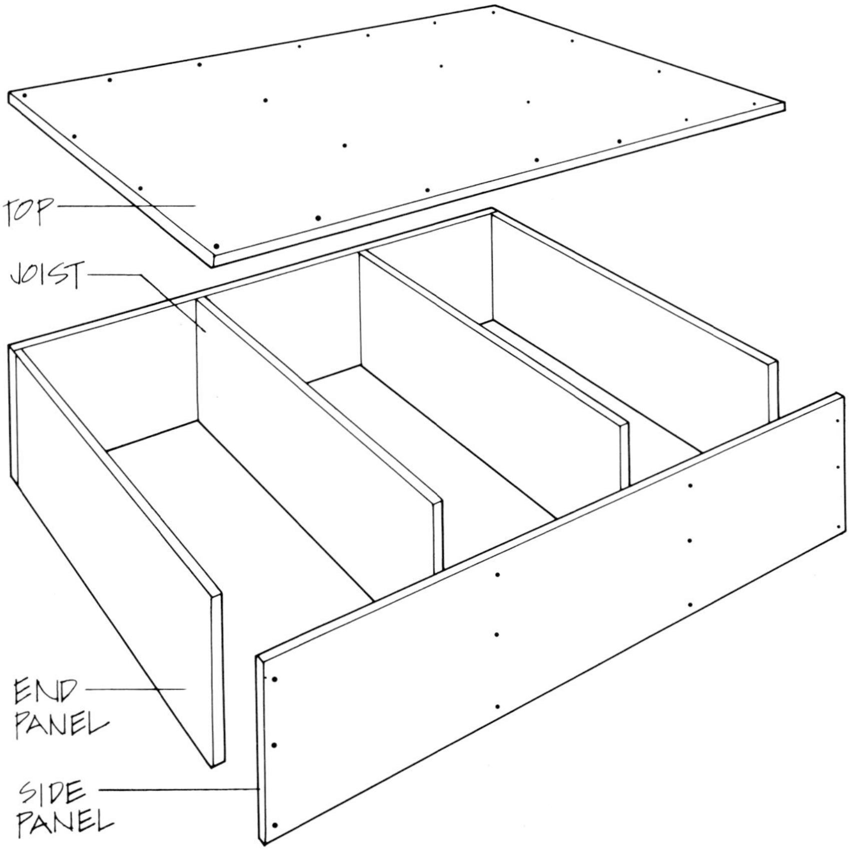

ASSEMBLY

It's possible to cut ¾″ plywood with a handsaw, but it's difficult to be neat about it. If a power saw (circular, saber, or table) is not available, it's worth paying the lumberyard to do it.

1. Cut two side panels 11¼″ × 60″. Cut two end panels and two joists 11¼″ × 34½″. Cut the top 36″ × 60″.

2. Apply glue generously to side edges of the end panels. Nail the sides to the ends with three evenly spaced finishing nails ⅜″ in from each end of the side panels. Set the nails.

3. Position the joists inside the open box so the space is divided into three equal-size "compartments." Measure carefully so that all joists are true perpendiculars, and all edges are flush. Mark each side panel where a joist butts against it. Repeat gluing and nailing procedure.

4. Mark the top with a pencil line ⅜″ from the four edges and one line marking the center of each joist. Start nails on these lines. Secure the top by repeating the gluing and nailing procedure.

5. No filling or sanding is necessary if you carpet the platform. Apply the carpet of your choice smoothly, working from one side over the top and down the other side—cutting to accommodate the end flaps. Fasten the carpet down with staples or carpet tacks. If you stain, polyurethane, or paint the platform, fill all nail holes and edges of plywood with wood dough or spackle, sand well, and apply finish.◇

A RAMP

A natural companion piece to a floor platform is a gently sloping ramp leading up to it. Not only are ramps often visually "right" with platforms, but they can heighten the theatricality of a room. And children love them. The project described here is 73″ long, 36″ wide, and rises to 12″ from the floor so that it fits perfectly with the preceding Basic Platform, but it could be altered to fit any space.

MATERIALS

For the end panel, side triangles, and joists, use ¾″ A/D interior plywood.

For the top, use ¾″ A/D plywood.

6-penny finishing nails.

White glue.

ASSEMBLY

1. Cut two right-angled side triangles 11¼″ high and 73″ long; cut one end panel 11¼″ × 34½″.

2. The two joists (as well as the end panel) will be fitted inside the side triangles, roughly dividing the space into thirds as indicated in the diagram, so cut joists 34½″ wide and to heights that will be flush with the top of the ramp. Bevel the tops of the joists and end panel to match the angle of the ramp.

3. Cut the top 36″ × 73″. Bevel its lower edge so that it will rest flat on the floor.

4. Assemble the ramp with glue and finishing nails, following steps 2–4 of instructions for the Basic Platform, page 115, except that here, of course, there is only one end panel. Carpet or finish the ramp following step 5 of instructions for Basic Platform.◇

A ramp is a logical way to reach a platform. See page 25.

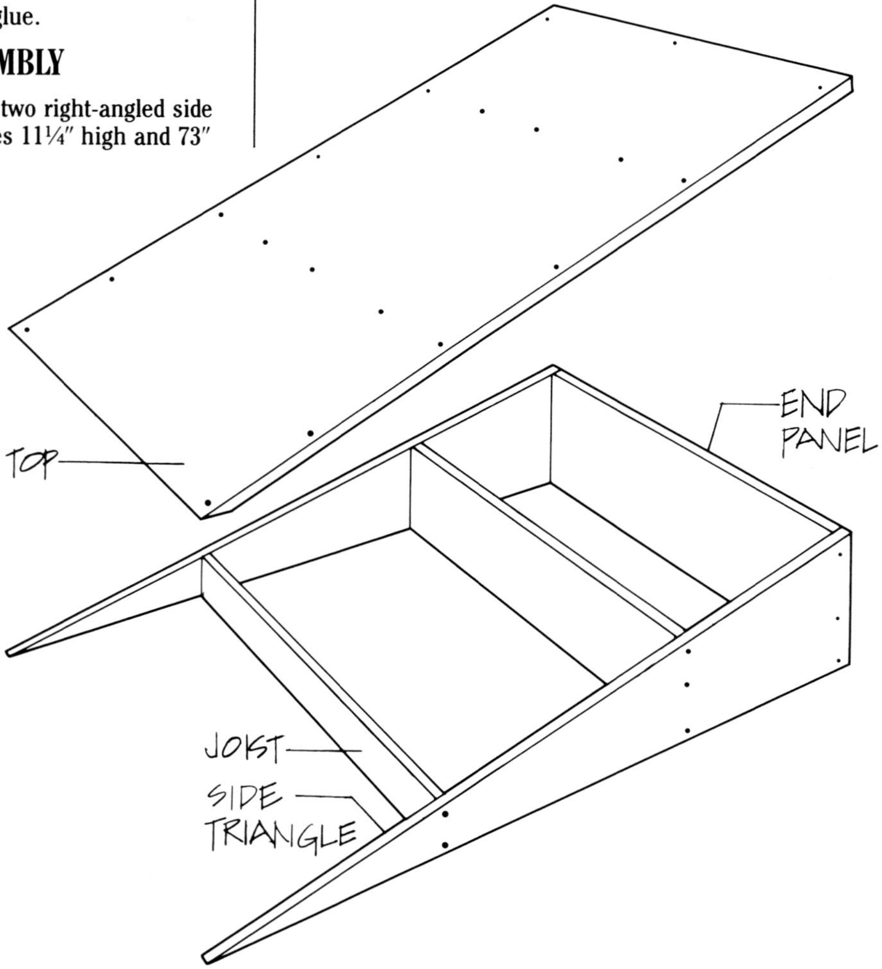

A TRIANGULAR PLATFORM

A simple flat platform can dramatically alter a room—especially if the platform appears to float on light. This variation is an isosceles triangle cut from half a 4′ × 8′ sheet of ¾″ plywood and measures about 68″ × 68″ × 96″. It rests on a triangular frame of on-edge 2″ × 6″ boards that are positioned about 6″ in from the platform's edges. It is faced with 1″ × 4″s and it is carpeted.

MATERIALS

For the top, use ¾″ A/D plywood.

For the frame and joist, use 2″ × 6″ fir or 2″ × 6″ hem-fir.

For the facing strips, 1″ × 4″ clear pine.

White glue.

10-penny common nails.

6-penny finishing nails.

Spackle.

Paint.

Carpeting.

Cup hooks and staples.

Christmas tree lights in the color of your choice.

ASSEMBLY

1. Assemble a triangular frame of 2″ × 6″s that measures 49⅞″ × 49⅞″ × 70¼″ with a center joist about 32″ long. Bevel the ends of the frame pieces so that they come together flush; fasten together the frame, including the joist, with glue and 10-penny nails. Paint the outside of the frame black so that it will be less visible.

2. Cut a 48″ × 48″ square of plywood; then cut the square diagonally in half to create two triangles. Position the two triangles over the frame so that two of the 48″ sides butt against each other over the joist to form a large triangle that is centered over the platform and overhangs the frame evenly on all sides. Attach the top to the frame with glue and 6-penny finishing nails. Set the nails.

3. Measure and cut three 1″ × 4″ facing strips to fit around the edges of the plywood top. Miter the ends of the facing strips to make them fit snugly together. The top edges of these strips should be flush with the top of the carpet on the finished platform, so be sure that the facing is as far above the plywood top as the carpet you are using is thick. Attach the facing with glue and 6-penny finishing nails. Set the nails.

4. Fill all nail holes and joints with spackle and sand the platform smooth. Paint the facing strips white or a color of your choice.

5. Cut the carpet to the exact size needed and staple it to the plywood top. Screw a series of cup hooks to the underside of the plywood top near its perimeter. Suspend strings of Christmas tree lights from the hooks.◇

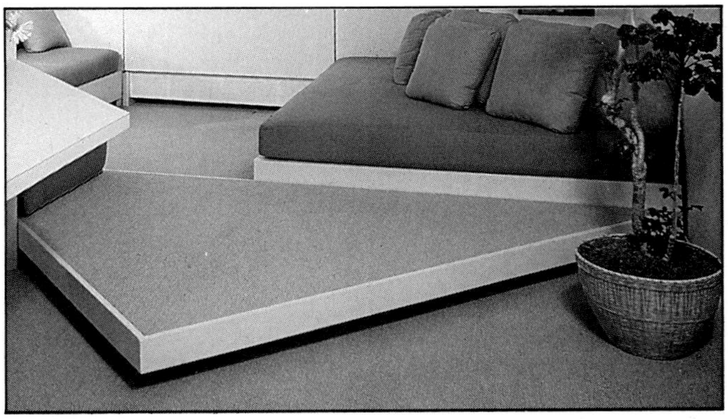

The floating platform in Susan Zevon's apartment was made from hollow core doors; it could just as easily have been constructed from plywood, as suggested here. *See page 13.*

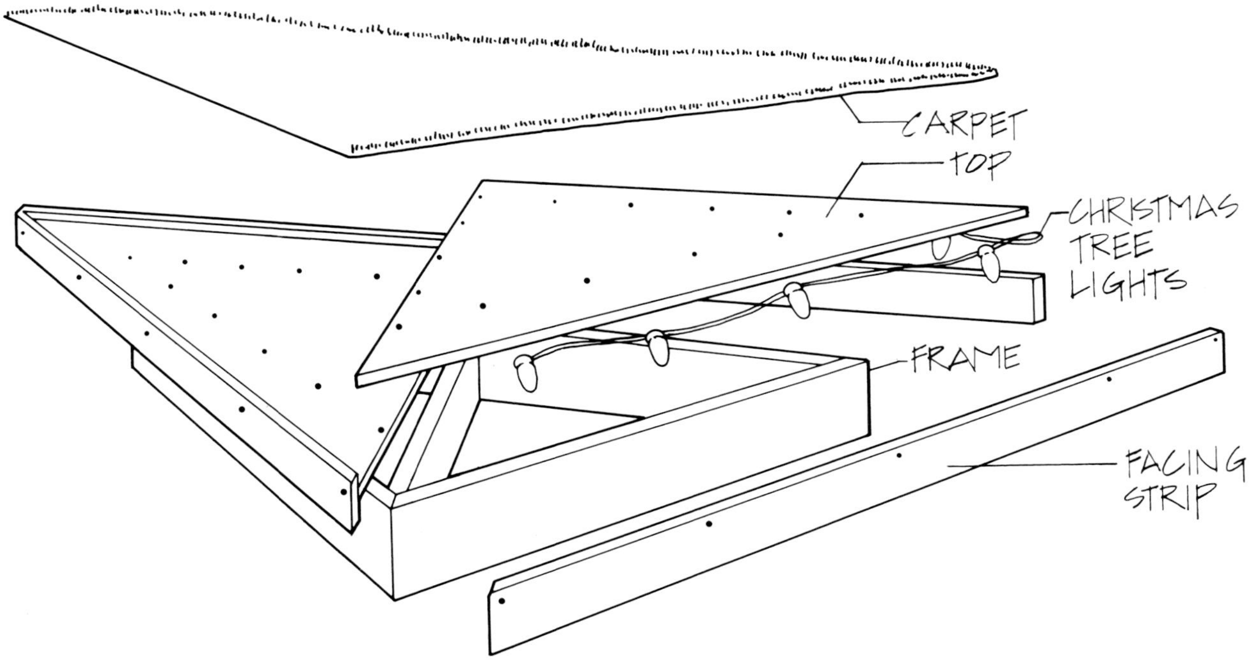

A PLATFORM BED

A platform bed is, at heart, a big low box. It must be sturdy enough to support the weight of two (or more) adults and tightly assembled, to resist squeaking. The bed should rise to average seating height of 18″ to 20″. Any lower, it'll be a strain to make up; any higher, shoe-tying will be awkward. One advantage of the design described here (which will accommodate a standard 54″ × 75″ full-size mattress) is that it can be disassembled with relative ease. The platform bed in the basic form as shown should cost no more than $125—compared with commercial products ranging from $300 to $1,000.

MATERIALS

For the side and end panels, use ½″ A/D plywood, or for more costly finished-furniture look, use birch veneer plywood.

For the top, use ½″ construction-grade plywood (it'll be under the mattress and won't show).

For the supports and the cross brace, use 2″ × 2″ fir or hem-fir.

For the top trim, use ½″ window screen lath.

Carriage bolts, 2½″ long and ¼″ in diameter, with nuts and 1″ flat washers.

No. 12 roundhead wood screws, 3″ long.

No. 10 flathead wood screws, 1¼″ long.

2-penny finishing nails.

Wood dough or spackle.

Stain or finish of your choice.

ASSEMBLY

For not very much extra, a lumberyard will cut the lumber for this project to size, but if you must do this step yourself, your best bet is to use a table saw.

1. Cut two 20″ × 77″ side panels. Cut two 20″ × 55″ end panels.

2. Cut four corner supports 16½″ long. Cut two side supports 76″ long and two end supports 52″ long.

3. Cut a cross brace (to support the place where the two top pieces meet) approximately 52″ long.

4. Cut two pieces of plywood 37¾″ × 54½″ to achieve a total top surface of 54½ × 75½″. (This allows for a ¼″ clearance all around.)

5. With a pencil, draw a line 2¾″ down from the top edge of the side panels and along this line drill four evenly spaced ¼″ holes. (Note: Plywood should always be drilled from the finished side to the rough side.) Mark and drill corresponding holes along the 76″ side supports, centering the supports between the side edges of the side panels. Then, using carriage bolts, bolt the supports to the insides of the side panels, always placing the washer and nut on the inside. Carriage bolt heads should be tightened snugly against—but not dimpling—the plywood surface.

6. Similarly, drill three evenly spaced ¼″ holes in the end panels and end supports. The end supports must be centered to clear the side supports. Bolt supports to the insides of the end panels.

7. Drill two ¼″ holes about 1″ in from the sides of the end panels and 1½″ in from the

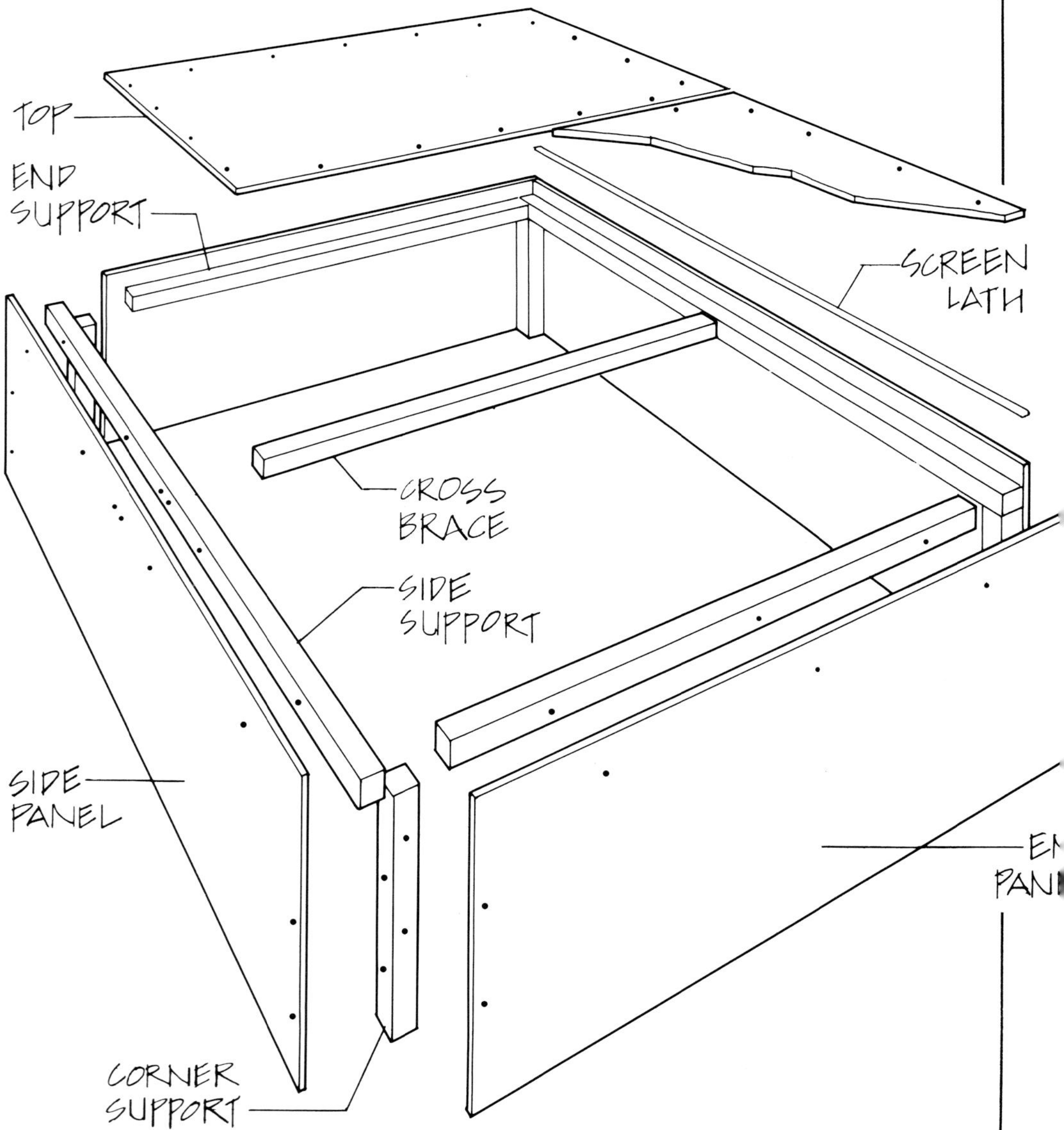

sides of the side panels, staggering the holes as shown in the diagram. Position the panels and corner supports to allow the end panels to butt against the inside of the side panels. Mark and drill corresponding holes through the corner supports. Insert carriage bolts and tighten all four panels firmly together.

8. Drill two 3⁄16″ holes through the side panels and side supports and with No. 12 roundhead wood screws mount the cross brace so that it is centered directly below the point at which the two top panels will meet.

9. Place the pieces for the top on the side and end supports and the cross brace. Countersink and drill 1⁄8″ holes 3⁄4″ in from the outside edges of the top pieces. The holes should be evenly spaced, about 9½″ apart, around the edges. Countersink and drill four evenly spaced 1⁄8″ holes ½″ from each of the two edges of the top panels where they meet over the cross brace. Secure the top pieces to the supports and cross brace with No. 10 wood screws.

10. Cut the window screen lath to fit the top edges of the side and end panels. Cut the corners on a 45-degree miter for a neater appearance. Glue and nail the lath into place with 2-penny finishing nails.

11. Fill over all the flathead wood screws with wood dough or spackle. Sand entire piece; then stain, paint with semigloss enamel, or apply your choice of finish.

VARIATIONS

Other platform bed sizes. The double bed (to accommodate a 54″ × 75″ mattress) shown may be built as a single (39″ × 75″) or a queen-size (60″ × 80″) bed by changing a few of the dimensions. (A king-size bed requires significant changes in material and design.) For a single, keep the same length, but reduce the end panels to 40″, the top surface to 39½″ × 75½″, reduce the end support pieces and the cross brace to 37″. For a queen-size bed, increase the side panels to 82″, increase the end panels to 61″, increase the top surface to 60½″ × 80½″, increase the side supports to 81″, and increase the end supports and cross brace to 58″.

Platform bed with door or drawers. To utilize underbed storage space, cut a door in one side panel and mount it on cabinet hinges. For a double bed, the door should measure about 12″ × 24″, to admit small suitcases. Similarly, large storage drawers can be incorporated under the sleeping surface if the platform is built high enough to accommodate them. One method of assembling and installing large drawers can be found on page 114. That method works as well in a platform bed, although for the bed you should use 3⁄4″ plywood in place of the ½″ plywood. Drawers should probably not exceed 32″ in depth. If a platform bed is to be freestanding, drawers could be built into both sides.◇

Tim Romanello's platform bed has rounded corners and doubles as a two-sided sofa. See page 51.

BED WITH OPEN STORAGE SPACE

Because this platform bed is lower than the standard height, it does not require box construction—instead, a plywood top rests on a frame of 2″ × 10″ uprights and long 2″ × 4″s, which results in open spaces ideally suited for storage. This variation by Austin Chinn is 11½″ high, 75″ long, and 54″ wide—standard double bed size.

MATERIALS

For the base supports, use four 2″ × 4″s, 75″ long.

For the uprights, use three 2″ × 10″s, 52½″ long.

For the top, use two pieces of ¾″ A/B fir plywood, each 37½″ x 52½″.

For the back supports, use four 9¼″ × 35¼″ pieces of ¼″ construction-grade plywood.

For the floor of the storage spaces, use four pieces of ¼″ construction-grade plywood, each approximately 17¾″ × 35¼″.

For the facing, use approximately 30′ of 1″ × 2″ clear pine.

No. 10 flathead wood screws, 3″ long.

No. 10 flathead wood screws, 1½″ long.

Small steel L brackets, with screws.

6-penny finishing nails.

White glue.

Wood dough or spackle.

Paint or other finish.

ASSEMBLY

1. The job of attaching the 2″ × 4″s to the 2″ × 10″s will best be done "upside down." First line up the 2″ × 10″s (uprights) on their edges, approximately 35″ apart. Place the 2″ × 4″s perpendicularly (lengthwise) on top of the uprights, broad sides down. Starting with either the "head" or the "foot" upright, position the 2″ × 4″s so that the two outer ones are flush with the corners of the upright and all are flush with the side and equally spaced (about 16″ apart, center to center). Using glue and countersunk 3″ wood screws, attach the 2″ × 4″s to the upright.

2. Move to the upright at the opposite end and attach the 2″ × 4″s to it in the same manner as step 1.

There are handy storage spaces on both sides of Austin Chinn's double bed. See page 41.

3. Making sure that the center upright is precisely in the middle (37½″ in from either end), screw and glue it in place there.

4. Turn your frame right side up so that the 2″ × 4″s are flat on the floor. Using the L brackets and screws, install the four back supports along the centers of the two inside 2″ × 4″s as indicated in the diagram. Then nail or screw down the flooring to the 2″ ×

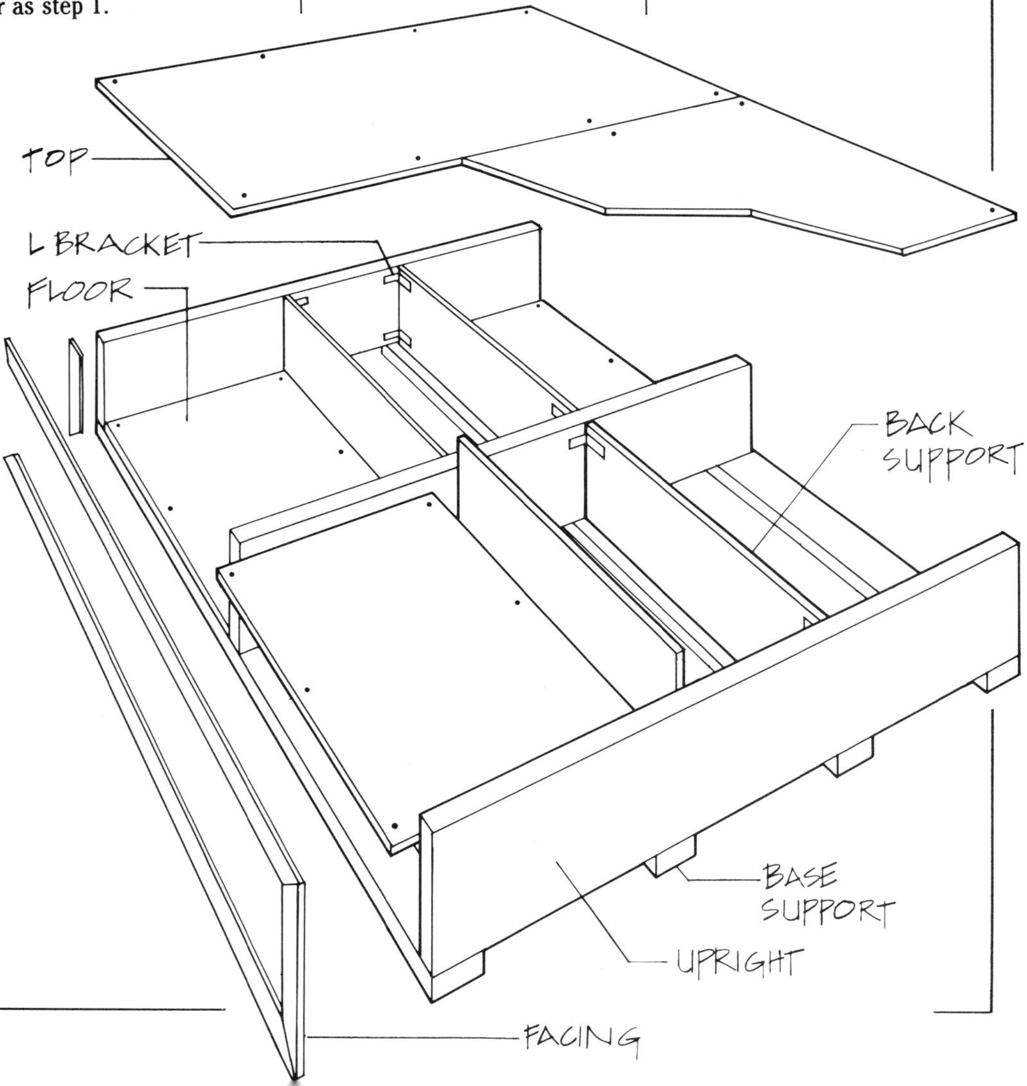

4″s in all four storage spaces, butting the plywood floor sections against the back supports.

5. For the top, fasten the ¾″ plywood to the uprights with glue and 1½″ wood screws. The two pieces should join at the center of the middle upright. Keep all edges flush with the edges and ends of the uprights.

6. Cut 1″ x 2″ clear pine into four 75″-long pieces and four 11½″ pieces for the facing around the storage openings. Miter all corners and attach on both sides of the bed by nailing into the uprights, into the 2″ × 4″s, and into the edges of the plywood top. Set the nails; fill the holes with wood dough or spackle.

7. Sand and paint, or give the bed a finish of your choice.◇

BOOKCASES & SHELVED UNITS

A BASIC BOOKCASE

A bookcase is just about the simplest object to assemble that qualifies as furniture. It's merely a narrow platform strong enough to support books or other objects. Depending upon its size and shape, it can function as a table, a desk support, a room divider, or in many other guises.

While a bookcase can be put together using a number of construction techniques, the Basic Bookcase described here is an unpretentious combination of lightness, strength, low cost, and portability that can be screwed together in short order. It is 33½″ wide, 30″ high, and 7½″ deep, and is nothing more—or less—than three pine boards screwed to two upright pine boards and backed (and further supported) by a sheet of thin plywood or Masonite.

MATERIALS

For the shelves and vertical supports, use 1″ × 8″ No. 2 common pine. (A better grade—clear B or better—could be used if you so choose.)

For the back, use ¼″ fir plywood or ¼″ Masonite.

4-penny finishing nails.

No. 6 flathead wood screws, 1¼″ long.

White glue.

Spackle or wood dough.

Paint or finish of your choice.

ASSEMBLY

1. Cut the shelves 32″ long and the two vertical supports 30″ long. Cut the back 29¼″ × 33½″.

2. To make accurate center lines for the three shelves, make a pencil mark on one vertical support ⅜″ down from the top, another mark 1⅛″ up from the bottom, and another halfway between the two. Carefully align the vertical supports and hold or clamp them tightly together; then, using a square, draw a circumferential line around them at each of the three marks. The top plank will be flush with the top of the supports, the bottom plank will be raised ¾″ of an inch (to prevent rocking on an uneven floor), and the middle shelf can be positioned to accommodate books of various sizes.

3. Tack the unit together temporarily with 4-penny finishing nails. Don't drive the nails all the way—you will need to remove them after screwing.

4. Countersink and drill three holes in the vertical supports along the center lines of the shelves. Glue and screw the unit together with the 1¼″-long wood screws.

5. Withdraw the finishing nails.

6. Glue and nail the back on with finishing nails, holding it ¾″ off the floor. Fill all screw holes and edges of plywood with spackle or wood dough. Sand all surfaces and paint or give the bookcase the finish of your choice.◇

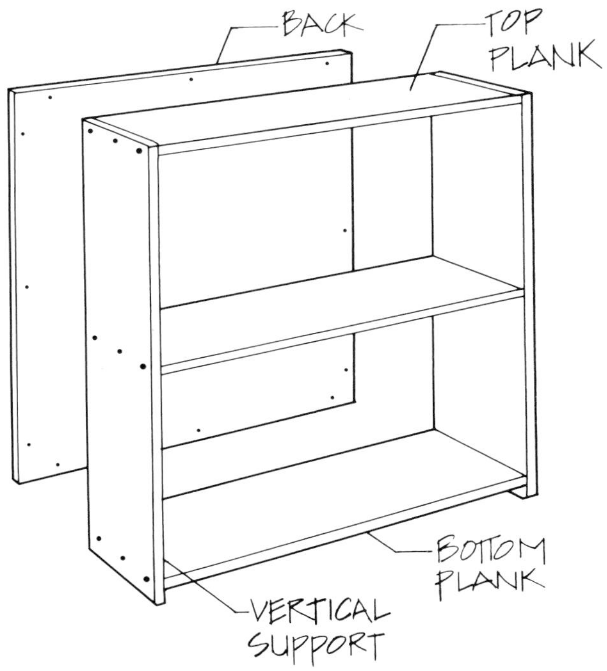

A NOT-SO-BASIC BOOKCASE

More complicated to construct, but a lot more interesting to look at, is this streamlined bookcase with recessed shelves and lots of rounded corners. It can be built in sections to fit any wall, and the vertical dimension between the shelves can be whatever suits your needs; if you own more short paperbacks than tall art books, for instance, you can adjust the shelf heights accordingly. Dadoes cut into the vertical supports hold up the shelves at one end; protruding rounded cleats support the opposite ends. This recipe is for four sections of six shelves; overall dimensions are: 79½″ high, 82¼″ long, and about 12″ deep. The bookcase is backless and the shelves are 7¼″ deep.

MATERIALS

For the vertical supports, use 1″ × 10″ No. 2 common pine, selecting boards that are free from warps and large knotholes. (You can also use No. 1 pine or redwood, but it will cost more.)

For the shelves and top and bottom planks, use 1″ × 8″ No. 2 pine.

For the cleats, use 1′ lengths of 1¾″-wide pine or 1″ × 2″ furring strips, or shelf scraps.

No. 10 flathead wood screws, 1¾″ long.

3-penny finishing nails.

White glue.

ASSEMBLY

All major cuts can be made with a crosscut saw, but to radius the top corners of the vertical supports and the ends of the cleats, a jigsaw or saber saw is necessary. For dado cutting, a router, a radial-arm saw with a dado blade set, or a circular saw with dado blade are best. Otherwise, dadoes can be cut with a backsaw and chisel.

1. Cut five vertical supports 78″ long, twenty shelves 20″ long, one top and one bottom plank 81½″ long, and 20 cleats 12″ long.

2. Using a pair of compasses, radius the top corners of the vertical supports and the front ends of the cleats. Cut with a jigsaw, smooth with a file, then sand.

3. Carefully measure and pencil mark all vertical supports for cleats and dadoes by following these steps:

a. Stack all five vertical supports, carefully aligning the edges and ends. Clamp them or tape them so they can't shift position.

b. Beginning at the bottom edge, measure and mark alternating spaces of 12¼″ and ¾″, 12¼″ and ¾″, and so forth. You will end with the last 12¼″ space at the top edge of the support. Using a square, mark these points all around the faces and edges of the vertical supports. Separate the stacked pieces and continue squaring the marks around the faces of all the pieces. You now have all the lines the shelves must fit between.

c. Cut ¾″-wide, ⅜″-deep dadoes between the lines on only one face of four of the five vertical supports so that the dadoes will always

A variation of the basic bookcase that involves dado cuts and rounded cleats.

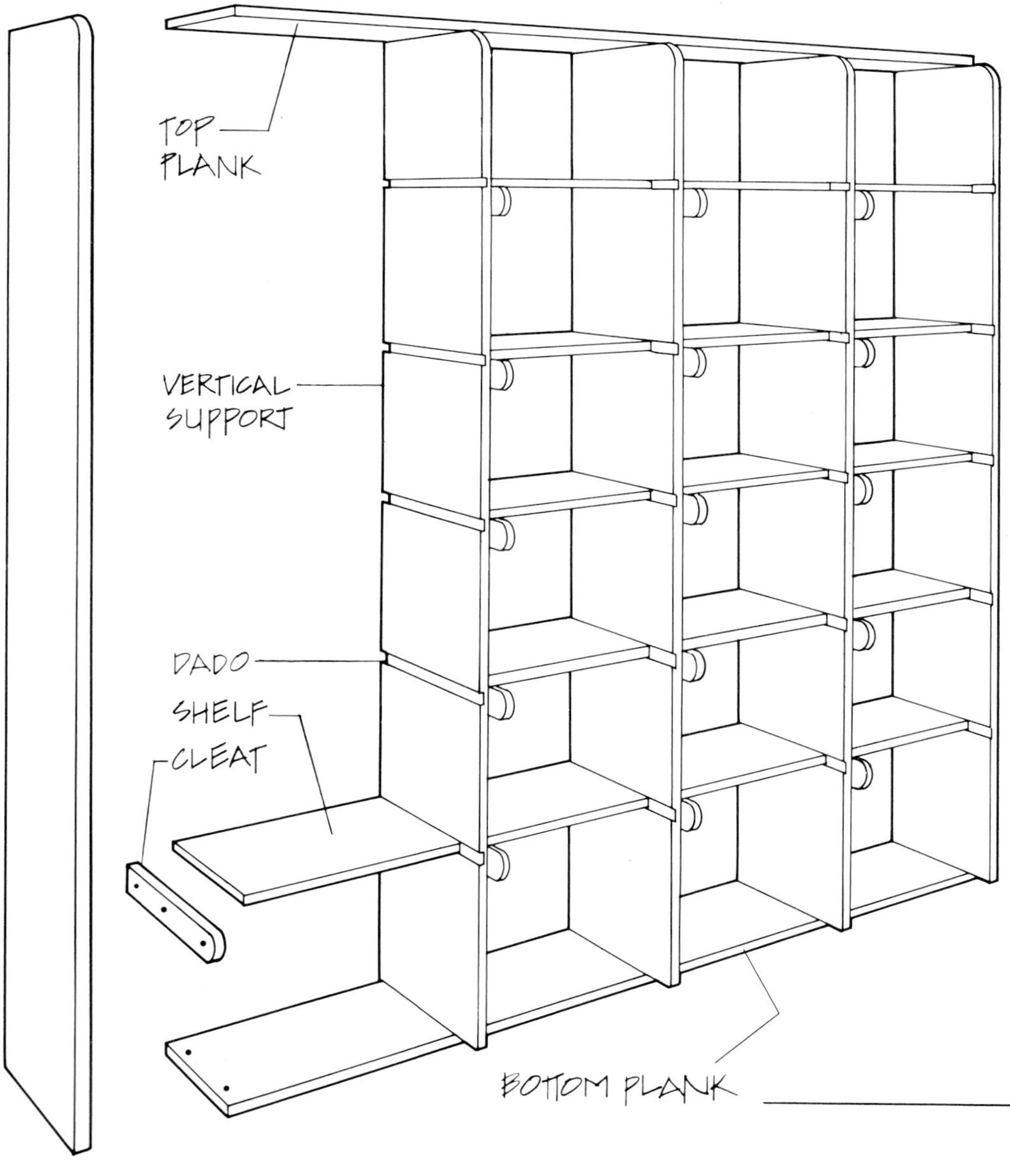

be on the right side of the shelf space.

4. If dadoes must be cut by hand, use a backsaw or other straight finishing saw and cut each line down to ⅜″, or halfway through the face of each vertical support. Use a sharp ¾″-wide wood chisel and a hammer to cut out the section of wood between the cuts, thus forming the trough or dado. Apply the chisel blade to either edge of the plank and cut against the grain of the wood.

5. Position the cleats on the vertical supports opposite the dadoes. The tops of the cleats should be flush with the lines marking the position of the bottom of the shelves. The rounded ends of the cleats should protrude out about 2¾″. Fasten each cleat to its support with glue and 3-penny finishing nails.

6. To attach the vertical supports to the top and bottom planks, first mark, countersink, and drill two $^{3}/_{16}$″ holes ⅜″ in from each end of the top and bottom planks. Then measure the distance remaining along the planks and divide it into four equal sections (each section will be about 20″ wide) and mark, countersink, and drill two $^{3}/_{16}$″ holes at each of those divisions. Holes in both top and bottom planks should match accurately. With the bookshelf on its back, screw the bottom plank to the base of each of the five vertical supports. Fasten the top plank loosely to the top of each vertical support. Stand the bookcase up, insert all shelves to be sure they fit properly, then tighten the screws in the top plank.

7. Sand the bookcase, leave it unfinished or apply a finish of your choice.◇

BOOKCASE WITH ADJUSTABLE SHELVES

One handsome example of a bookcase with adjustable shelves is the unit described here. It has a plywood backing and shelves supported by small pegged metal brackets. The brackets are available at hardware and lumber stores and require only the precise drilling of parallel ¼″ holes.

This bookcase is 32″ long, 78″ high, and 7¼″ deep. Of course, these dimensions can be varied somewhat to fit the dimensions of your room, but units should not exceed 32″ in width. That's about the limit for an unsupported ¾″ pine shelf.

MATERIALS

For the vertical supports, top, bottom, and shelves, use 1″ × 8″ pine.

For the kickplate, use 1″ × 2″ pine.

For the back, use ¼″ A/D plywood.

No. 6 flathead wood screws, 1¼″ long.

6-penny finishing nails.

Shelf brackets or library pegs (four per shelf).

White glue.

Spackle or wood dough.

Paint or finish of your choice.

ASSEMBLY

1. Cut two vertical supports 78″ long, one top plank and one bottom plank 30½″ long, and five or six shelves 30¼″ long. (This length will allow ⅛″ clearance on each side and facilitate insertion and removal of shelves.) Cut the kickplate 30½″ long and the back 32″ × 78″.

2. Along the inside surface of each vertical support, measure and draw lines for the ¼″ shelf bracket holes. These should be 1″ in from both the front and back, and aligned meticulously. The holes should be marked and drilled 1½″ apart vertically, and ⅜″ deep. Drill all the holes precisely; it's surprising how a slight variation can make the whole job look wobbly. An inexpensive adjustable drill stop can be used to ensure accurate and uniform depth and that you don't accidentally go through the entire vertical support. To be sure of accu-

(continued on next page)

Shelves can be moved up and down—or removed entirely.

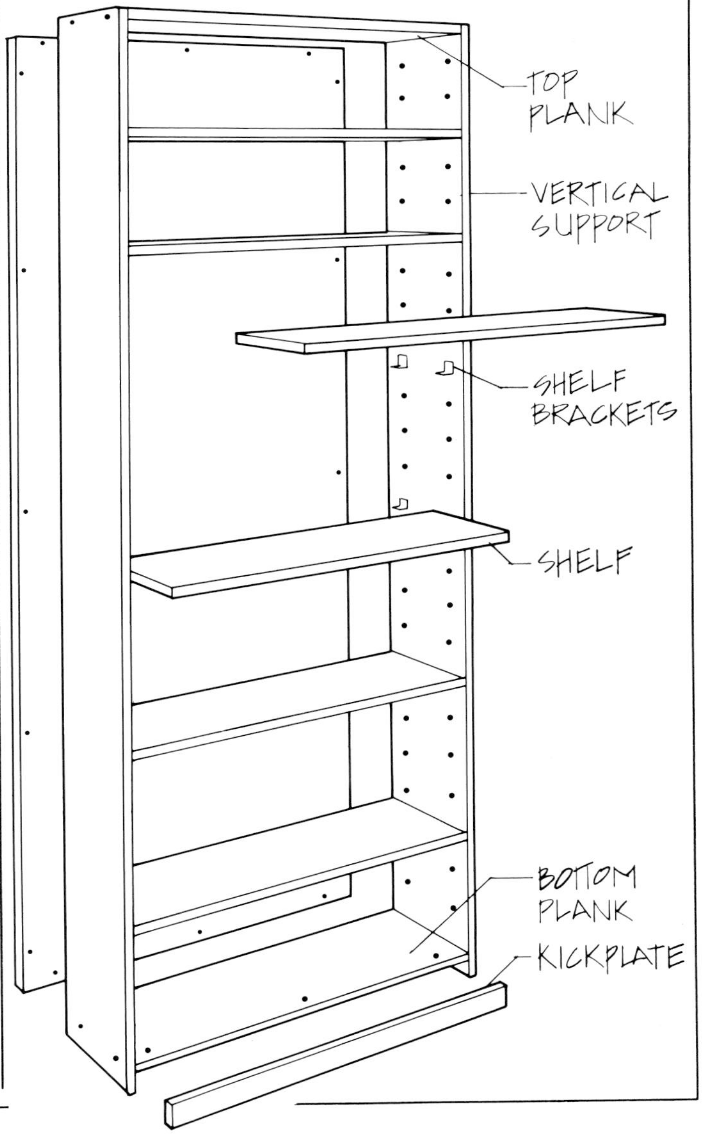

rate drilling a jig can be made by first laying out the holes to be drilled on a piece of scrap stock. Drill the holes all the way through the jig, then clamp or temporarily tack it to the vertical supports, always starting from the same end (top or bottom, doesn't matter). By doing this, even if your jig is a little off, all the holes will be at the same height.

3. Assemble the bookcase, gluing and screwing it together, with the top plank butting inside the tops of the vertical supports. The bottom plank should be mounted about 1½″ up from the bottom of the vertical supports, to allow clearance for the 1″ × 2″ kickplate, which can be fastened into place with glue and finishing nails. Fasten the plywood back (with the smooth side facing into the room) to the vertical supports and to the bookcase top and bottom with glue and nails or wood screws.

4. Fill all screw or nail holes, the plywood edges, and the joints around the kickplate with spackle or wood dough. Sand and paint the bookcase and shelves or apply a finish of your choice. Insert shelf brackets into the precisely drilled holes at appropriate intervals, then set in the shelves.◇

STEPPED DIVIDER BOOKCASES

A bookcase unit can sometimes do additional duty as a room divider. It might go all the way up to the ceiling, or perhaps only to eye level to act as a visual barrier. Simple bookcases can be grouped in a staggered line to form a stepped wall—these by Ken Sanden form a wall 94½″ long. Besides being more visually interesting, the stepped configuration provides more stability than an end-to-end straight-line arrangement; still, you must screw them each to the floor or anchor them to a wall at one end.

MATERIALS

For the vertical supports, top and bottom planks, and shelves, use 1″ × 12″ common pine.

No. 8 flathead wood screws, 1¼″ long.

6-penny finishing nails.

Six stove bolts, 2″ long and ¼″ in diameter, with large washers and nuts to fit them.

Molding of your choice, 3½″ wide.

White glue.

Spackle or wood dough.

Paint or finish of your choice.

ASSEMBLY

1. Cut six vertical supports, two of them 90″ long, two of them 80″ long, and two of them 70″ long (or however high you want the respective bookcases to be). Cut three top planks, three bottom planks, and about eighteen other shelves 30″ long.

2. Following the method outlined in step 3 of the Not-So-Basic Bookcase, page 122,

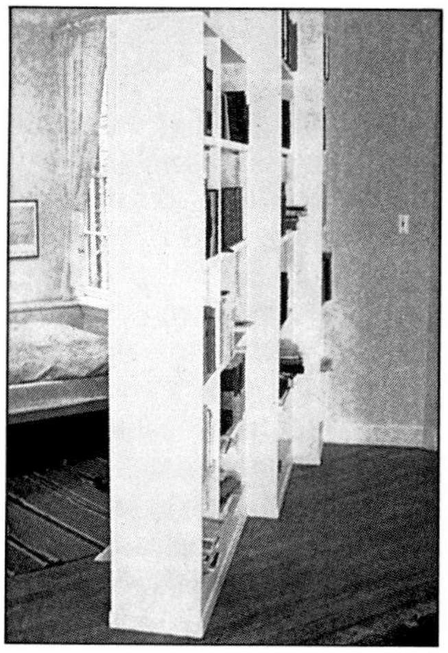

Ken Sanden's bookcases are backless to give an open, airy look. See page 39.

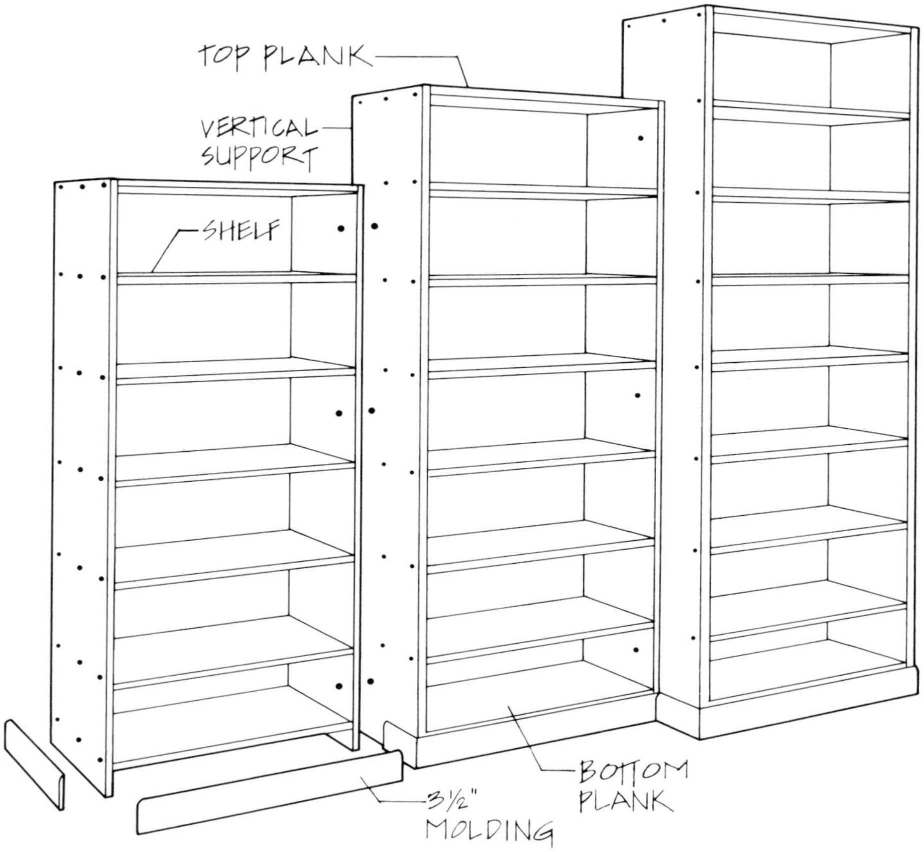

mark the location of the center lines of all shelves and planks. Using a square, mark the center lines all around each vertical support. The top surface of the bottom planks should be 3½″ up from the bottom of the vertical supports; the top planks should be even with the tops of the vertical supports. The shelves can be spaced as you desire.

3. Tack the units together temporarily with finishing nails, then countersink and drill three ⅛″ holes along all the center lines. Glue and screw each unit together. Remove finishing nails.

4. Arrange the three units side by side the way you want them. Fasten each unit to the next with stove bolts, washers, and nuts at top, center, and bottom. (Drill ¼″ holes through adjacent vertical supports to accept the bolts.)

5. Secure the units with L brackets screwed into the vertical supports and the floor, or with molly bolts, toggle bolts, or another fastening system into a wall.

6. Measure the exposed parts of the bases on all sides and cut sections of molding to cover them. Fasten the molding into place with glue and finishing nails. Set the nails. Fill all screw holes, joints, and nail holes with spackle or wood dough, and sand. Paint or give the bookcases a finish of your choice.◇

A PEDIMENTED WALL WITH SHELVES

Seeming to be quite complicated at first glance, this divider wall is formed basically of three 28″-wide bookcases flanking a 28″-wide opening, with two bookcases on one side and one bookcase on the other. Most of the shelves face the larger, nursery side of the divided room, but the upper part of one unit is "flipped," and four shelves there face the smaller section of the room on the other side. The backing material for the shelves is Homosote covered with fabric, which can double as a bulletin board.

The unit pictured here is 10′ 2″ wide and 11¾″ thick overall; the two shorter bookcases are 72″ high, the taller bookcase and door opening are 80″ high, and the point of the pediment is 90″ from the floor. Depending upon the size and proportions of your room, all these measurements, as well as the pitch of the pediment, can change to fit the space.

Sturdy 2″ × 12″s are used for the vertical supports; shelves, top planks, and the pediment are made from 1″ × 12″s. You will have to rip about ½″ from the backs of all the shelf 1″ × 12″s so that there will be room for the Homosote backing to fit flush with the vertical supports and the top planks.

After deciding on how the shelves will be spaced, assemble the three units following the general procedure for the Basic Bookcase, page 121, for making the center lines, tacking, and gluing and screwing together all vertical supports, shelves, and planks.

When screwing in the shelves that are directly opposite one another, first fasten the shelves in one side of the unit by screwing straight through the vertical supports into the edge of the shelves. To fasten the adjacent shelves,

(continued on next page)

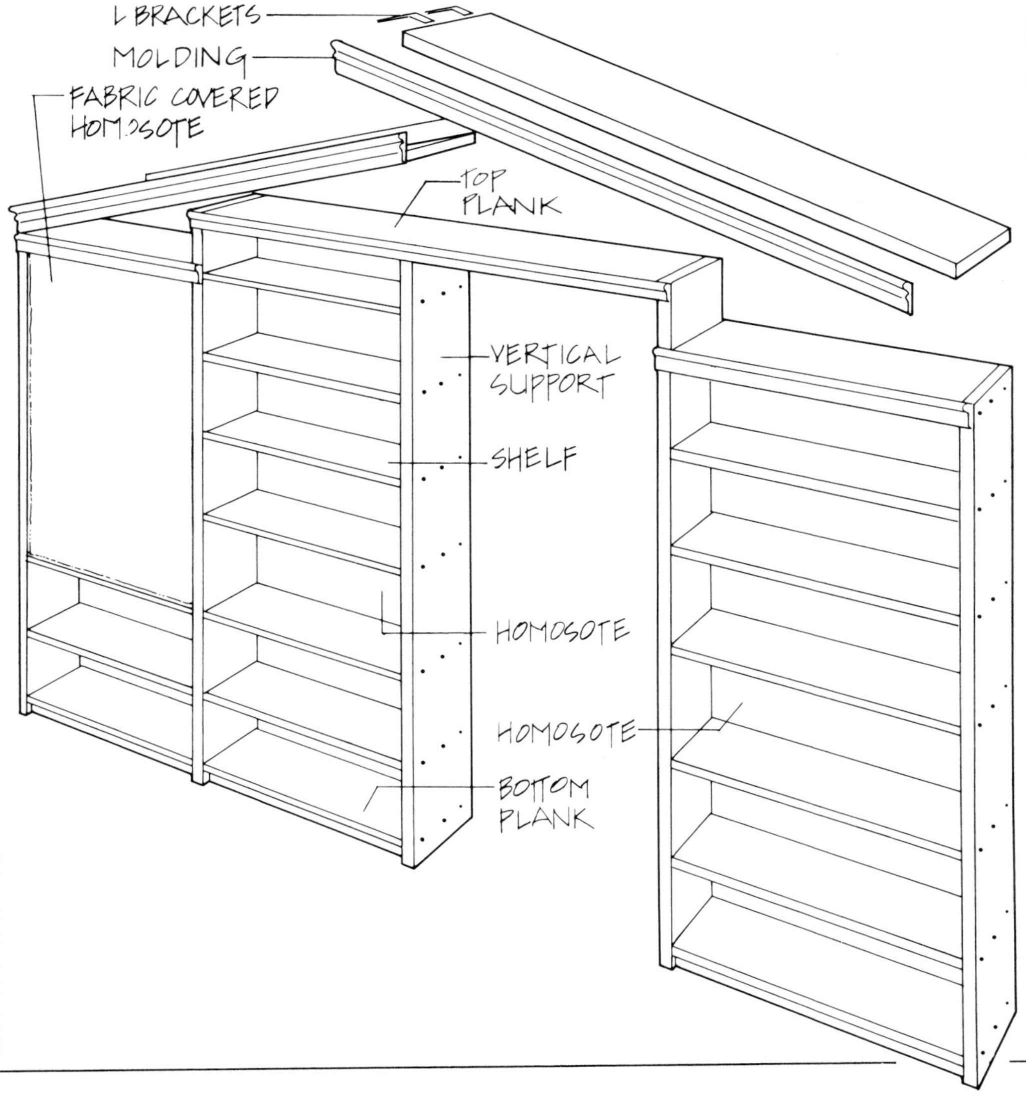

The playful spirit of this pitched-roof divider wall is well suited to a child's room. *See page 17.*

start just below the edge of the already in-place shelves, then carefully countersink and drill up at a slight angle through the vertical support into the edges of the shelves. Be sure that the angle is such that the screws do not cut across the bottom edges of the shelves or come out the top.

Fit the 1″ × 12″s for the pediment into place over the bookcases and mark them for cutting. Cut them to size, beveling the ends so that they fit together flush when set at the desired angle and fit flat against the wall.

Partially unbend the L brackets to the angle of the pediment, and fasten the halves of the pediment together by screwing the brackets to them. Screw the pediment to the bookcases.

For a recessed kickplate, nail lengths of 1″ × 2″s below the bottom plank of each unit on the open sides. Attach 1″ × 4″ molding, in any pattern of your choice, to both sides of the top planks and the pediment. This molding should be nailed in place with its lower edge flush with the lower edge of the pediment and planks to give added weight and height to these elements.

Finally, measure the bookcases for the Homosote backing, taking the thickness of the covering fabric into consideration. Cut the Homosote with a mat knife or saw; staple on the fabric. Secure the backing in place with cement-coated box nails hammered through the vertical supports into the edges of the Homosote. If these panels need further support, add small L brackets to the vertical supports here and there.

This wall is too tall and slender to be freestanding, so it will have to be secured at either end. If there is a stud in the existing wall at the spot where you want to position your pedimented wall, it is a relatively simple matter to screw through the outside vertical supports and directly into the stud. If no stud can be found, you will have to use molly bolts, toggle bolts, or whatever fastening system is appropriate for your wall.

Fill all screw holes and joints with spackle; sand the unit and paint to match the rest of the room.◇

BASIC WALL SHELVING

A shelf is a horizontal shape in need of vertical support. The fundamental problem to be solved is how to hold it up. Many solutions come to mind: hang it from a ceiling; rest it like a beam on posts; suspend it like a bridge between two facing walls. In most instances, though, a shelf is attached at a right angle to a wall.

The most elementary shelf is a board that is screwed on to L-shaped brackets. Not too stylish, but this is the least expensive and quickest shelf system. To make sure your shelf will support a reasonable weight without the brackets pulling out of the wall, insert plastic or lead anchors into the wall before you screw in the brackets, or use molly or toggle bolts. Ask at your hardware store which securing system will be best suited to your wall. To make sure shelves are horizontal, a level is more reliable than mere eyeballing or measuring from nearly always crooked ceilings or floors. Several different kinds of L brackets are available, and many materials can function as shelving—softwood, hardwood, plywood, plastic, glass, steel—as long as it has enough support to prevent sagging.

A kitchen can never have too many shelves.

Another type of bracket shelving is slightly more complicated, and its big advantage is its flexibility it provides. In this method, called "track and bracket" shelving, two or more slotted metal tracks are aligned and mounted verti-

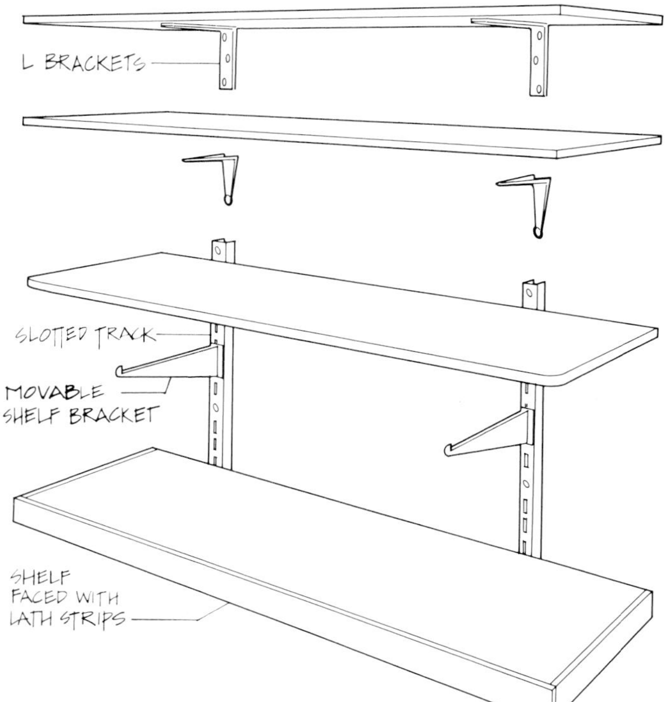

cally on a wall and long metal brackets are hooked into the slots. Shelves are then simply placed across these brackets and are kept in place by a lip at the end of the brackets. The distance between the shelves can easily be changed by moving the brackets up or down as you wish.

Besides making certain that the tracks are securely attached to the wall, the only hitch in installing this system is to make certain that the tracks are hung at exactly the same height so that the slots are lined up; if they aren't, the shelves won't be level.

Shelves can be any length, but the tracks should be spaced about 2½–3′ apart—about the optimum length a shelf should extend without support. Tracks and brackets come in a wide variety of finishes and price ranges, as well as many different lengths and widths.

A shelf is one of the easiest carpentry projects to dress up. Not only do single lath strips tacked to shelves with finishing nails instantly make them look more substantial, but this facing also hides some of the hardware.◇

A KITCHEN STORAGE CLOSET

One solution to the problem of never having enough storage space in a kitchen is to build a closet with shelves. The basics here are the same as for bookcases with adjustable shelves, but considering that the average can is shorter than the average book, more shelves can be fitted more closely together.

These shelves are contained in what is really just a Basic Box, with the verticals drilled with holes to accommodate the ¼″ pegs on which the shelves rest; the framework is rigid and the shelves are movable. All is concealed by tall flush doors.

Actual dimensions will be determined by the space available, but the unit described here is 80″ high, 40″ wide, and about 9″ deep. If the unit is any higher than this, the upper shelves will be out of reach of the average person. Since 96″ is a low standard/average ceiling height, the ceiling above this cabinet may have to be dropped a bit for a more finished look.

This closet is divided into two sections (each 20″ wide) and are identical except for the swing of the door. Any number of sections may be made, or only one (to any width, depending on the amount of room you have in which to swing open a door). This recipe is for one 20″-wide single section.

MATERIALS

For the top plank, bottom plank, shelves, and vertical supports, use 1″ × 8″ common pine.

For the back, use ¼″ A/D fir plywood.

For the top apron and bottom kickplate, use 1″ × 2″ pine.

For the door, use a 1⅜″ × 1′ 8″ × 6′ 8″ hollow flush door.

One set, top and bottom, pivot hinge or other hinges of your choice.

One magnetic or friction catch.

One pull.

Shelf brackets or library pegs (four per shelf).

6-penny finishing nails.

4-penny coated box (or common) nails.

White glue.

One piece of ¼″ plywood or Masonite scrap about 3″ wide and 80″ long.

ASSEMBLY

1. Cut top and bottom planks 18½″ long; cut nine shelves 18¼″ long; cut two vertical supports 80″ long. Cut the back panel 80″ × 20″. Cut the top apron and the kickplate 18½″ long.

2. The key to success with this project, as with bookcases, is making sure that the holes for the shelf supports are meticulously aligned. To do this, make a jig and drill holes in both vertical supports, following instructions for the Bookcase with Adjustable Shelves, page 123.

3. With the white glue and finishing nails, fasten the top and bottom planks to the inside of the vertical supports—keeping the top flush with the top of the verticals and the bottom 1½″ up from the bottom of the verticals. To the underside of the top and bottom planks fasten the top apron and bottom kickplate flush with the front edge of the top and bottom planks and vertical supports.

By joining shelves with brackets to both sides of common vertical supports, these bookcases can be duplicated and made to fit a space of any width.

4. Glue and nail (with the 4-penny coated box or common nails) the back panel in place, being careful that none of the nails penetrates the shelf support holes.

5. The unit—and the shelves—can be sanded, painted or otherwise finished, and placed in position at this time. Be careful not to load up the shelf support holes with paint.

6. Attach to the wall with molly bolts, toggle bolts, or whatever fastening system is appropriate for your wall.

7. To mount the door, follow instructions packed with the hinges.

8. Mount catch on underside of top plank or to vertical support (not to movable shelf) and mount pull about 40″ above the floor.

9. When paint or other finish is dry, insert pegs and drop in shelves.◇

A SALVAGE BOOKCASE

Almost every type of furniture used for storage—chest, wardrobe, bureau, or breakfront—is essentially a vertical box. So a piece that's too far gone for reasonable refinishing can be transformed into another kind of box—a bookcase.

MATERIALS

For the host unit, find or somehow acquire an appropriate piece—such as a wardrobe—that is structurally sound.

For the new cleats, if needed, use 1″ × 1″ or 1″ × 2″ common pine.

For the new shelves, use 1″ No. 2 common pine of whatever length is appropriate.

White glue.

Finishing nails.

Stain, paint, or appropriate finish.

ASSEMBLY

1. Remove all doors, drawers, hardware, and internal fittings. If drawer supports happen to be where you'd like shelves, and they are still strong, leave them in place. Otherwise, measure for shelf heights (measure vertical dimensions *carefully* so that the shelves will be level), and fasten 1″ × 1″ or 1″ × 2″ pine cleats with glue and finishing nails to the inside walls of the wardrobe. Depending on the width of the wardrobe, cut shelves to length from 1″ × 8″ or 1″ × 12″ No. 2 pine planks.

2. Sand the shelves smooth, set them in place, and finish them in a way that harmonizes with the original or restored finish of the host unit.◇

A found cupboard was transformed into useful open shelving for books and other objects. See page 15.

PARTITIONS

CANVAS DRESSING ROOM

In one corner of their loft, Stan and Roanne Peskett made a nifty dressing room cum closet by partitioning off shelves and a clothes rack with large— 4′ × 8′— expanses of cotton artists' canvas. The individual sections of the partition are constructed just as an artists' canvas is made, and as such they can be (and were) painted. They are lightweight and relatively inexpensive—the cost will depend somewhat on what quality canvas you purchase. To support the canvas, the Pesketts used regular artists' stretcher bars. While this would be the easiest method, stretchers as long as 8′ might be somewhat difficult to find. If your local artists' supply store does not carry stretchers this long, you can use 1″ × 3″s bought at a lumberyard.

Depending upon what kind of walls you have, you can attach the partition to them with L brackets, cleats, or even hinges. The Pesketts left a 3′-wide opening between their two sections and spanned the space with a rod on which they hung a sailcloth curtain for privacy.

The following recipe is for one 4′ × 8′ section of this partition.

MATERIALS

One set of stretcher bars—two 4′ long, two 8′ long (or 1″ × 3″s of the same lengths).

One cross brace (or one approximately 4′-long 1″ × 3″).

Pieces of ⅛″ or ¼″ plywood scrap.

6-penny finishing nails.

No. 4 flathead wood screws, ½″ long.

One piece of artists' canvas, primed or unprimed, at least 4½′ × 8½′.

Staples or carpet tacks.

Staple gun or tack hammer.

METHOD

1. Assemble the premitered and notched stretcher bars. If using 1″ × 3″s, miter the corners and nail the four lengths together through the edges at the corners with finishing nails.

2. Cut four triangular pieces of plywood for corner braces (the long side of the triangles should be about 12″ long), and screw them into the corners so that their edges are about ¼″ in from the edges of the stretchers or the 1″ × 3″s.

3. Install the cross brace. The system of installation of these braces for ready-made stretcher bars differs from manufacturer to manufacturer. If you are using 1″ × 3″s, cut the 4′ length to exactly fit between the two long (8′) sides of the frame and toe the brace in place with finishing nails. Cut two more triangular pieces of ⅛″ plywood and screw them down to secure the cross brace; there should be at least two screws through each piece of plywood into the brace and two into the 8′-long side pieces, for strength and stability.

4. Roll out the canvas on the floor and place the frame on top, braced side up, so that there is an equal amount of fabric all around the frame. Beginning in the middle of one of the long sides, start stapling or tacking the fabric into the back side of the frame. When two or three staples or tacks are in place, move around to the opposite side and, keeping the canvas taut, install two or three staples or tacks in the back of the other long stretcher.

5. Next, move to one of the shorter sides and, still keeping the fabric tight, put in another tack or two. Do the same in the opposite short side. Move back to the longer sides and, alternating sides and making sure you have enough material to work with, but always keeping the fabric tight, continue stapling.

6. When you get to the corners, make neat "hospital" corners as if you were making a bed, and staple the folds down securely. If the canvas is wrinkled or floppy, sprinkle or mist water onto the back; this will shrink the canvas slightly and tighten it up nicely.

7. Paint the canvas (priming it first if you are using unprimed fabric). You may want to paint it to match your walls, or you can try your hand at working out—as the Pesketts did—an abstract design, perhaps with paint rollers of two or three different widths, using several different colors. Note: If you used 1″ × 3″s to build your frame, you may want to give your partition sections a painted border the same width as the frame to help disguise the "line" that might appear. Unlike regular stretcher bars, the 1″ × 3″s will not be beveled, therefore you will probably be able to detect a crease at the inside edge of the 1″ × 3″s where it presses against the underside of the canvas. Painting a border that meets this line will make it less noticeable.◇

These partitions, of artists' canvas, make a handsome dressing room. See page 52.

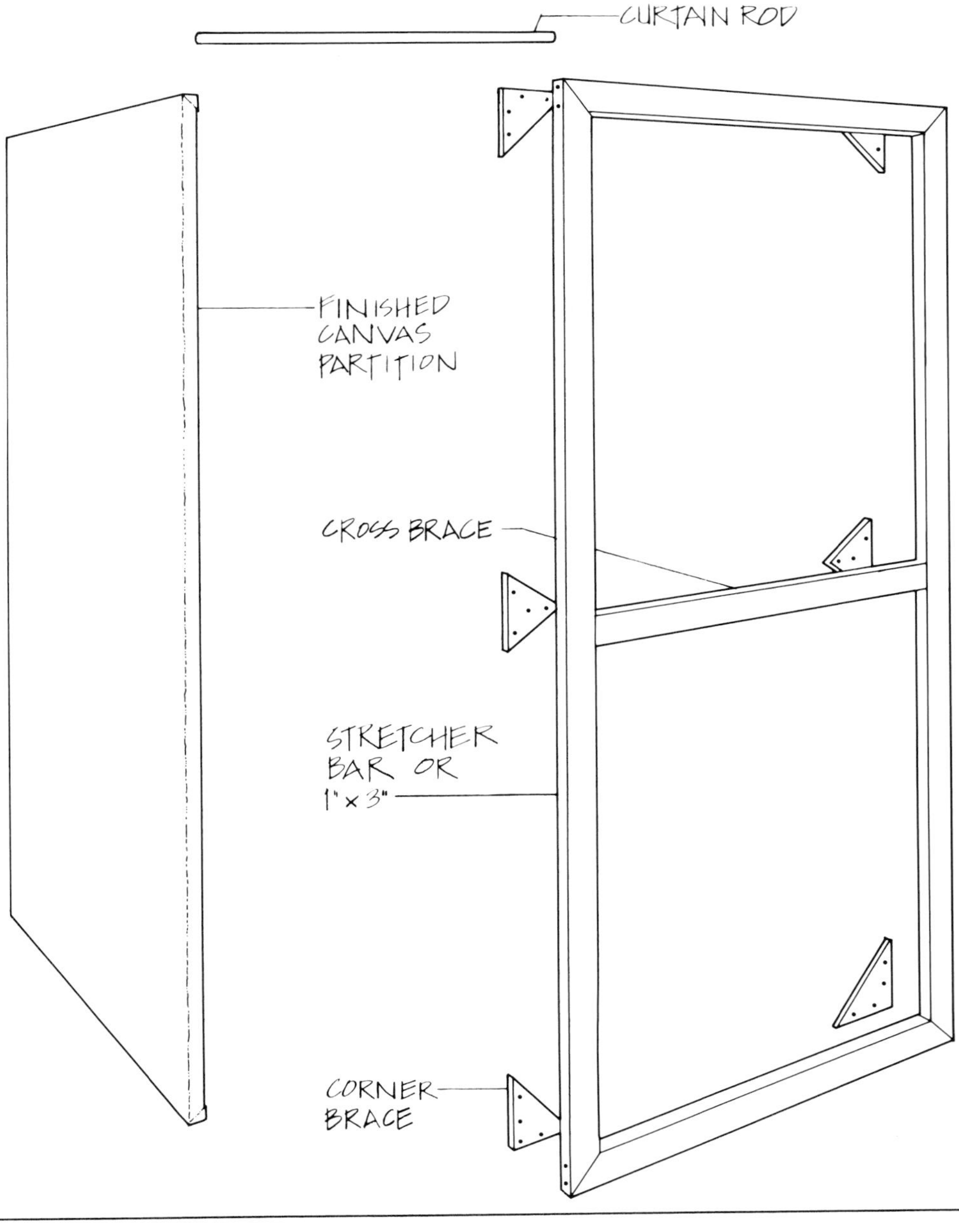

OTHER WAYS TO USE STRETCHER-BAR PARTITIONS

- In a small room, use two narrow panels to make a closet in one corner. If you hinge them to abutting walls so they meet at right angles, they could latch with a magnetic catch or two, and if you use hinges, the whole thing could open wide for easy access.
- Instead of artists' canvas, use the same fabric that is used elsewhere in the room.
- Make three or four narrow panels and hinge them together to make a screen. Use large-patterned fabric with a Far Eastern motif and you've got an Oriental-look screen; a bold colorful fabric could hide piles of toys in a kids' room.

DRYWALL SCREEN

Because it is fabricated almost like an actual wall, from drywall and galvanized metal studs (sometimes called steel 2″ × 4″s), this partition is almost like a built-in fixture; it isn't permanent, but you probably wouldn't want to move it very often. This is a good idea when a sturdy, solid-looking barrier in a large space is in order.

Metal studs were used rather than wood 2″ × 4″s because the metal ones are lighter weight and make for a good industrial-look contrast with the drywall. The drywall is used in its full 4′ width, so the prefinished edges can remain on three sides; a foot and a half was sliced off the top, so the panels are 78″ high. The panels are placed at angles to one another and hinged together at the top corners with twisted together loops of 12-gauge steel wire. Holes will have to be drilled for this wire if there are no conveniently positioned openings in the studs. For further stability, once a location is decided upon for the partition, drive a pair of 6-penny common nails into the floor to line up with openings on the bottom of each panel.

No special tools or skills are needed for this project; the following recipe is for one panel of the multisectional divider.

MATERIALS

Three 1½″ × 1½″ galvanized steel studs, each 96″ long.

Metal shears or hacksaw.

Two 4′ × 8′ sheets of ⅜″ drywall.

Pencil and ruler.

Drill.

Mat knife.

Self-tapping drywall screws.

Screwdriver.

METHOD

1. Using metal shears or a hacksaw, cut two studs to 78″ long; cut the other stud in half (resulting in two 48″ lengths).

2. Measure 18″ down from the top on the finish side of each sheet of drywall and draw a line all the way across. With the mat knife, make a deep cut along this line. Bend this "flap" backward and then make a clean cut with the mat knife on the back side along the resulting fold.

(continued on next page)

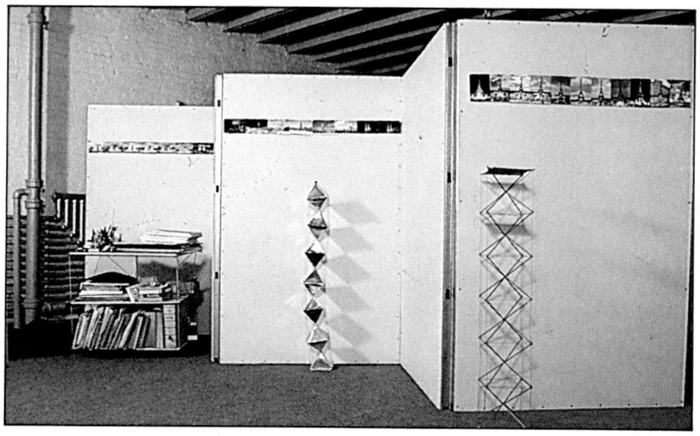

These partitions can be tailor-made for any space. See page 60.

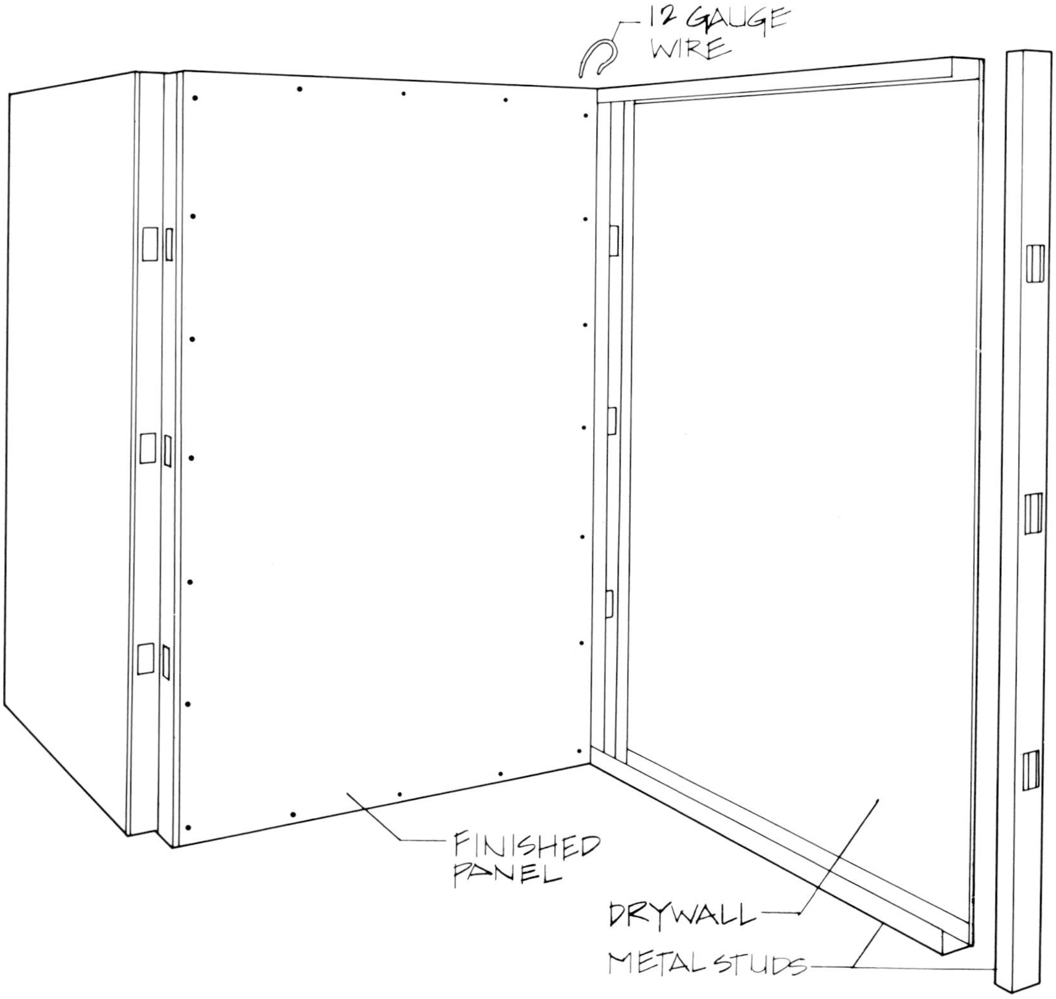

3. Measure and mark the finish side of drywall for placement of screws. They should be ¾″ in from the edge and at intervals of not more than 12″.

4. Place the studs on the floor in a rectangle (it may be necessary to miter the corners to make them fit properly), then place the drywall on top.

5. Using a drill bit about half the diameter of the screws, and making sure that edges of drywall and studs are lined up, drill three holes along each side—one in the middle and one at each end—through the drywall and into the studs. Insert screws and tighten them. Drywall will be held in position. Continue drilling and inserting screws all around the panel. When all screws are securely in place, turn panel over.

6. Cut second panel as you did the first, lay it on top of the studs, and mark and screw as in steps 3 and 5.

VARIATION

Place just two of these panels in a V shape or at right angles to each other and then butt the edge of one panel against a wall to create a small "room" with one open side. In either configuration, you might want to secure the panels to the floor with L brackets.◇

CANVAS PARTITION "DOORS"

To give a clean, contemporary look to an entrance hallway, designer Tim Romanello devised some clever "manually operated" fabric partitions that function like floor-to-ceiling sliding doors in the openings of the entryway. He chose beige duck (a heavy material works best here) and the walls were painted to match.

To install a panel like Tim Romanello's over any opening, all that is needed is a length of fabric, a couple of steel rods, a sewing machine, a clear expanse of wall that adjoins and is at least as wide as the opening, and a narrow traverse rod stripped of its pull mechanism. The traverse rod should be a bit longer than twice the width of the opening.

Cut a length of fabric that is about 8″ longer than the distance from floor to ceiling (to allow for hems). Hem the fabric at the sides; the material should be wide enough so that even with these hems it will completely hide the doorway or window.

Hem the fabric at the bottom in the usual way, with a 1½″ hem. At the top make a "double-looped" hem (or heading) to form a trough that will cover the traverse rod. The trough should be about 1½″ deep. For stability, insert a ¼″ steel or wooden rod in one of these top hems. Sew up the ends.

Remove the hanger glides that ride in the track of the traverse rod and sew them into the bottom of the trough about every 3″ or so.

Install the traverse rod on the ceiling close to the wall above the opening; it should extend in whichever direction—left or right—you want the panel to slide open. Fit the glides back into the track and let the panel hang free.

When closed, Tim Romanello's floor-to-ceiling fabric doors give the appearance of a solid wall. See page 50.

Slip another ¼″ steel rod into the bottom hem; sew up the ends.

For easier operation and to keep the fabric cleaner, you may want to attach a wooden or plastic dowel to the heading. This can be painted to match the wall.◇

PARTITION WALL WITH WINDOW

To create this partition wall with a half-round opening takes no special expertise—just careful planning, careful assembly, and careful finishing. The wall itself is of drywall construction. If you're daunted by working with this material, you can just as readily use plywood, Masonite, or some other wall material.

Obviously, a window wall such as this cannot fit into every room, and it cannot stand by itself. It must be securely attached to the floor and/or to existing walls, depending upon how it is placed. In the apartment Janice Gewirtz designed, the 8′ × 8′ wall was built as one half of an L-shaped partition and the whole thing was secured to the floor.

MATERIALS

Exact sizes and proportions will vary with individual needs and the size and shape of the room that will be divided, but to build it as shown:

Fifteen 8′ fir 2″ × 4″s.

Two 4′ × 8′ sheets of ½″ A/C plywood.

Approximately 9′ of ⅛″ Masonite, 4″ wide.

One 26″ fir 2″ × 2″.

Four 4′ × 8′ sheets of ⅜″ drywall.

Drywall tape and joint compound.

1⅜″ drywall nails.

4-penny common nails.

4-penny and 6-penny finishing nails.

No. 6 flathead wood screws.

Spackle.

An ingenious solution for creating a space within a space. See page 35.

White glue.

Paint.

ASSEMBLY

The wall is framed out in the standard house-construction method. Top and bottom 2″ ×

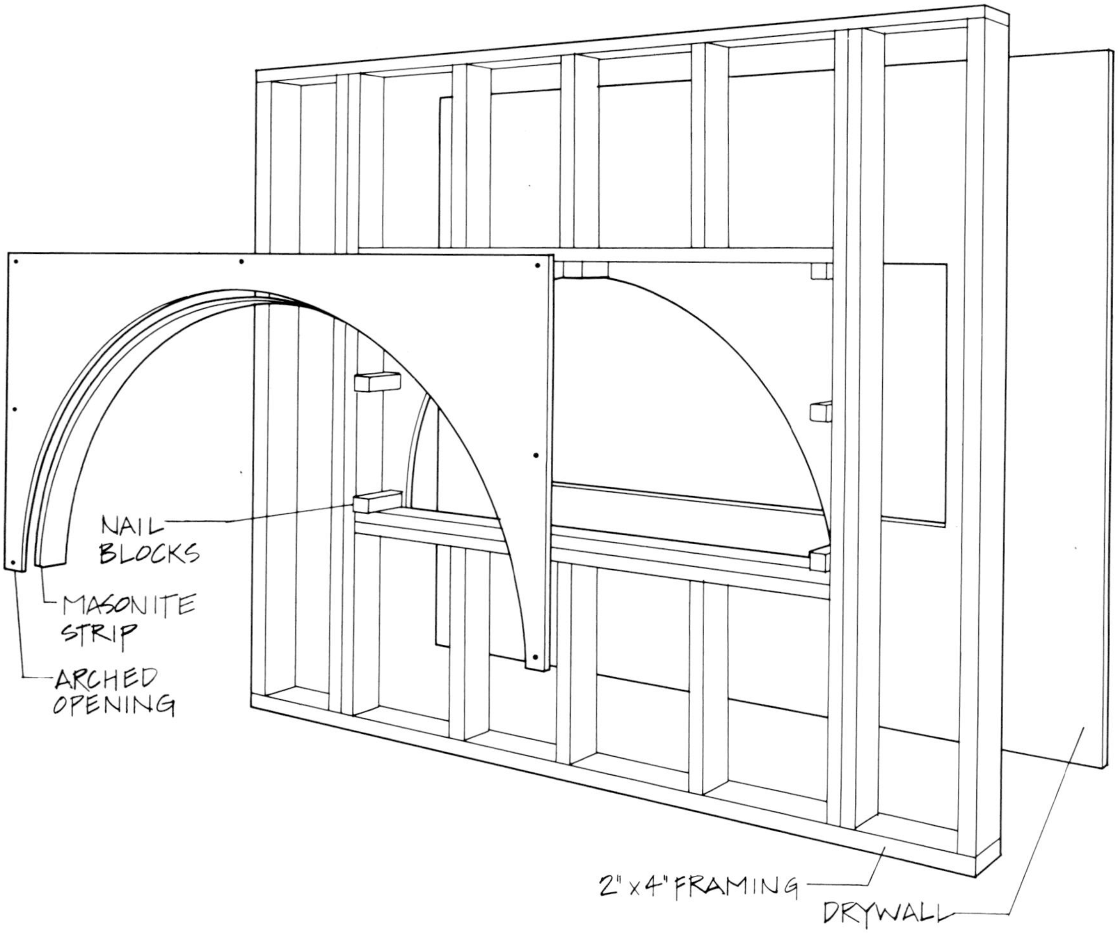

4″ rails are joined by seven vertical 2″ × 4″ studs 16″ on center (that is, spaced 16″ from center to center) with extra, doubled studs for added strength on either side of the opening.

1. Build the wall frame with a rectangular opening for the half-round window to fit into. Construct the bottom sill of the opening from doubled 2″ × 4″s; the bottom of the lower 2″ × 4″ should be 32″ above the floor. The opening itself should measure 36″ high, 77″ wide, and 3½″ thick.

2. Cut two ½″ plywood pieces 36″ × 77″. Carefully mark a semicircle with a radius of 34″ on these plywood rectangles. To do this, find and mark the exact centers of the long edges of the rectangles. Next, drive a small nail through one end of a yardstick or length of lath; then exactly 34″ away from the nail, drill a hole just large enough to admit the point of a pencil. Place the nail point at the mark on the bottom edge of one piece of plywood, and with the pencil in the hole, carefully draw a semicircle. Repeat on the second plywood rectangle. Then make careful cuts along the lines with a saber saw.

3. These panels should *not* be mounted flush with the framing surface. Instead, they should jut out ⅜″ on either side of the wall so that their surfaces will be flush with the face of the ⅜″ drywall that will cover the frame. To accomplish this ⅜″ offset, cut seven nail blocks of 2″ × 2″s, each one exactly 3¼″ long. Position each of these nail blocks around the rectangular opening and nail them down, one in each corner and one in the center of the top and the sides, as indicated in the diagram. Nail the arches to the 2″ × 2″s with 4-penny common nails.

The new room created by the partition wall becomes a bedroom. See page 34.

4. The inside of the arched opening is completed by the 4″-wide Masonite strip. It should be just slightly less than 107″ when in position. Hold it in place and trim it to fit. The Masonite strip is fastened in position with white glue and 4-penny finishing nails. Set the nails once the glue is dry.

5. Fill all the joints, cracks, and rough edges of the arch with spackle, and sand down any high spots along the edges of the Masonite.

6. Nail the drywall flush around the plywood, carefully dimpling the heads of the drywall nails below the surface of the face-paper without breaking it. A final square blow with the face of the hammer will accomplish this. Tape and joint-compound the drywall, feathering over the drywall/plywood junction. Sand smooth, then finish like the rest of the room or to your taste.◇

TABLES, COUNTERS, & MISCELLANEOUS PROJECTS

A THREE-PIECE TABLE

This good-looking unit can serve as a low divider, a work surface, an end table, or many other functions. In artist Bill Engel's apartment it acts as a telephone table. It should be attached to the wall with steel angle irons or screwed into a wooden cleat that is bolted into the wall. A table such as this can be built to varying dimensions, but Bill Engel made his 60¾″ long with an 11¼″-wide top and a 24″-high end support. The top is 18¾″ from the floor.

MATERIALS

For the top, use 1″ × 12″ pine, 60″ long.

For the end support, use 1″ × 12″ pine, 24″ long.

For the vertical support under the shelf, use a piece of ½″ A/B plywood, 18″ × 60″.

White glue.

Finishing nails.

Spackle or wood dough.

Paint or finish of your choice.

ASSEMBLY

1. Find the vertical center of the end support, then glue and nail the plywood vertical support to it along that center.

2. Find the center of the 1″ × 12″ pine top. Glue and nail the top to the vertical support along that line, butting it against the end support. Glue and nail the top horizontally through the end support.

3. Set the nails, fill the holes with wood dough. Sand and paint or apply a finish of your choice.◇

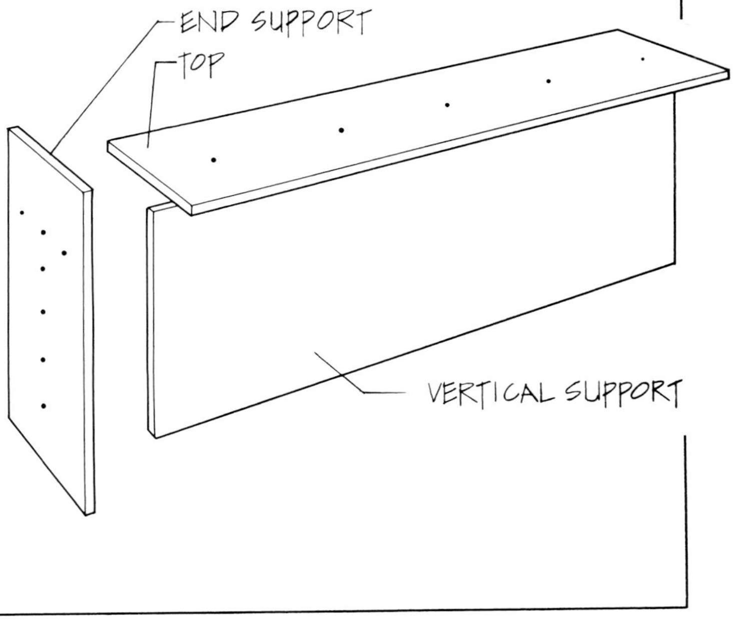

A WALL & PEDESTAL TABLE

This handsome plywood table is attached to a wall at one end by means of an angle iron; a sonotube supports the other (rounded) end. The tabletop utilizes two matching pieces of plywood glued together—one piece is furniture-grade birch veneer, the other is A/D plywood. Before the panels are glued, two sections are sawed out of the underside piece—one rectangular (to get rid of some weight) and one round (to accept the leg).

MATERIALS

For the top panel, use ¾″ birch veneer plywood.

For the lower panel, use ¾″ A/D plywood.

For the leg, use a sonotube 9″ in diameter and 29¼″ long.

A drilled angle iron 24″ long.

No. 10 flathead wood screws, 1¼″ long.

White glue.

Semigloss varnish or finish of your choice.

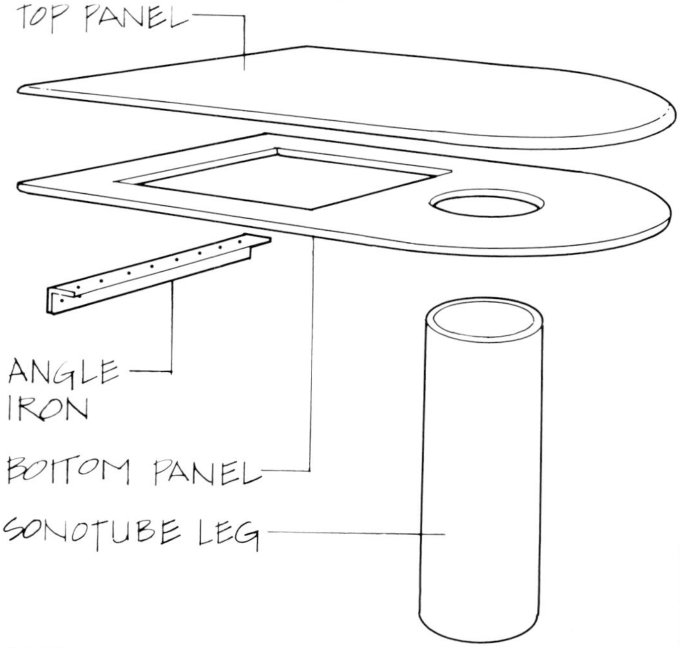

ASSEMBLY

1. Cut two 30″ × 48″ plywood panels. Draw a circle on what will be the bottom panel with the same diameter as the outside of the sonotube leg. The center of the circle should be 15″ from one end of the panel and 15″ from each side of it. Use a saber saw to cut out the circle. Next cut a rectangular area out of the panel as shown in the diagram.

2. Apply a generous amount of glue to the bottom panel, then lay the other panel on top, making sure both are aligned. Place heavy books or canned goods on top for weights and allow to dry for several hours or overnight. When glue is dry, mark a semicircle with a radius of 15″ on the leg end of the tabletop. Cut this half-circle with a saber saw.

Plywood and a sonotube combine for a versatile table. See page 37.

3. Round the edge of the table, except for the side that will be against the wall. This can best be done with a rounding bit and a heavy-duty router. Run the bit around the edge of both the top and the bottom. Sand the rounded edge smooth.

4. Birch veneer requires a careful finishing. Sand it smooth, then apply semigloss varnish or the finish of your choice.

5. When the finish is dry, glue the sonotube to the inside of the circular socket in the underside of the table.

6. Fasten the angle iron to the wall with molly bolts, toggle bolts, or whatever fastenings are necessary; attach the table to the angle iron with wood screws.◇

A CURVED KITCHEN COUNTER

Shelf and counter space seem ever at a premium in apartment kitchens, but this variation by architect Richard Oliver demonstrates that kitchen space need not be difficult to achieve. This shelf runs along one wall, creating storage space for a bicycle and a food preparation/breakfast counter; also, its curved shape and molding add some visual life in an otherwise plain kitchen.

The shelf is supported at one end by a plywood bookcase. For your unit, use an existing bookcase or build the Basic Bookcase, page 121 to meet your needs. While Richard Oliver's counter is 12″ wide at the narrow end, curving to 18″ at the other, the exact dimensions of this project will again depend on the size and shape of your kitchen.

MATERIALS

For the counter top and front posts, use 3/4″ A/B plywood.

A plywood bookcase.

For the cleat, use 1″ × 2″ pine.

No. 8 flathead wood screws, 1 1/2″ long.

Steel L brackets, with screws.

1 3/4″ wooden molding.

White glue.

Finishing nails.

Spackle or wood dough.

Paint or finish of your choice.

ASSEMBLY

1. Since you will cut a long shallow curve into the 3/4″ plywood for the counter top, the piece you buy should be as wide as you want the shelf to be at the curved end. With a saber saw, cut the plywood into the curved shape (see diagram).

2. Cut a cleat from the 1″ × 2″ pine. Since the counter will be held up at one end by the bookcase, the cleat need only be long enough to support the remaining section.

3. Screw the cleat to the wall using molly bolts, toggle bolts, plastic anchors, or other appropriate fastening method.

4. Cut two front posts from 3/4″ plywood 4″ to 6″ wide and to the same height as the bookcase, then screw the posts to the underside of the counter top using the L brackets, positioned as indicated in the diagram.

5. With the bookcase against the wall, position the counter top so that its narrow end rests on the bookcase and the wider end on the cleat. Mark, countersink, and drill a series of 1/8″ holes 3/8″ in from the back edge of the counter top, and with the 1 1/2″-long screws, glue and screw the counter to the cleat. Screw the front posts to the floor with L brackets.

6. Glue and finish-nail the 1 3/4″ molding (Oliver used a pattern called nose-and-cone) to the facing edge of the counter top. Set the nails.

7. Fill all nail holes, screw holes, and plywood edges with spackle or wood dough. Sand and paint or apply the finish of your choice.◇

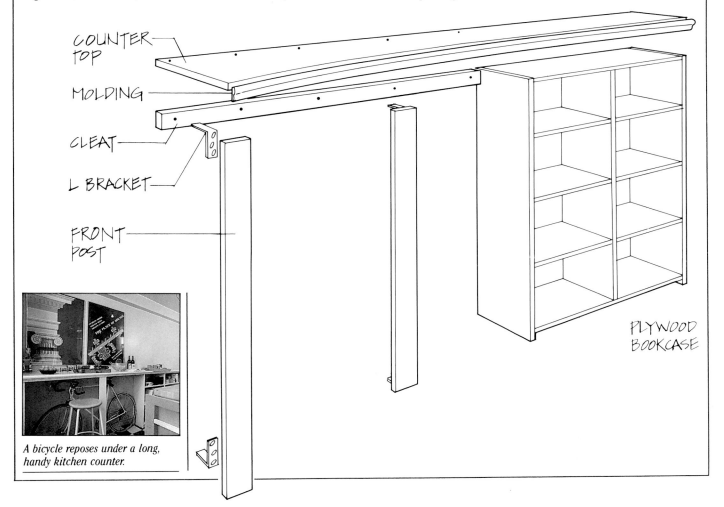

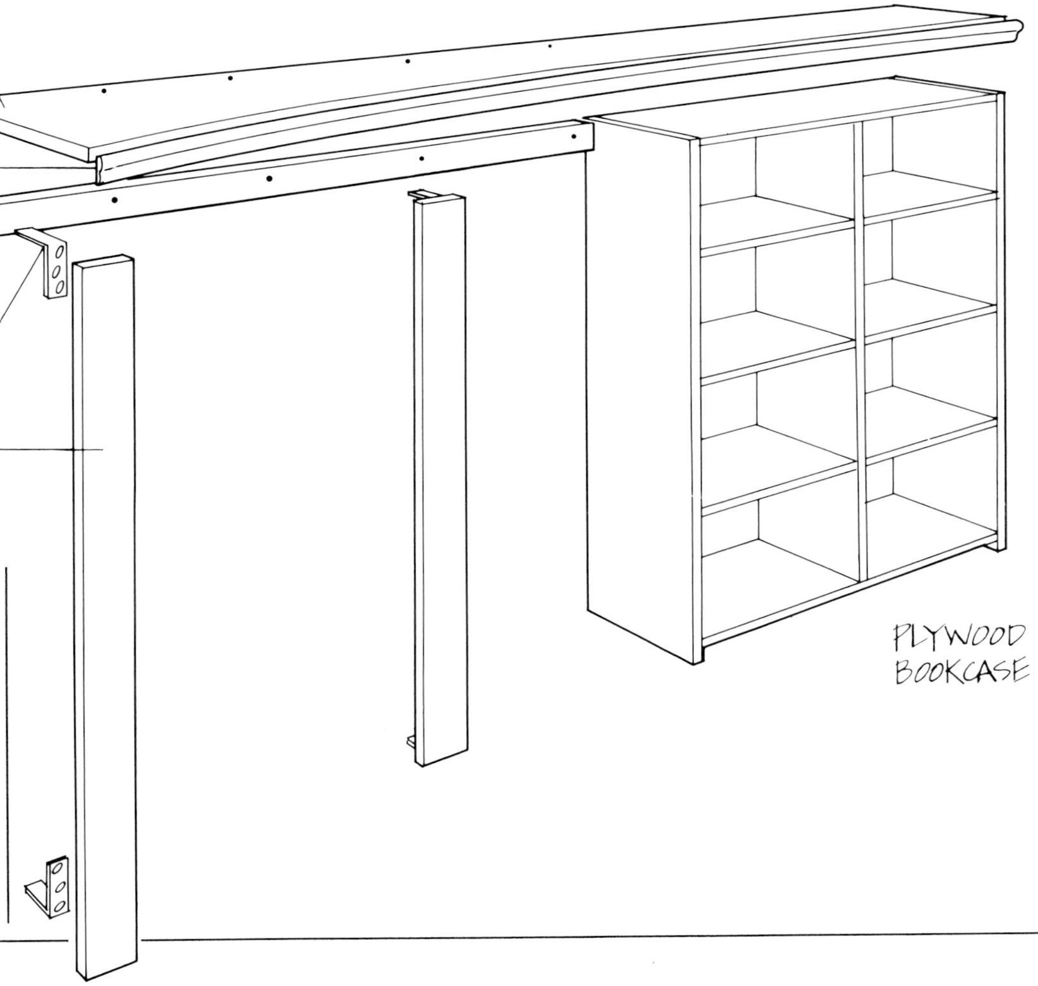

A bicycle reposes under a long, handy kitchen counter.

MULTIPURPOSE L-UNIT

A combination of basic bookcases and platform beds results in a multifunctional piece that becomes an environment in itself. Dimensions may be varied to suit your space, but the instructions here reflect how it was done in the apartment of architect Richard Oliver. Essentially, there are two platform beds, plus two deep bookcases—one with a kneehole that makes part of it a desk. Birch veneer plywood is used throughout; the edges are left unfinished after very precise cuts. All butt joints are made with glue and countersunk No. 10 1¼″ flathead wood screws.

Overall dimensions of the longer banquette are 9½″ high, 78″ long, and 30″ wide; the shorter banquette is 9½″ high, 60″ long, and 30″ wide. Overall, the bookcase with desk measures 30″ high, 94″ long, and 26″ wide; the smaller plain bookcase measures 30″ high, 90″ long, and 16″ wide.

Each bookcase has a solid plywood back that doubles as a backrest for the cushions. To make the kneehole in the long bookcase, build two topless cases (one 2′ long and one 4′ long), position them 22″ apart, and join them with a common 94″ top and back. Reinforce the banquettes with joists of ¾″ plywood—one in the shorter banquette and two in the longer one. Again, make careful and precise cuts for a professionally finished "furniture" appearance. If you cannot make such cuts at home, have them done by a lumberyard or cabinet shop.

MATERIALS

¾″ birch veneer plywood is used throughout.

Finishing nails.

White glue.

No. 6 flathead wood screws, 1¼″ long.

Wood dough or spackle.

Stain or finish of your choice.

ASSEMBLY OF THE BANQUETTES

1. For the longer banquette: cut two side panels, each 78″ × 8¾″; cut two end panels and two joists, each 28½″ × 8¾″; cut the top 78″ × 30″.

2. Glue and screw the sides to the ends so that the sides cover the ends of the end panels at the corners. Space the joists equally and glue and screw them in place.

3. Glue and screw the top to this frame. Fill screw holes and edges with wood dough, then sand all exterior surfaces.

4. For the shorter banquette: cut two side panels 60″ × 8¾″; cut two end panels and one joist, each 28½″ × 8¾″; cut the top 60″ × 30″.

5. Assemble the short banquette in the same way that you did the long one.

ASSEMBLY OF THE BOOKCASE WITH DESK

1. Cut four vertical supports, each 29¼″ × 25¼″; cut two shelves 22½″ × 25¼″; cut two shelves 46½″ × 25¼″; cut the back 94″ × 30″; cut the top 94″ × 25¼″.

2. Assemble the bookcases, one 24″ wide, the other 48″ wide, following steps 2–5 in the directions for the Basic Bookcase on page 121 (omitting the top plank).

3. Place the half-formed

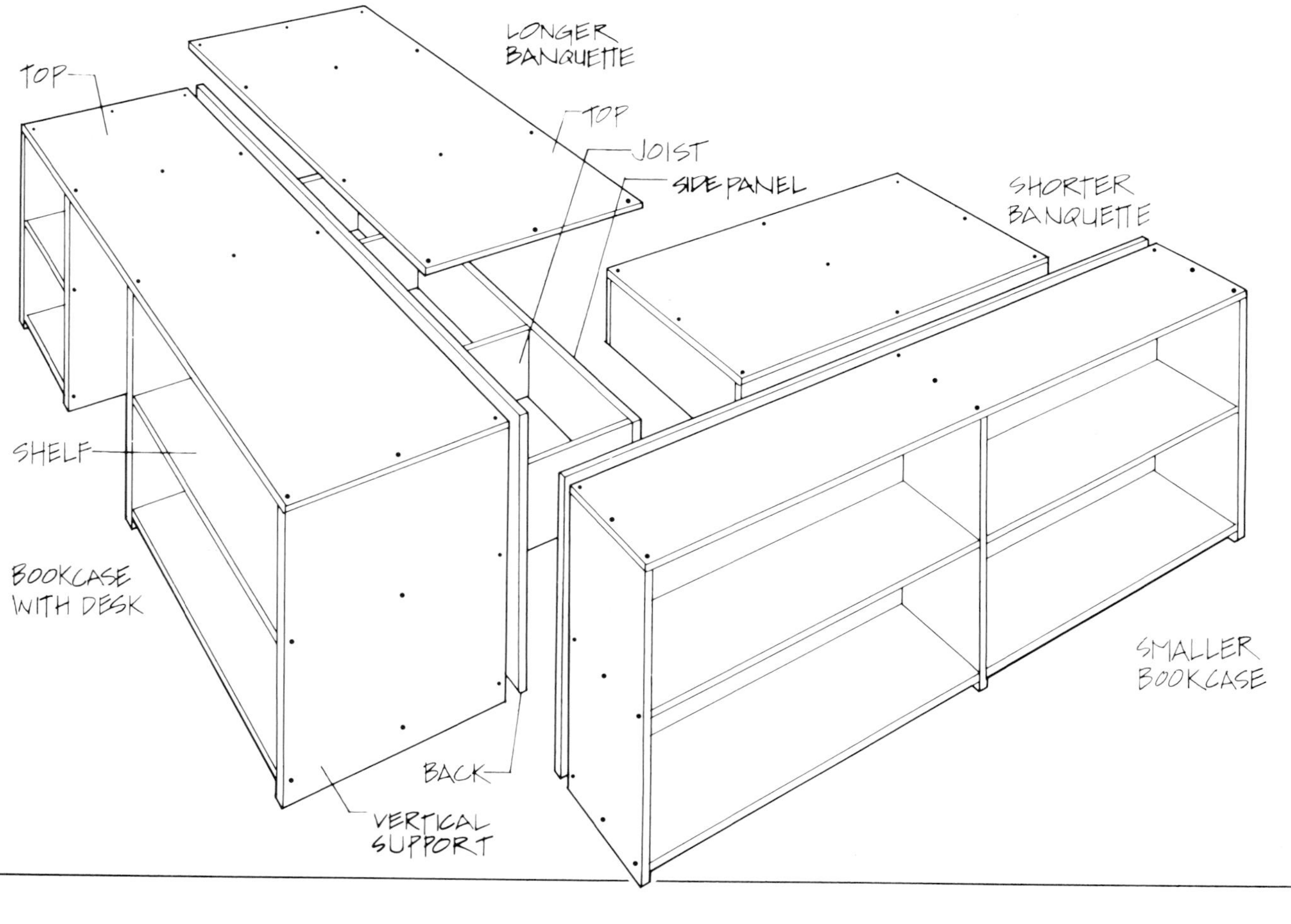

bookcases 22″ apart. Glue and screw the back to both units, keeping the edges of the back flush with the edges of the bookcases' vertical supports.

4. Glue and screw the common top onto both bookcases.

ASSEMBLY OF THE SMALLER, PLAIN BOOKCASE

1. Cut three vertical supports 29¼″ × 15¼″; cut four shelves 43⅞″ × 15″; cut the back 90″ × 30″; cut the top 90″ × 15¼″.

2. To assemble, again follow the instructions for the Basic Bookcase, except that here there is a vertical support in the center because the bookcase is so long. The only tricky part is screwing the center shelves to this support. Since these shelves are exactly opposite each other, fasten either the left- or right-hand one first by screwing straight through the vertical support into the edge of the shelf. To fasten the adjacent shelf, start just below the edge of the already in-place shelf, then carefully countersink and drill up at a slight angle through the vertical support. Be sure that the angle is such that the screw does not cut across the bottom edge of the shelf or come out the top.

3. When all components are assembled, fill all holes and edges with wood dough or spackle, then stain, paint, or give them whatever finish you choose. Place them in their proper configuration and screw them together. The screws should go through the backs of the bookcases into the backs (side panels) of the banquettes and through the back of the shorter bookcase into the vertical support of the longer bookcase/desk.◇

This slick all-in-one unit is easy to make. Its modules can be adapted to almost any space. See page 57.

LESLIE ROBERTS' FIRELESS FIREPLACE

While a real fireplace is a wonderful thing, not all apartments and houses have them. The next best thing to a working fireplace is a fake one, which does have the advantage of being smokeless, ashless, and fuel-less. This one was made for Leslie Roberts' apartment, and even without flames it generates warmth.

To build a fireplace, start with the tiles; the size and number to be used as hearth and "flue" liner will determine the actual overall dimensions. Here, 5″-square, ¼″-thick tiles are employed. They are spaced to allow about ½″ of grout between them.

Essentially, this fireplace is made of two Basic Boxes: one (four-sided) is lined with tiles and placed inside the second, larger (five-sided) box that forms the fireplace itself and mantel. The overall dimensions are 69½″ long, 46¼″ high, and 13¾″ deep.

MATERIALS

For the inner, tiled box, use ¾″ A/D plywood.

For the larger, outer box and the sides and top of the mantel, use ½″ A/D plywood.

For the back of the larger box, use ¼″ A/D plywood or ¼″ standard Masonite.

For the bottom molding, use quarter-round pine.

For the top molding, use pine molding in a pattern of your choice.

For the trim around the opening, use 1″ lath.

For the glue blocks, use 1″ × 1″ pine.

Seventy-two 5″-square ceramic tiles.

No. 10 flathead wood screws, 1¼″ and 1½″ long.

3-penny finishing nails.

White glue.

Mastic.

Grout.

Spackle.

Paint.

ASSEMBLY

1. For the smaller, inner box, cut two side panels 33½″ × 11½″; cut the back 35″ × 34¼″; cut the bottom 35″ × 11½″. Position these panels to butt against the sides, not edges, of the back and bottom. Assemble the box using countersunk 1½″ screws. Do not use glue blocks. Leave open the front of the box (the part facing the room) and the top, or "chimney." The inside dimensions will be 33½″ high, 33½″ wide, and 11½″ deep.

2. Measure and mark a grid pattern on the inside of the inner box to guide the exact placement of the tiles. Fasten down the tiles, using a caulking gun cartridge of construction adhesive, such as PL200 or Maxbond; it's neater and faster-drying than standard tile mastic. Begin with the twelve tiles that go on the bottom. Let these set completely before applying tiles to the two sides and the back wall. Apply grout to the cracks between the tiles and let it set.

3. While the grout is setting, build the larger, outer box. Cut the front panel of plywood 45½″ × 69½″, with a 33½″-square cutout located 18″ in from either end. Cut the back to the same overall measurements, with no cutout. Cut two side panels 13″ × 45½″, and the top panel 13¾″ × 69½″.

(continued on next page)

An inventive way to warm up a room. *See page 15.*

4. Position these panels to allow the side panels to butt against the inside of the front panel and the back. The top fits over the front, back, and sides. Assemble the outer box utilizing butt joints reinforced at the corners with 45″-long glue blocks. Fasten the pieces together with glue and countersunk 1¼″ screws. Fill all screw holes with spackle and paint the upper inside portion of the backing matte black.

5. Miter-cut the corners of the molding for the top of the mantel and fasten it on all three sides around the top with glue and finishing nails.

6. Set the outer box down over the inner one, then align the boxes carefully at the opening in front before fastening them together with three 1¼″ countersunk screws along either side of the opening—about ⅜″ in from the edges. Leave these screws unfilled so that the fireplace can easily be taken apart, if need be.

7. Cut and attach the quarter-round bottom molding as you did the molding for the top of the mantel. Mask the six screws on the front of the fireplace with 1″ lath, miter-cut at the corners. Fasten the strips in place with finishing nails so that they frame the opening.

8. Sand and paint the fireplace a color of your choice.◇

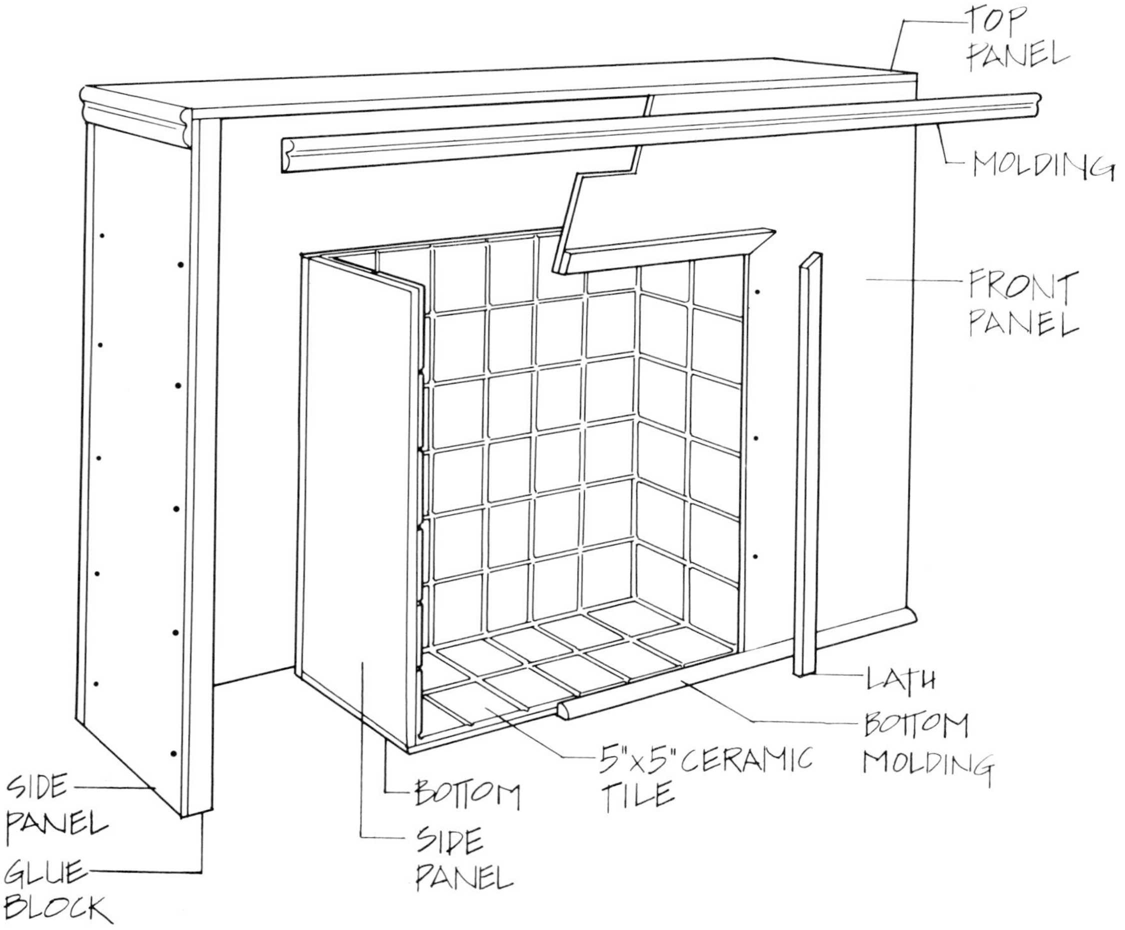

SAM NEUSTADT'S MODULAR SYSTEM

The word "modular" is excessively—and often erroneously—applied to furniture. But architect Sam Neustadt developed a system that fits the term precisely. That is, it employs a uniform component that is used repeatedly to construct various pieces of furniture. It is simple, neat, inexpensive, strong, and light.

Essentially, this is a tension-and-compression system using "struts" made from threaded rods placed inside hollow metal tubing to join surfaces of ¾″ plywood. The rod and tubing combine forces to hold the plywood simultaneously together and apart, as well as holding other plywood panels between them at right angles. Anything that has sides—a box, a table, a bed, a wardrobe—can be assembled this way.

At the point where there will be struts, holes are drilled in the plywood to admit threaded steel rods ⅜″ in diameter. (These rods are available in standard lengths of up to 72″ in most hardware stores.) Rods and 1¼″ tubing are cut to appropriate lengths; the rods are always a little longer than the tubing. Where the ends of the threaded rods protrude, on the outer faces of the panels, a ¾″ diameter steel washer is fitted, followed by a dome-capped nut, known as an acorn nut. When the nuts on either end are tightened down, they compress the tubing between the plywood, holding everything in place.

For greater ease of assembly, make a shallow depression 1½″ in diameter around each hole on the inside of the panels with a flat-bottomed Forstner bit. The hollow tubing will fit into these depressions and thus be positioned automatically.

The following directions apply this system to make a coffee table, a king-size bed, and a wardrobe.

WILLIAM P. STEELE

All sorts of furniture pieces can be put together using architect Neustadt's tube-and-rod assembly system. See page 21.

THE MODULAR COFFEE TABLE

The coffee table is the easiest of these units to build. Try it first, then apply the same principles to build the other two pieces or pieces of your own design.

MATERIALS

For the top panel and two side panels, use ¾″ A/B plywood.

About 12′ of hollow metal tubing (aluminum clothes rod, conduit, chrome plumbing pipe, or mild steel tubing) 1¼″ in diameter.

About 12′ of threaded steel rod ⅜″ in diameter.

Steel washers ¾″ in diameter.

Chrome-finish acorn nuts with ⅜″ threads.

Spackle or wood dough.

Paint or finish of your choice.

ASSEMBLY

1. Cut the side panels 17″ × 32″. Cut the top panel 32″ × 33″. Radius all the corners of the side panels and top, using a circle with a 1″ radius.

2. Clamp the threaded rod securely in a vise and use a hacksaw to cut the threaded rod into four sections 35″ long. Be sure to clamp the rod at a point well inside the ends where the nuts will fit, since clamping will damage threads. Because it's impossible to cut threaded rod with a hacksaw without doing *some* damage to

(continued on next page)

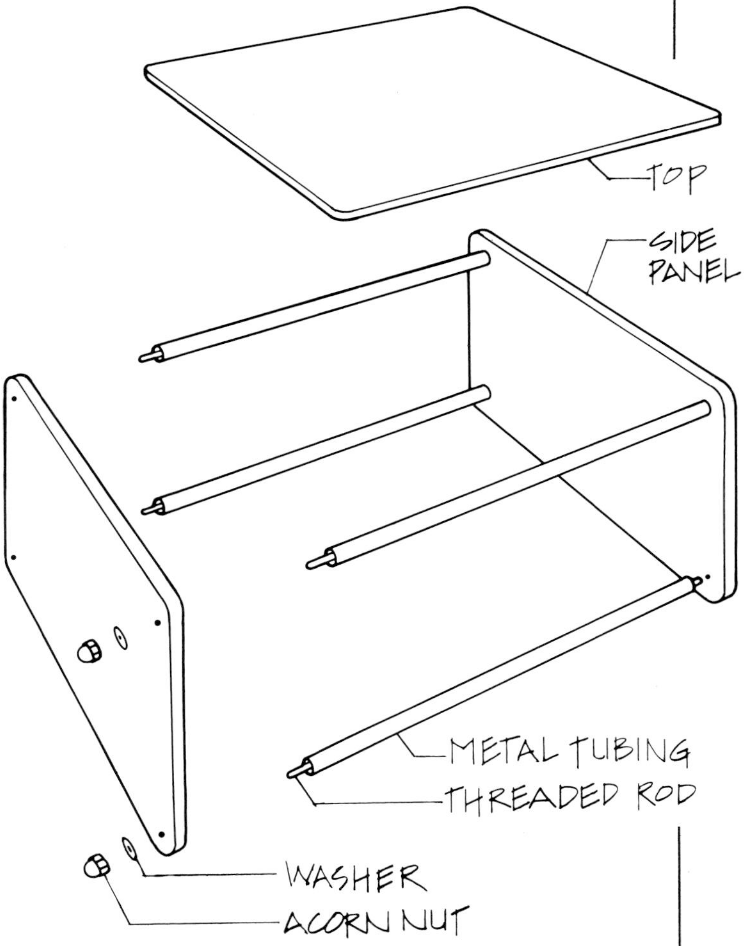

the threads near the cut, inspect the cut. If it is very rough, or if you experience difficulty in screwing on a nut, clean up—"dress"—the threads with a small triangular file. Another way to clear the threads is to spin a regular ⅜″ nut past the point to be cut *before* cutting. Then back the nut off after the cut is made.

3. Cut four sections of tubing 33″ long. You can do this with a hacksaw, if you must, but you will get neater results if you use a simple pipe cutter, a hand tool that is available in hardware stores for a few dollars.

4. Drill a ½″ hole in each corner of the side panels. The holes should be evenly spaced about 2¼″ in from the corners so that the holes correspond exactly on each side.

5. Fill all the plywood edges and gaps with spackle or wood dough. Sand the piece smooth and paint or apply finish of your choice. Let the finish dry thoroughly.

6. Working with one corner at a time, hold a length of tubing in place and insert rod through the first side panel, through the length of the tube, and out through the second side panel. Fit one washer and one acorn nut to each end of the threaded rod, tightening the nuts just enough to hold the assembly together. Repeat for the other three corners. Check to see that the tubes are centered around the threaded rod and that the two sides are not racking but are sitting squarely on the floor.

7. Set the top panel in place, resting it on the tubes. Tighten the nuts until the ends of the tubes just begin to "bite" the plywood and the top panel is "trapped" securely in place.◇

Threaded rods are slipped into holes in side panels and through tubing.

Rods are first held loosely in place with acorn nuts.

Top panel is dropped into place before nuts are tightened completely.

The completed modular coffee table.

THE MODULAR WARDROBE

As can be seen here, Neustadt's system works well with upright pieces of furniture as well. This wardrobe can be combined with other such units of the same design (as long as sets of tubes and rods are offset from one another) or similar units housing various other storage systems to create a modular wall system. This wardrobe is 78″ high, 30″ wide, and 24″ deep. A fold-down table is concealed in an adjoining unit, which is double this width and forms the headboard for the king-size bed.

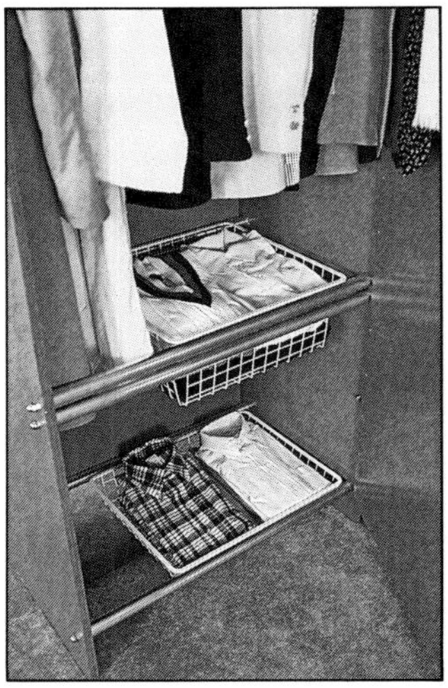

Wire baskets resting on tubing hold neatly stacked shirts.

WILLIAM P. STEELE

MATERIALS

For the door, back, and side panels, use ¾″ A/B plywood.

About 23′ of hollow metal tubing (aluminum clothes rod, conduit, chrome plumbing pipe, or mild steel tubing) 1¼″ in diameter.

About 23′ of threaded steel rod, ⅜″ in diameter.

Steel washers, ¾″ in diameter.

Chrome-finish acorn nuts with ⅜″ threads.

Continuous (piano) hinge 72″ long, with ¾″ leaves.

Handle for the door.

Set of magnetic catches.

Spackle or wood dough.

Paint or finish of your choice.

ASSEMBLY

1. Cut the two side panels 24″ × 78″, then radius all the corners of the two panels, using a circle with a 1″ radius. Cut the door panel 28″ × 72″ and radius all its corners. Cut the lower back panel 28½″ × 25¼″, and radius its lower corners. Cut the upper back panel 28½″ × 46″ and radius its upper corners. Cut nine sections of threaded rod 30½″ long. Cut nine sections of metal tubing 28½″ long.

2. Drill nine ½″ holes in each side panel, taking care that the holes in the two panels correspond exactly, about 1½″ in from each side edge. The top holes should be evenly spaced and about 3″ down from the top edge of the plywood. The four center holes should be about 28″ and 30″ up from the bottom edge and the two bottom holes should be about 5″ up from the bottom edge.

3. Fill all the edges and gaps with spackle or wood dough. Sand all the plywood panels smooth. Paint or apply finish of your choice. Let the finish dry thoroughly.

4. Hold the two side panels parallel. Starting at one corner, insert one section of tubing between the panels and hold it in place, then insert a section of rod (with a washer and a nut already on one end of the rod) through a hole in the second side panel. Then attach a washer and a nut to the other end of the rod. Repeat for all tubing-and-rod assemblies, but don't tighten any of them until all are in place and the panels are "true." Hold the two back panels in place (with about a ¾″ horizontal gap between them) while tightening the nuts in order to trap the back panels into place.

5. Mount the continuous hinge on the right-hand side of the door. Screw one leaf of the hinge to the inner surface of the right side panel and the other leaf to the ¾″ edge of the door, keeping the bottom edge of the door 4″ up from the bottom of the side panel. Screw on the magnetic catches and the pull handle. ◇

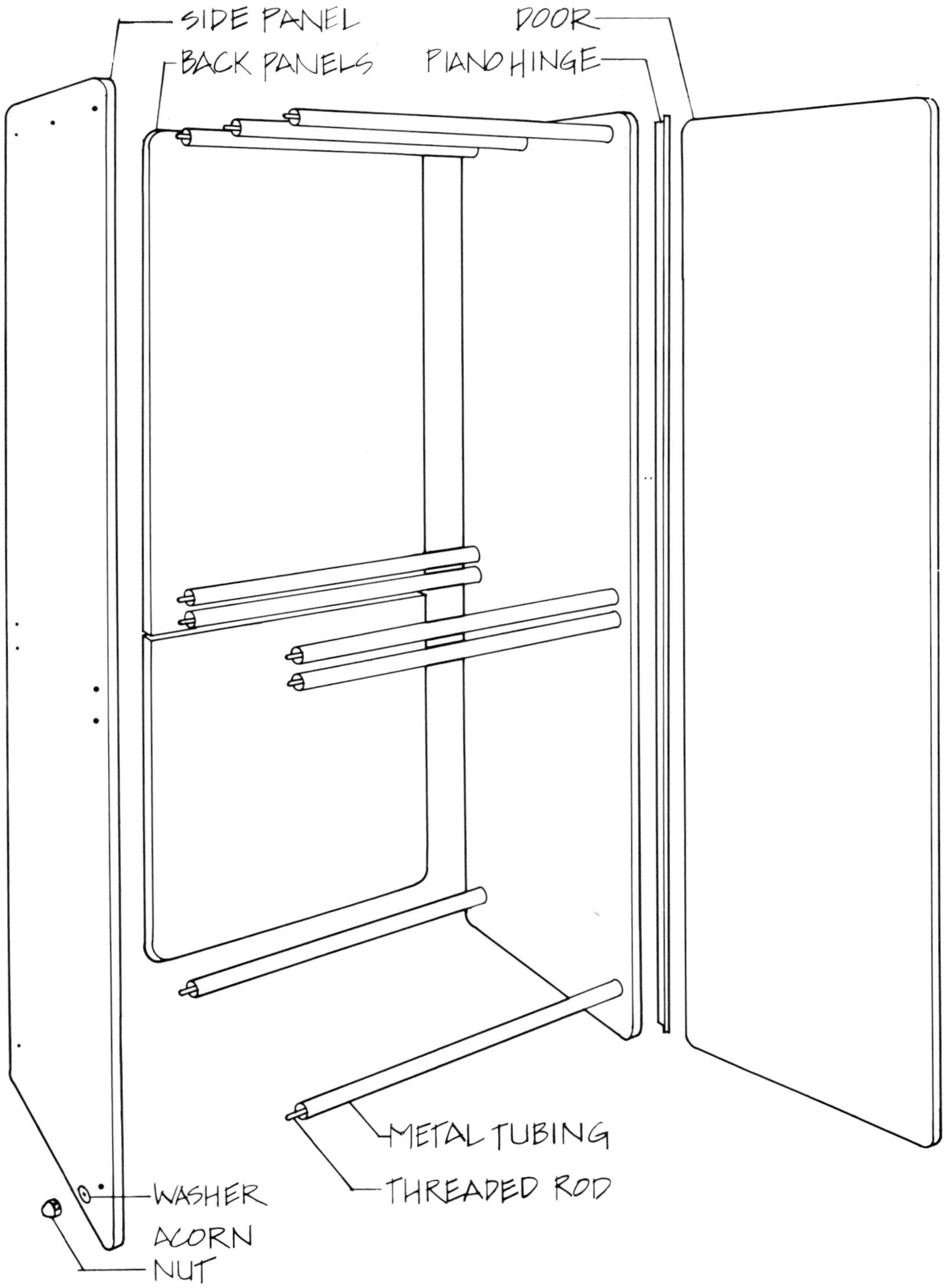

THE MODULAR PLATFORM BED

While the principle of building a platform bed is the same as that for building the coffee table, it is essential to use more lateral braces of tubing and rod for the bed. For a finished appearance, this double bed has solid plywood end panels, which are held in place by the pressure of the side panels.

MATERIALS

For the side, end, and top panels, use ¾″ A/B plywood.

About 41′ of hollow metal tubing (aluminum clothes rod, conduit, chrome plumbing pipe, or mild steel tubing) 1¼″ in diameter.

About 41′ of threaded steel rod, ⅜″ in diameter.

Steel washers, ¾″ in diameter.

Chrome-finish acorn nuts with ⅜″ threads.

Spackle or wood dough.

Paint or finish of your choice.

ASSEMBLY

1. Cut the two side panels 12″ × 79″. Radius all the corners of the side panels, using a circle with a 1″ radius. Cut the two end panels 12″ × 60½″. Cut two plywood panels to serve as a top, or mattress platform, each about 77″ × 30″. Cut eight sections of tubing 60½″ long. Cut eight sections of threaded steel rod 62½″ long.

2. In each side panel, drill eight evenly spaced ½″ holes for the rods. The five top holes should be about 2½″ down from the top edge and the three bottom holes about 2½″ up from the bottom edge. The holes for the two sides must correspond exactly. To accomplish this, line up the two panels exactly, then clamp them together, "good face" to "good face" and drill. The holes closest to the ends of the side panels should be about 2½″ in from the ends of the panels.

3. Once all the holes have been drilled, fill all the edges and gaps with spackle or wood dough. Sand the panels smooth and paint or apply finish of your choice. Let the finish dry thoroughly.

4. Assemble the tubing and rods as described in instructions for the modular coffee table, "trapping" the two end panels between the sides. Place the two top panels between the ends, resting them on the five top sections of tubing. Since top panels will not be seen, the only finish they need is a good sanding.◇

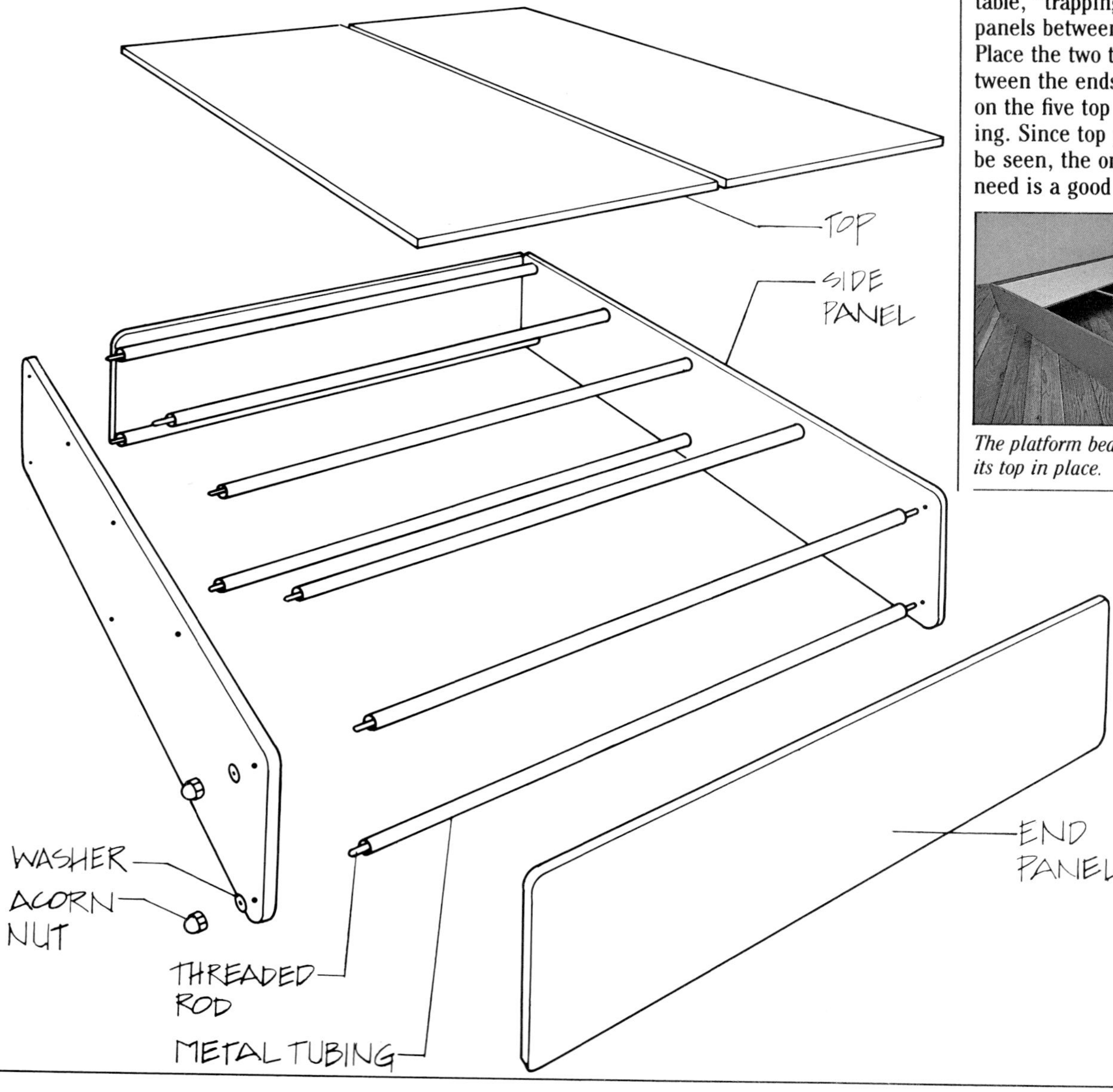

WILLIAM P. STEELE

The platform bed with just half its top in place.

FURNISHING SPACE

Whether moving into a new home or apartment, or launching into doing over your present one, very few people have the burden—or the opportunity—of starting with a completely empty room to furnish. Most of us have a few hand-me-downs or former purchases to build upon (or to contend with, depending on your point of view). But whether you have a lot to start with or almost nothing, it is difficult not to panic about how to put it all together, how to choose new pieces, and—perhaps most daunting of all—how to pay for everything.

The simplest piece of advice is to decide in the beginning where to spend and where to save. You clearly have to have certain anchor pieces: something to lie on, something to sit on, something to eat from, something to work on. And you need a few ancillary pieces—chests of drawers, side tables, perhaps a cocktail table—to put things on or in as well as to fill the gaps and add your own particular stamp of character. But none of it need cost the earth if you have the time, the patience, and the interest either to make the basic pieces yourself (see previous chapter); to forage around looking for used furniture that you can redo; or to find objects that you can modify, transform, or otherwise utilize.

The restoration of really fine furniture is a craft bordering on an art—it takes years of training and practice, and involves a great deal of care and attention. Any truly distinguished piece should always get such treatment.

The restorative techniques I'm suggesting are for structurally sound used furniture with basically good lines, or brand-new items—also basically with good lines—from an unpainted-furniture store. This is not to say that these less-exalted methods of renewal are not effective; a piece of properly painted or antiqued furniture can look absolutely wonderful. Done correctly and with a bit of care, you won't recognize the poor bedraggled thing you found on the street a few weeks before.

Another way to come by low-cost home furnishings is to alter found objects or objects that were never meant to be furniture. This perhaps requires a bit of daring, but once you've tried your hand at it and been successful, you will start to see possibilities everywhere for transforming all sorts of non-furniture items into things sittable, storageable, or otherwise usable in your home.

One final word of warning: Bargain hunting and transformations can become almost a disease. You may start snapping things up simply because they are bargains, not because you need them or have a use for whatever they might be turned into. So beware. Try not to let the bargain bug get the upper hand.

THINGS YOU SHOULD KNOW ABOUT FINDING FURNITURE

There are as many places to find pieces of furniture as there are ways to refinish or transform them when you get them home. You might think that many of the following suggestions for useful foraging grounds are obvious, but it is interesting how people do forget the obvious. One thing to remember is that prices can vary staggeringly from one source to another and from one geographical location to the next. Furniture from the 1950s, for example, might be almost worthless in the country and very valuable in a major city; the same applies to old Depression or utility furniture, as well as to golden oak and Mission pieces.

ANTIQUE SHOPS. You should not be put off by antique shops, thinking that they are always too expensive. Sometimes you can find real bargains in shops that specialize in a particular period but have had to buy a whole household in order to obtain things especially wanted—they often sell the unwanted items at far below their real value. It is worth paying regular visits on the chance you may get lucky.

CLASSIFIED ADVERTISEMENTS AND BULLETIN BOARDS. It is always worthwhile to check newspaper classified ads and bulletin boards at your local supermarket, library, or community

(continued on next page)

center for notices of apartment sales, garage sales, and the like.

SECOND-HAND AND JUNK SHOPS. There are basically two varieties of these stores: those that buy job lots, whole households, or generally unselected merchandise, and those that are somewhat classier that sell particular items and have old, if not yet antique, furniture and other objects. The best times to visit these is in the fall—especially if they are in well-known antiquing areas or vacation spots—just after the summer season, or in the early spring when the pockets of the owners are usually somewhat emptier.

GARAGE, YARD, TAG, PORCH, LAWN, RUMMAGE, JUMBLE SALES. Whatever they are called, there are enough of these family or group-sponsored sales these days to keep one busy every weekend, all weekend.

ESTATE AND HOUSEHOLD LIQUIDATION SALES. When the contents of a house are sold on the premises, a professional auctioneer or auction company is usually on hand to do the selling. The advantage of sales of this kind is that there is generally a preview at which you can look over the selection and find out what the price of anything you are interested in is likely to be. Also, on the last day of the sale there is usually an "everything must go" atmosphere.

CITY STREETS. Keep your eyes open for dumpsters. I have found bathtubs, sinks, nice old chairs, and even marble fireplaces in them. On sidewalks the night before garbage collections there are often all sorts of discarded pieces to be found. Prosperous neighborhoods are the most fertile hunting grounds.

FLEA MARKETS. There are three types of these: permanent, transient, and special. The permanents are often indoor markets with regular stallholders who sell items that other stallholders and dealers have certainly picked over first. Transients, on the other hand, are normally outdoor markets, sometimes hovering around the perimeters of permanents. If you can get to these at dawn, and I mean literally at dawn, you stand as good a chance as the dealers of getting a bargain. Specials are just transient fleas that have been well-advertised. You can find out about all of them by looking in newspapers, observing road signs, and seeing ads in antique magazines.

WRECKING COMPANIES. When any sort of public building such as an old theater, hotel, or office building is being demolished, the contents are either sold right on the site or will be summarily thrown out to the benefit of any keen and alert scavenger. These sales are usually announced in the local newspapers, and if the building is of national interest, on radio and TV as well. In any event, sales like these are marvelous sources for fireplaces, moldings, paneling, old baths and sinks, doors, hardware and a whole host of architectural fittings. I have known people to get whole staircases and mantels for almost nothing.

STRIPPING AND REFINISHING SHOPS. Some sell second-hand furniture or else have unclaimed pieces to sell. It is certainly worth inquiring.

THRIFT AND CONSIGNMENT SHOPS. These stores sell furniture and odds and ends for private owners on a commission basis and are generally operated for the benefit of charity or religious organizations. Prices are usually pretty reasonable and many of them hold markdown sales on all items not sold by the end of the month.

MOVING AND STORAGE COMPANIES. Many companies hold an annual sale of unclaimed goods, and these can be gold mines for bargain hunters if they are prepared to wait for the sale of endless packing cases of old kitchen utensils and gardening tools before the real stuff makes an appearance.

MARBLE AND GLAZE

Glazing and marbleizing, those terrific paint finishes for walls and floors (see pages 75–76 and 93, respectively), are both very effective on furniture. As on walls, glazes add depth and richness, and can be used to pep up or change the color of a base coat. Marbleizing is almost as good as antiquing for hiding knicks and scratches, but it should be reserved for flat surfaces such as the tops of tables, chest, and cabinets—it usually doesn't look great on things that cannot be made of marble (spindly or slatted chairs, for example). If you do any marbleizing on vertical surfaces, take special care that the paints do not run, or else tip the piece on its side so you are working on a horizontal area. Once you get the hang of marbleizing you can make your own pieces of "marble" from simple pine boards from the lumberyard—and there is almost no flat surface, from kitchen work areas to living room cocktail tables, on which a piece of marble is not appropriate.

Rag-rolled glaze on a chest of drawers is almost like marbleizing.

REFURBISHING FURNITURE

PAINTING FURNITURE

One can almost always spot a piece of home-painted furniture. The job is usually done with enamel, and enamel rarely looks great as a finish on furniture. Not only is the choice of colors extremely limited, but the finish itself has an undesirable thick-ish look. It would be nice if one could duplicate at home the lacquer finish found on much store-bought furniture, but this kind of lacquer is tricky to use, it's not readily available and is just not suitable for domestic do-it-yourselfers. It must be sprayed on and demands the use of special equipment, including a spray booth.

There is, however, an excellent and easy way to paint furniture that provides a good-looking finish in any color. Give the piece a coat or two of oil-base flat wall paint in whatever color you want (remember, you can "fine tune" your color choices with universal tinting colors), sanding between coats. When the final coat is completely dry, sand it again with fine-grain sandpaper until it is completely smooth. Wipe the surface well with a tack cloth and then give the whole thing a coat or two of varnish—matte, semigloss, or gloss, depending upon the look you want. Regular varnish works better on furniture than polyurethane.◇

An old drop-leaf table gleams with a finish of crisp white paint.

ANTIQUING FURNITURE

One of the really great ways to fix up an old piece of wooden furniture is to antique it. In fact, the technique works *best* on a slightly beaten-up piece—the pits and pockmarks of worn wood fill up nicely with the glaze that is applied, instantly adding decades of graceful age. Unlike stripping and refinishing—which can be a long, tedious process—antiquing is quick, cheap, and easy. (Refinishing, of course, is worth the effort with furniture made from fine, costly woods, but for pieces of more humble origins, antiquing is a good solution.)

Basically, what you do is apply a coat or two of eggshell or semigloss oil-base paint and, when it is dry, put on a coat of glaze; the glaze is then gone over with a rag, sponge, or steel wool. A lot of glaze will be removed, but an interesting patina will remain. The trick is to leave enough glaze in corners and other nooks and crannies to simulate the appearance of years of tender loving wear. The edges of tabletops, for instance, usually have more patina than the center, as do the backs and fronts of chair arms and the centers of rungs of chairs. Take a good close look at actual antiques in museums and shops to get an idea of the real effects of age.

Besides figuring out how best to manipulate the glaze, you will have to decide what glazing medium you want to use (there are several choices) and what color and/or tone combination you want. Traditionally, antiquing involved putting an earth color coat of glaze over a lighter base coat, and perhaps this remains the wisest choice, particularly for a beginner. Endless contrasts are, however, possible. An off-white

MICHAEL DUNNE

All the nooks and crannies make this hutch ideal for antiquing.

glaze on a dark gray base, for instance, would give a bleached, driftwoody finish. Other possibilities: red base with an almost black glaze; green base with dark brown glaze; blue base with dark green glaze.

As for the glazing medium itself, you can use ready-made glazing compound (Pratt & Lambert's Lyt-All or McCloskey's Glaze Coat, for instance); a homemade mixture of linseed oil, mineral spirits, and driers; or very thinned-down artists' oil paint. (You will have to color glazing compounds and the homemade glazes with tinting colors.) You can also use very thinned-down oil-base interior paint, if you can find the "old-fashioned" kind that does not contain acrylic. The acrylic tends to make the glaze "ball up" as it is being worked.

Since there are so many different ways to antique and so many choices to make, it is almost imperative that you experiment a bit, if you are unfamiliar with the technique. Try your hand on scrap wood that more or less resembles the piece you will do your finished work on. You will probably want to try a couple of different base coats and two or three glaze colors, besides seeing how the glaze moves

(continued on next page)

around using the various "tools" (rag, sponge, whatever).

Paint stores sell boxed antiquing kits, which contain a can of base coat and a can of glaze, the colors of which have been "precoordinated" to achieve a particular finish. A color photograph of the way this finish will look usually appears on the box. These kits are perfectly fine, but they are comparatively expensive, and they remove much of the sense of adventure and fun that antiquing can have.

MATERIALS

Oil-base paint, eggshell or semigloss finish.

Paintbrushes.

Glazing medium (glazing compound, artists' oil paint, homemade glaze, oil paint).

Mineral spirits.

Tinting colors, if needed.

Rags, sponges, steel wool.

Polyurethane varnish.

METHOD

1. Paint the piece of furniture with oil-base paint in whatever color you choose. If the finish already on the piece is in reasonably decent shape, you can paint right over it.

2. If you are not using thinned artists' oils or regular interior paint for your glaze (and perhaps even if you are) tint your glaze. See Tinting a Glaze, page 75.

3. When you are certain that the base coat is thoroughly dry, apply your glaze. Work on one area (top, one side, a single drawer front, for instance) at a time; you don't want the glaze to dry out too much or it will be difficult or impossible to remove. Be sure to get the glaze into all corners, cracks, and crannies; it is really more important that you get the glaze into the out-of-the-way places than on the broad expanses.

4. As the glaze begins to dry, begin wiping it off with whatever you have chosen to remove it with, starting in the areas where you want to remove most glaze and working toward the areas where more will remain. Use care not to take off *too much* glaze; you want to be sure it stays to highlight (or lowlight) indentations, many of which may have been invisible before.

5. After the glaze is completely dry (artists' oil paint will take longest), protect your new finish with two or three coats of varnish.◇

COLLEEN BABINGTON'S FAUX GOLD LEAFING

Over the centuries, the art of gold leafing has been used in countless ways. Museums are full of illuminated manuscripts that employ gold leaf; entire domes (inside and out) of enormous buildings have been covered with it; whole statues are sheathed in it. These days, with the price of gold at sky-high levels, one sees it used most often on expensive picture frames and such domestic items as small trays and boxes. However, gilding is a handy thing to know about when trying your hand at redoing old furniture, for even sparing use of it can add a rich, distinctive touch to an otherwise ordinary piece.

To do really exquisite goldleafing takes years of training and practice. It involves patiently putting down a base—layers of plasterlike gesso or a red clay called "bole"; it takes a steady hand to lift the thin-as-air sheets of pure gold with a special wide brush known as a gilder's tip; and it takes a lot of money. Happily, there is a look-alike alternative material that is easier to apply and a lot less expensive. This material is called Dutch metal—an alloy of zinc and copper—and it is about one-tenth the price of gold leaf.

While Dutch metal can be laid down on many different types of surfaces, one of the best places for a fledgling faux gilder to try his or her wings is the trim or molding on a piece of furniture—it is a traditional use of gold leaf, it is relatively simple, and the results can be striking. Here's how to go about it:

Find a small table, chest, or cabinet that has a relatively complicated trim. The only materials you will need (all available at art supply stores) are a couple of brushes, a bottle of quick-drying synthetic size (adhesive), and the Dutch metal leaf itself. Paint the entire piece of furniture if necessary (see Painting Furniture, page 145) and/or paint the trim a contrasting color. You will apply the Dutch metal to the curved surfaces of the molding, and since the paint underneath will always show through a bit, you may want to paint that area either yellow or red, depending upon the effect you want. Red showing through will look a bit like bole and will impart an instant antique look; yellow will brighten the work.

COLLEEN BABINGTON

A face-in-the-sun motif was metal-leafed on this painted cabinet. See page 69.

Now you are ready to lay down the Dutch metal. Decide exactly what areas you want to cover and apply a thin layer of the varnish-like quick-drying size. "Quick-drying" may sound like a misnomer, since it takes an hour or so to harden to the required tackiness, but oil size takes a lot longer. Size is really the "glue" that will hold the metal in place, so it goes wherever you want the metal to go.

Dutch metal leaf comes in

sheets separated by thin sheets of paper, all bound in booklets, just like regular gold leaf. With a scissors, cut strips of the metal that are just a bit wider than the area you will be covering, leaving the metal between the paper in the booklet. When the size is almost dry and tacky to the touch, pick up the metal with your fingers and carefully lay the strips onto the size. Using a soft brush, pounce the metal gently. This will fix it in place and ensure good adhesion. Any cracks or spaces can be covered immediately with another layer of leaf.

After the size is completely dry (overnight) you can wipe off any bits and pieces of excess metal with a soft cloth, and/or you can clean up and straighten the edges with the corner of a piece of cloth dipped in turpentine.

Since Dutch metal tarnishes if left unprotected, you must now give it a coat of varnish and antique it, using a glaze just as in the instructions on page 145. (Antiqued Dutch metal looks more like real gold than it does in its "raw" state, which is quite bright and shiny.) If you used a red undercoat, you might want to rub off a bit of the metal to let the color show through before antiquing it.◇

DEALING WITH SPACE

Faced with an empty room, a room you want to redo, a featureless, boxlike room, not enough room, a rental, a temporary accommodation, or a combination of any or all of these, what can you do? People are usually so relieved to have found a place to live that is fairly affordable and reasonably convenient that they simply accept and adapt to whatever space they have—however cramped or awkwardly laid out it is—without too much thought. All too often they rush to assemble basic decorations and furnishings without ever seriously considering the space and how it could be manipulated to the best advantage. Yet with a little planning, most spaces can be made to work in ways that are out of all proportion to the time, trouble, and money spent.

At the very simplest level, you can make rooms and furniture much more multifunctional than they usually are. Instead of thinking in conventional terms—living room, dining room, study, den, bedroom—try to figure out what would be most practical for your style of life in terms of allowing rooms to serve more than one purpose. If you have the luxury of an extra room (one more than a living room and the number of bedrooms you need, that is) you might turn it into a combination dining room/guest room/study/home office by furnishing it with a table that doubles as a desk, a bed that functions as a sofa, shelves that can hold almost anything, and a closet that can be used for china and glassware as well as for files—and even clothes.

With a little reorganization, a bedroom might well be big enough to hold a desk, bookshelves, and judiciously incorporated filing cabinets—if you

Like any geometric pattern, lattice will always add depth to a space.

rethought closets and furniture placement. Or could you put a table-cum-desk in a hallway, or under the stairs, or in a good-size bathroom, and fit extra filing cabinets under or near that?

This all may sound quite obvious, but visiting other people's homes all the time as I do, I find it interesting how rarely the obvious is put into practice.

MAKING SPACE COSMETICALLY

Well-thought-out colors, patterns, and textures can make a space *seem* much larger than it really is. It might sound dull to advise making everything in a room—walls, floors, and large pieces of furniture—the same pale, neutral tone, but this treatment will make the most confined area seem lighter and airier, and will make bulky objects such as sofas, armchairs, and beds recede into the background. And you needn't worry about too much blandness, for the pace can be varied to quite a remarkable degree by using different textures and spots of color from things such as throw pillows, books, and plants.

Diagonal designs, whether painted right on the floor itself or woven into carpets, will always seem to push walls back. Anything on the walls themselves that lends a sense of perspective—photo murals or trompe l'oiel murals, garden lattice (from a lumberyard), or any geometric-pattern wall covering—will seem to give extra depth. And shiny or reflective walls, ceilings, and floors will also make a space seem much bigger both from the extra reflected light and the fact that that kind of light tends to blur and soften a room's lines, making things feel less constricting.

MAKING SPACE WITH FURNITURE ARRANGEMENT

Built-in furniture—window seats, closets, and wall units all along one wall, for instance—will always take up less space than "free floating" pieces, and the space beneath a window seat or built-in seating along a wall can be used for storage. You need only to hinge the seat part so it can be lifted or put shelves underneath, and you have immediately doubled the usefulness of the piece.

In a small room, use as much transparent and fold-up furniture as possible. Desks and tables of all kinds made of plexiglass or glass and metal will appear to take up much less space. And fold-up furniture can easily be stashed away when not in use or even hung on a wall and turned into an instant sculpture. Cane and wicker will look lighter than wood; white-painted pieces will always be less conspicuous than dark. The conventional wisdom is to place large pieces of furniture around the sides of a room to get them as much out of the way as possible, but there are exceptions. Two sofas placed back to back in the center of a space can often define divisions of a room very well. And in a one-room apartment a large bed placed in the middle can be used as an island lounging unit. By positioning a bolster in the middle instead of at the end, the bed will be divided into two separate areas.

TRANSFORMING CASTOFFS

A PALLET SOFA

Taking the concept of a platform bed to what is perhaps the ultimate ready-made simplicity, Mark Hulla created a functional sofa based, literally, on found objects—two wooden pallets, the timber frames designed to support stacked cargo and allow it to be fork lifted. Pallets are often discarded in warehouse districts or in dumpsters at construction sites. While pallets come in many different widths, lengths, and heights and their strengths vary a lot, for the purpose here you need to find pallets that are quite sturdy and also quite high (the ones Hulla used were made to hold heavy construction materials and are 10″ high). With the plywood top, a foam mattress, and some well-chosen fabrics, this sofa is a stylish variation on the platform theme.

MATERIALS

For the top, use ¾″ construction-grade plywood.

Two wooden pallets.

Burlap fabric for the plywood top.

A 4″-thick foam mattress, covered in wide-wale corduroy.

6-penny finishing nails.

Staples.

ASSEMBLY

1. Place the pallets next to each other and measure their combined width and length, then cut the top so that it will overhang the pallets by 6″ to 8″ on all sides. Since dimensions of pallets vary, you might have to experiment a bit with their placement, depending on how long and wide you want your sofa to be. (Hulla's is 43″ × 75″, slightly larger than a standard single bed.) The pallets do not necessarily need to butt together.

2. Sand the plywood top lightly, then wrap it in burlap, folding it neatly at the corners, underneath. Staple the burlap to the underside of the top.

The sofa's humble beginnings are hardly recognizable. *See page 18.*

3. Place the plywood top on the pallets and nail it in place through the burlap with 6-penny finishing nails into the timbers of the pallets.

4. Cover the platform with the mattress in its cover.◇

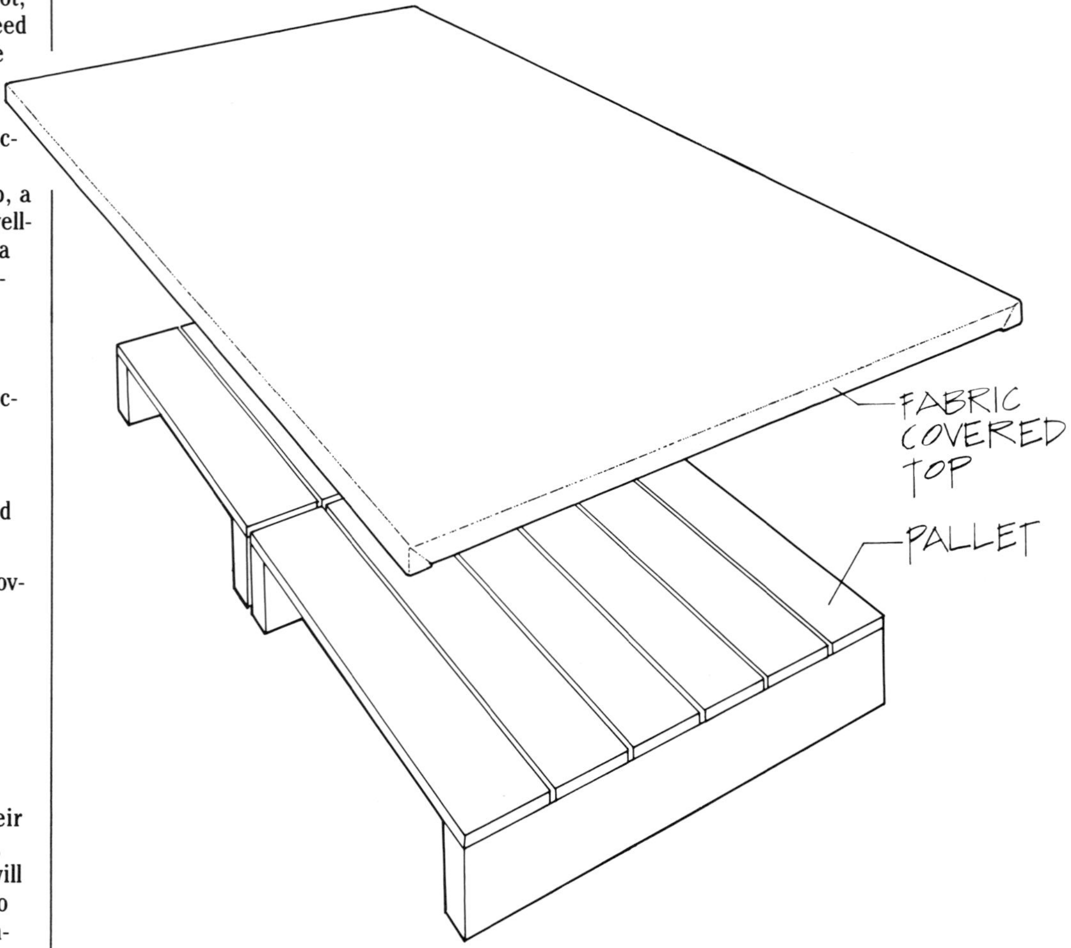

GLASS-TOP TABLES

A glass-top table hardly qualifies as an innovation among furniture ideas. The types of objects that will support a piece of glass in style, however, is virtually without limit.

For a decent-size table, the glass should be at least ¼″ thick. Half-inch plate glass has a more substantial look, but it is much more expensive. Beveled edges and smoky tints also increase the cost, but they also add to the appearance. Whatever your choice, the possibilities for a "base" are nearly infinite. ◇

Four sections of drain pipe. A clean look, with a hint of the Mediterranean.

Two large clay flowerpots—filled with sand for stability.

A sturdy box of any kind can be covered with carpeting for a smooth look.

Objects as humble as wire milk crates can be pressed into service.

Attractive wood-and-metal wine racks look good—and keep bottles handy.

MICHAEL DUNNE

SONOTUBE CONSOLE TABLE

While most sonotube applications are vertical—posts or pedestals and such—this console table capitalizes on the sculptural qualities of sonotubes, here used in the half round.

A long (84″ in this case) 14″ diameter sonotube is sliced in two lengthwise, forming two semicircular half tubes. Note: It is essential that the tube be cut exactly in half, or else the halves will not seat flat. It could be a tricky job at home, but it can be done with careful measuring, a plumb line or tape measure, and a good saber saw.

The sonotube halves are then mounted lengthwise on an 84″ × 30″ panel of ½″ plywood using white glue or epoxy, leaving a ½″ gap between them to allow for carpeting. The panel will hang from the wall by means of an 84″-long jamb cleat, and thus can be made to "float" a few inches off the floor, if so desired, by correctly positioning the portion of the cleat that is attached to the wall. A 1″ × 2″ should be glued to the plywood panel near the bottom as a spacer so the panel will hang vertically.

The top of the table—an 11½″ × 94″ piece of ½″ plywood—is glued and screwed to the upper portion of the jamb cleat and to the upper edge of the plywood panel. A ¾″ dowel is wedged and glued in place beneath the plywood top and the upper sonotube half to stabilize the top and keep it from sagging. A 3″ plywood edging is then butt-jointed, glued, and screwed all around the plywood top.

The ends of the sonotube halves are "capped" with plastic laminate (3″-wide strips on the curved surfaces, "B"-shaped for the open ends), as is the top of the table and its edging. The remaining exposed surfaces of sonotubes are then carpeted.◇

One could never guess at the origins of this table. *See page 32.*

TUBULAR METAMORPHOSIS

Sonotubes, a product of the Sunoco Company, are sturdy fiberboard tubes. These tubes, which come in a whole range of sizes, were originally designed for industrial use—to form concrete columns for freeways, factories, and other heavy-duty industrial use. But in the last few years these tubes have been popping up in many different guises in lofts, apartments, boutiques, and all manner of interiors from coast to coast. They are also very handy in that they can be painted or covered with fabric, carpeting, canvas, plastic laminate, or any other flexible material; they are relatively lightweight and easy to cut with a saber saw, yet they are strong enough to drive nails and screws through.

Sonotubes are not the only useful cylindrical objects around. Don't overlook the possibilities of fiberboard barrels and drums, or the tubes that fabric and carpeting are wrapped around.

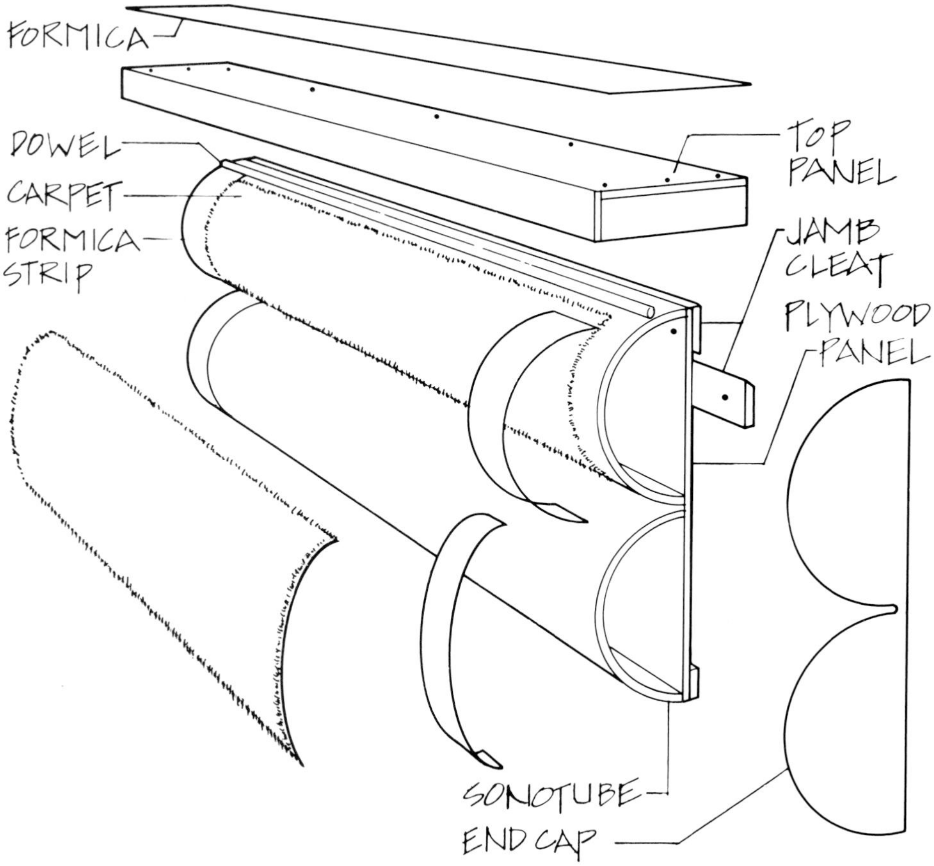

A REVOLVING STORAGE WALL

Demonstrating that there is no end to the ways of working with sonotubes, interior designer Joan Regenbogen devised 8′-high rotating columns that, placed side by side, create a wall that can be "closed" to appear as a rank of stolid pillars, or "opened" to reveal handsome *objets* and home entertainment equipment. Such a configuration may not be practical or even possible in many homes, but two of these units might be placed in opposite corners of a room. Or they might be made of small-dimension sonotubes. The columns were made this way:

Sections of 31″ diameter sonotubes are cut away with a saber saw (each tube has a different-size opening), and the columns are covered inside and out with plastic laminate. Each sonotube is "floored" with ¾″ plywood, and then lazy Susan-type turntables are mounted on the bottom, and the turntable is in turn mounted on a thick wooden base. The base is also covered with plastic laminate. The entire column can rotate 360°—now you see the shelves, now you don't.

The top of each cylinder contains two incandescent light fixtures above a lens of white translucent plastic. Along the vertical margins of each opening, ¾″ L-shaped pine molding strips provide support and conceal the electrical wiring. And the shelves? Chromed wire mesh shelves are refrigerator-style, but are of custom-made size and shape. The shelves are mounted on threaded clips screwed to the inner walls.◇

The wall in its completely open position. *See page 32.*

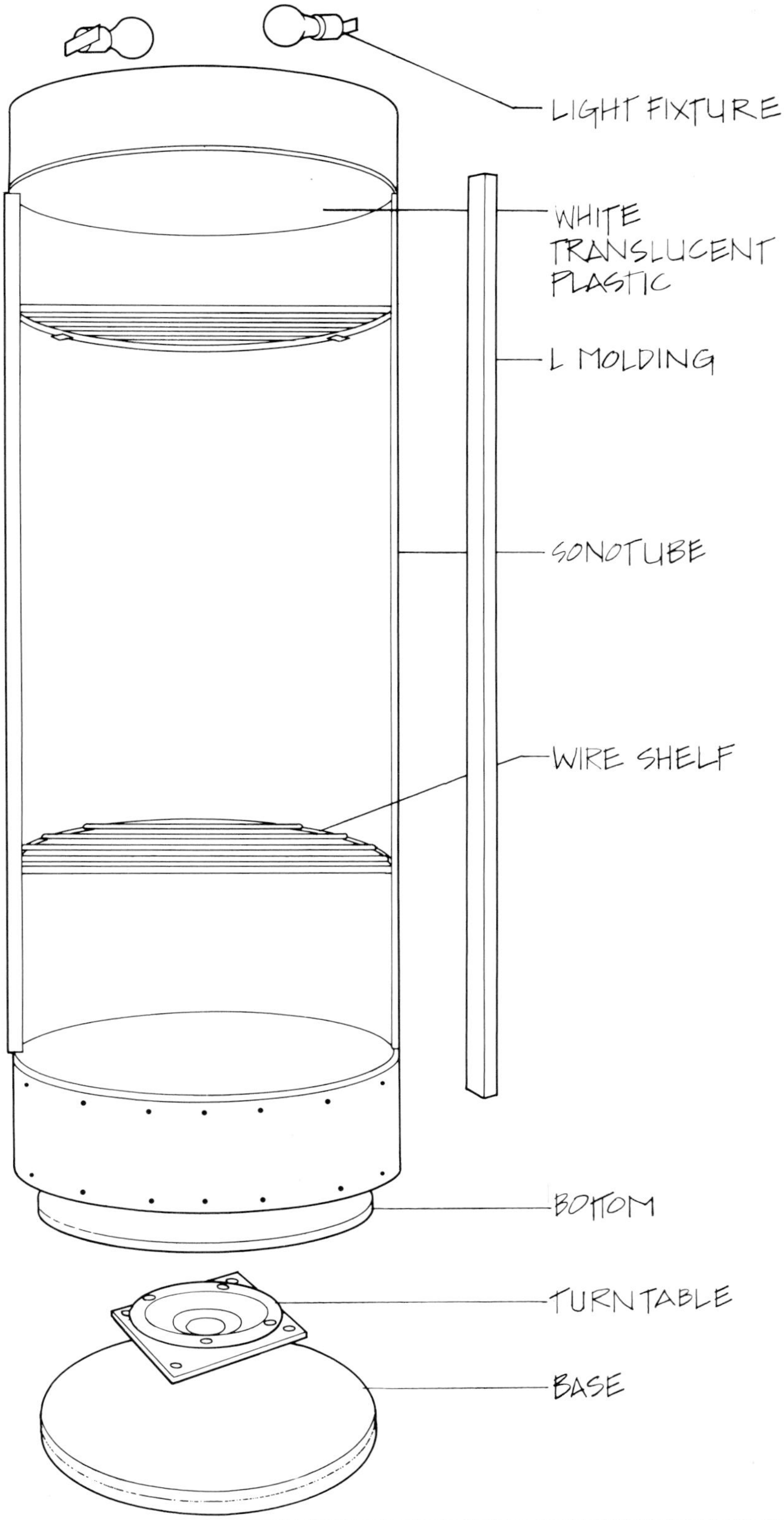

A SMALL PEDESTAL TABLE

Stan and Roanne Peskett have made something of a specialty of tables made with sonotubes, but the cylinders are so altered that the origins are not readily apparent.

The height of this table and the width of its top can vary according to the needs and tastes of the builder. The diameter of the sonotube should be in proportion to the table's height (the length of the tube) and the diameter of the top.

A circular piece of ¾″ plywood is fitted into one end of a length of sonotube like a flat plug and secured with glue and screws through the sides of the tube into the wood. A second, larger, circular piece of plywood is centered over the sonotube and attached to the first piece of plywood with countersunk wood screws.

A length of medium-weight artists' canvas is cut to the length of the circumference of the tabletop and as wide as the height of the sonotube plus 8″. One edge of the canvas is folded over and stapled to the underside of the tabletop about ⅛″ in from the edge all around. The staples should go up through the underside of the fold through only one thickness of canvas; they will thus be hidden.

The canvas is then dampened thoroughly and stretched down, a bit at a time, trimmed if necessary, and securely stapled inside the open bottom of the sonotube.

The canvas is primed, painted with acrylics, and then given several coats of polyurethane as a sealer. The top is painted to match.◇

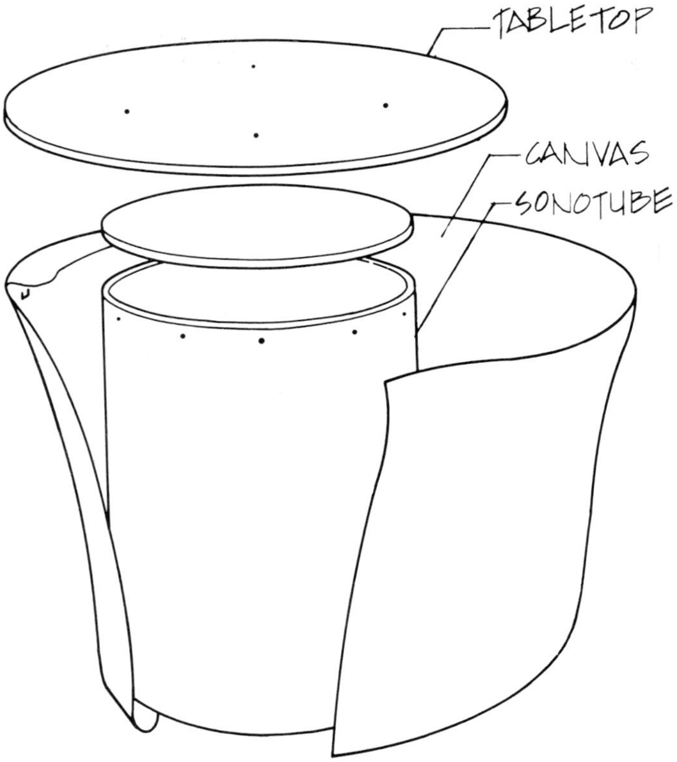

A table like this could be painted any color. See page 53.

SOURCE GUIDE

This selected Source Guide is divided into four main categories—Fabrics and Household Textiles; Floor, Wall, and Window Coverings; Lighting and Furniture; and Miscellaneous Good Buys. Within individual states, chain stores, if any, are indicated as such and listed first, followed by independent stores. States and towns are listed alphabetically; not all states are represented in all categories. If a listing includes a mail order service, a ◆ precedes the store name.

Because of space limitations, it was impossible to list individual paint and artists' supply stores, lumberyards, hardware stores, and electrical suppliers. For good local sources, check the white pages of your telephone book for Goodwill and Salvation Army stores; check the yellow pages under Thrift Shops, Second-Hand Stores, and Flea Markets.

FABRICS & HOUSEHOLD TEXTILES

CALIFORNIA

◆ **THE FACTORY STORE**
1900 Norris Rd. (near Airport Dr. & U.S. Hwy. 99)
Bakersfield 93308
(805) 399-3300
All bed comforts at 40–70% discount. Also sleeping bags, fabrics, draperies.

POPPY FABRIC
2072 Addison St.
Berkeley 94704
(415) 841-2100
Enormous selection of elegant and casual fabrics. Not discounted, but excellent quality for the price.

CONNECTICUT

◆ **HOME FABRIC MILLS, INC.**
882 South Main St.
Cheshire 06410
(203) 272-3529
Discount draperies, slipcovers, upholstery supplies, fabrics.

COLCHESTER MILL FABRICS
Broadway & Clark La.
Colchester 06415
(203) 537-2004
Discount upholstery fabrics, draperies, remnants, and closeouts.

DANIELSON FACTORY OUTLET
Danielson 06239
(no phone)
Discount bed and bath supplies; also lawn furniture and kitchen accessories.

JOY'S FABRIC CORNER
676 West Main St.
New Britain 06053
(203) 225-5043
Brand name fabrics at discount.

DELAWARE

◆ **EVERFAST, INC. MILL STORE**
9 Rockford Rd.
Wilmington 19806
(302) 654-8831
Designer fabrics at discounts of 50–90%.

FLORIDA

TEXTILE OUTLET
3337 First St.
Bradenton 33508
(813) 748-7545
Discount bedspreads and draperies.

LUCKY LINEN OUTLET
1854 U.S. Rt. 19, North
Clearwater 33572
(813) 799-3314
Discount bed and bath supplies.

◆ **CORONET FABRIC MILLS**
4502 N.W. Sixth St.
Fort Walton Beach 32549
(904) 373-3666
Designer upholstery fabrics at discount.

◆ **MARUSHKA FACTORY OUTLET**
Coastland Center Mall
Nuggets Arcade
Naples 33940
(813) 263-1662
Marushka and hand printed fabrics; seconds and discontinued designs.

YARDAGE UNLIMITED
6013 East Colonial Dr.
(Rt. 50, one half mile east of Rt. 436)
Orlando 32807
(305) 277-2755
Drapery and upholstery fabrics at discounts.

ILLINOIS

STORY, INC. QUILTING CO. OUTLET
790 West Chicago St.
Algonquin 60102
(312) 658-5626
Quilted and unquilted bedspreads, fabrics, and draperies. Stuffing materials at discount.

SPIEGEL OUTLET STORE
9950 Joliet Rd.
Countryside 60513
(312) 352-3370
Discount household textiles, furniture, and home accessories.

LINENS PLUS, INC.
8760 Dempster St.
Dempster Plaza
Niles 60648
(312) 296-5330
Name brand bed and bath textiles at discount.

INDIANA

CHERRY'S BED & BATH & TABLE TEXTILE MILL STORE (*chain*)
Tablecloths and bed and bath textiles at discount.

460 East Carmel Dr.
Carmel 46032
(317) 844-1884

6838 Madison Ave.
Indianapolis 46227
(317) 788-0888

BLUEGRASS BEDDING FACTORY OUTLET
Youngstown Shopping Center—Hwy. 62
Jeffersonville 47130
(812) 288-7925
Bedding at discount.

KENTUCKY

BLUEGRASS BEDDING FACTORY OUTLET (*chain*)
Bedding at discount

2325 Nashville Rd.
Bowling Green 42101
(502) 781-8349

North Dixie
Elizabethtown 42701
(502) 765-6892

439 Southland Dr.
Hopkinsville 42240
(606) 277-0376

2502 Plantside Dr.
(in Bluegrass Industrial Park)
Louisville 40299
(502) 491-2308

5001 Preston Hwy.
Louisville 40213
(502) 964-8512

1655 South Highway 27
Somerset 42501
(606) 679-6400

MAINE

◆ **MILL FABRIC CENTER**
2 Ridge St.
Lisbon 04250
(207) 353-8421
Bedding at discount. Catalog available.

MARYLAND

A. W. HURT DISCOUNT FABRIC
1505 Forest Dr.
Annapolis 21403
(301) 263-3093
Decorator fabrics at discount; also slipcovers, draperies. Labor available.

MASSACHUSETTS

◆ **HOME FABRIC MILLS**
Rt. 202
Belchertown 01007
(413) 232-6321
Upholstery fabrics and supplies; also draperies and pillows at discount.

LOUISHAND FACTORY OUTLET
847 Pleasant St.
Fall River 02723
(617) 674-2326
Bed and bath textiles at discount; also lawn furniture and kitchen accessories.

THE FABRIC PLACE
136 Howard St.
Framingham 01701
(617) 872-4888 or 237-9675
Upholstery fabric and supplies at discount. Designer and basic.

BEDSPREAD MILL OUTLET & NEEDLEPOINT CENTER
21 Cove St.
New Bedford 02744
(617) 992-6600
Bedspreads at discount. This is the main store. Save 30–50%.

MICHIGAN

THE COTTON MILL (*chain*)
Famous maker linens at discount.

22133 Eureka Rd.
Detroit 48234
(313) 287-3722

27302 Plymouth Rd.
Detroit 48239
(313) 937-2140

MISSOURI

THE LINEN CLOSET
Route 63
Northlake Shopping Center
Kirksville 63501
(816) 665-8522
Closeouts, discontinueds, overstocks, and remainders at discount. Also bed and bath accessories.

ARTISTIC FABRICS
1234 North Lindberg
St. Louis 63132
(314) 997-2040
Upholstery supplies and fabrics. Also slipcovers, draperies, designer fabrics, and upholstery tools at discount.

◆ **SMITHSON INC. MILL OUTLET**
Box A
Stover 65078
(314) 377-2502
Drapery, bedspreads, pillows, decorator fabrics at discounts of 75%.

NEW JERSEY

EVERFAST, INC. MILL STORE (*chain*)
Designer fabrics at discounts of 50–90%.

460 West Rt. 70
Marlton 08053
(609) 983-4615

Rt. 34, Market Pl.
Matawan 07747
(201) 583-4222

RFD 4, Place Mall
Princeton 08540
(201) 297-6090

ALL-IN-ONE
690 High St.
Burlington 08016
(609) 387-0300
Bedspreads, curtains, draperies, shades, sheets, rugs, towels, pillows, blanket at discount.

THE DOMESTIC BIN
49 Quackenbush Ave.
Dumont 07628
(201) 385-1097
Comforters at 50% off. Also towels and sheets at 40% discount. Brand names like Wamsutta, Burlington, others.

NETTLE CREEK FACTORY OUTLET
35 Market St. at River Dr.
Elmwood 07407
(201) 791-8696
Nettle Creek bedding at discount.

THE BEDSPREAD OUTLET
Church St.
Flemington 08822
(201) 782-8677
Bedding, slipcovers at discount. Draperies to match many spreads.

LINENS 'N THINGS
Rt. 4 (Bergen Mall)
Paramus 07652
(201) 845-0680
Brand name linens, sheets, towels at discount.

DAYTON OUTLET
126 Dayton Ave.
Passaic 07055
(201) 471-2621
Bedding, linens, housewares at discount. No credit cards.

CASTLE CREEK MILL END SHOP
Brass Castle Rd. (Rt. 22–24)
Washington 07882
(201) 689-7848
Draperies, slipcovers, and tablecloths at discount.

LEACOCK AND COMPANY INC.
51 South Lincoln Ave.
Washington 07882
(201) 689-1900
Tablecloths, towels, place mats at discount.

NEW YORK

ASHIL FABRICS INC.
101 West Thirty-fourth St.
New York City 10001
(212) 560-9049
Job lots and closeouts on upholstery fabrics at 30–50% off.

EZRA COHEN CORP.
307 Grand St.
New York City 10002
(212) 925-7800
Enormous selection of sheets, towels, comforters, draperies, bedspreads at good discount.

ELDRIDGE TEXTILE CO.
277 Grand St.
New York City 10002
(212) 925-1523
Bedspreads, blankets, comforters, sheets, towels, draperies, at good discounts.

FRONTIER FABRICS CLOSEOUT WAREHOUSE
247 Church St.
New York City 10013
(212) 925-3000 or 925-6999
Silks, suedes (!), fake furs, sailcloth, satin, wool blends, gabardines, percales, etc. at 50% off.

INTERCOASTAL TEXTILE CORP.
480 Broadway
New York City 10013
(212) 925-9235
Decorator fabrics, slipcovers, draperies, upholstery, Haitian cotton, satin, velvet, crewel, brocade, linen, tapestries, excellent quality, brand name, designer fabrics at 75% off.

HOME FABRICS MILLS
Route 50, 443 Saratoga Rd.
Scotia 12302
(518) 399-6325
Upholstery fabrics, trims, and supplies. Pillows, slipcovers, draperies, foam at discounts of 30–75%.

NORTH CAROLINA

BEDSPREAD WORLD (*chain*)
Famous name brand bedding, towels, draperies at discount (to 60% off).

15-501 North Roxboro Rd.
Durham 27701
(919) 471-1668

535 West Elm St.
Graham 27253
(919) 584-1830

FIELDCREST OUTLET STORE (*chain*)
Fieldcrest linens at discount.

Highway 14
Eden 27288
(919) 623-8715

I-95, Brogden Rd.
Smithfield 27577
(919) 934-9441

HERITAGE QUILT FACTORY OUTLET (*chain*)
Bedding, draperies, and rugs.

Black Ave.
Bryson City 28713
(704) 488-9201

1906 South Chapman St.
Greensboro 27403
(919) 292-7505

3306 North Blvd.
Raleigh
(919) 876-2232

2317 South Seventeenth St.
Wilmington 28401
(919) 791-3501

MILL OUTLET VILLAGE (*chain*)
3201 Clarendon Blvd.
New Bern 28560
(919) 633-5675

Rt. 2, Hwy. 74 & 76 East
Whiteville 28472
(919) 642-2542

1827 Carolina Beach Rd.
Wilmington 28403
(919) 762-3775
Velvet, upholstery, drapes, canvas at discount.

MONEYTREE OUTLET
30 Haywood St.
Asheville 28801
(704) 258-9100
Linens and rugs at discount. Overruns, cancellations, irregulars.

◆ **LUXURY FABRICS/LUXURY CRAFTS**
2430 North Chester
Gastonia 28052
(704) 867-5313 or 865-7620
Upholstery, fabric, pillows, bedspreads. First-quality only. At discount.

◆ **MIDAS FABRICS OUTLET STORE**
880 Huffman St.
Greensboro 27405
(919) 274-3443
Upholstery, slipcovers, drapery, bedspread fabrics. Huge selection at good discount. Also accessories.

J. P. STEVENS AND CO.
5 Elm St.
Greensboro 27406
(919) 275-9851
Coordinating sheets and towels, spreads, curtains, quilts, carpets, and fabric remnants at discount.

WHITE SHIELD FACTORY OUTLET
107 West Main St.
Hazelwood 28738
(704) 456-3756
Linens and bedding at discount.

OAKLEY'S DRAPERY OUTLET
Hurdle Mills
Hillsborough 27278
(919) 732-3488
Famous name matching drapes and spreads, also curtains and blinds at discounts to 70%.

CANNON HOME FASHIONS
120 West Avenue
Kannapolis 28081
(704) 938-4651
Cannon linens; firsts, seconds, and thirds at discount from 50%. By the pound or separately.

WAMSUTTA OUTLET
Hwy. 181
Morgantown 28655
(704) 437-1403
Assorted fabrics by Wamsutta and Burlington at discount. Sheets by the pound. Also discount towels and spreads.

◆ **ALL AMERICAN FABRICS**
636 S. Lafayette St.
Shelby 28150
(704) 482-3271
Upholstery fabrics at discounts to 75%.

◆ **SMITHSON INC. MILL OUTLET**
North Hwy 1 Bypass
Southern Pines 28387
(919) 692-6709
Designer bedding/fabric at discount.

OHIO

TEXTILE MILL BEDSPREAD WORLD (*chain*)
Discount bedding, linens, rugs, cushions.

7617 Reading Rd.
Valley Theater Center
Cincinnati 45237
(513) 948-1100

9905 Montgomery Rd.
Cincinnati 45242
(513) 984-2233

4-POSTER BEDDING
11551 Grooms Rd.
Cincinnati 45242
(513) 489-0726
Closeouts and overruns. All kinds of bedding at discounts up to 50%.

DRAPERY OUTLET
5471 Mayfield Rd.
Cleveland 44124
(216) 442-9465
Quality decorator bedspreads and drapes at discounts. Overruns, cancellations, etc.

PENNSYLVANIA

COLUMBIA FACTORY OUTLET
225 Oswego Dr. & Rt. 462
Columbia 17512
(717) 684-6341
Bedspreads, draperies, linens, towels, pillows, rugs at discount.

AMES SHOWER CURTAINS
518 Main St.
Forest City 18421
(717) 785-5601
Shower curtains, window curtains, plasticware bathroom accessories. Good selection. Thirty-five percent off retail.

FACTORY DRAPERY OUTLET
17 Paoli Plaza
Paoli 19301
(215) 664-3337
Draperies and bedspreads at discount.

RICHARD TEXTILES-REMNANTS SHOP
North Seneca St. S.E.
Shippensburg 17257
(717) 532-4156
Upholstery, drapery fabrics at discount.

SOUTH CAROLINA

HERITAGE QUILT FACTORY OUTLET
520 Mills Ave.
Greenville 29605
(803) 235-5441
Bedding, draperies, and rugs.

TENNESSEE

HERITAGE QUILT FACTORY OUTLET (*chain*)
Bedding, drapes, and rugs.

959 Volunteer Pkwy.
Bristol 37620
(615) 968-4406

1618 East Fiftieth St.
Chattanooga 37407
(615) 867-9449

TEXAS

HANCOCK FABRIC OUTLET
436 Northlake Shopping Center
Dallas 75238
(214) 348-8020
Fabric at 50% discount. Good weekly specials.

LEGGETT FABRICS
2702 Capitol
Houston 77003
(713) 222-2471
Upholstery fabrics and supplies at discounts of 50–75%.

VIRGINIA

OLD STORE IN THE VILLAGE
Box 246
Rt. 60 West
Norge 23127
(804) 564-9604
Decorator fabrics, velvets, brocades, upholstery, drapery, slipcovers, hand screened Scandinavian cottons, hand embroidered crewel at 50% off.

CALICO CORNERS

A good place to find fabrics for the home is the Calico Corners chain; this coast-to-coast string of stores has consistently good prices and excellent sales. Besides a fine selection of home-decorating fabrics, Calico Corners' well-organized stores carry a complete line of upholstery and drapery hardware and notions.

ALABAMA

108 Loehmann's Village
Birmingham 35244
(205) 988-5533

ARIZONA

10401 North Scottsdale Rd.
Scottsdale 85253
(602) 991-1121

CALIFORNIA

5764 Paradise Dr.
Corte Madera 94925
(415) 924-2275

5753 Pacheco Blvd.
Pacheco 94553
(415) 825-2600

3830 East Foothill Blvd.
Pasadena 91107
(213) 792-4328

2700 El Camino Real
Redwood City 94061
(415) 364-1610

4619 Convoy St.
San Diego 92111
(619) 292-1500

5353 Almaden Expwy.
39-A Almaden Plaza
San Jose 95118
(408) 723-8200

COLORADO

6625 Leetsdale Dr.
Denver 80224
(303) 320-5338

(continued on next page)

7470 South University Blvd.
Littleton 80122
(303) 740-7252

CONNECTICUT

P.O. Box 117
Rt. 7, Danbury Rd.
Wilton 06897
(203) 762-5662

FLORIDA

20 South Dixie Hwy.
Boca Raton 33432
(305) 395-4244

4725 San Jose Blvd.
Jacksonville 32207
(904) 737-6930

16810 South Dixie
Miami 33157
(305) 253-5400

3702 Edgewater Dr.
Orlando 32804
(305) 299-2200

1 North Tamiami Trail
Osprey 33559
(813) 966-2117

2700 Northwest Federal Hwy.
Stuart 33494
(305) 692-1780

1711 South Dale Mabry Blvd.
Tampa 33629
(813) 251-2327

GEORGIA

4256 Roswell Rd.
Atlanta 30342
(404) 252-7443

ILLINOIS

896 South Waukegan Rd.
Lake Forest 60045
(312) 234-6800

18 West 050-22nd St.
Oak Brook Terrace 60181
(312) 629-2511

105 South Green Bay Rd.
Wilmette 60091
(312) 256-1500

INDIANA

165 West Sycamore
Zionsville 46077
(317) 873-3347

KANSAS

Loehmann's Plaza
9013 Metcalf Ave.
Overland Park 66212
(913) 381-9840

LOUISIANA

1820 St. Charles Ave.
New Orleans 70130
(504) 522-0005

MARYLAND

305 York Rd.
Towson 21204
(301) 821-9230

MASSACHUSETTS

444 Great Road-2A
Acton 01720
(617) 263-8549

716 High St., Rt. 109
Westwood 02090
(617) 326-4981

MICHIGAN

1933 South Telegraph Rd.
Bloomfield Hills 48013
(313) 332-9163

21431 Mack Ave.
St. Clair Shores 48080
(313) 775-0078

MINNESOTA

Leisure Lane Center
7101 France Ave. South
Edina 55435
(612) 925-5600

2325 Fairview Ave. North
Roseville 55113
(612) 636-5112

MISSOURI

10440 German Blvd.
Frontenac-Ladue
St. Louis 63131
(314) 993-1388

NEW JERSEY

323 Rt. 10
East Hanover 07936
(201) 887-3905

Rt. 34, The Marketplace
Matawan 07747
(201) 583-5223

NEW YORK

681 East Main St.
Mt. Kisco 10549
(914) 666-4486

1040 Mamaroneck Ave.
Mamaroneck 10543
(914) 698-9141

NORTH CAROLINA

520 North Spring St.
Winston-Salem 27101
(919) 724-6306

6631 Morrison Blvd.
Charlotte 28211
(704) 365-1483

OHIO

P.O. Box 177, Rt. 43
196 South Chillicothe Rd.
Aurora 44202
(216) 562-8558

Gold Circle Mall
Ridge and Highland Sts.
Cincinnati 45213
(513) 631-8778

OKLAHOMA

6149 South Peoria Ave.
Tulsa 74136
(918) 743-9911

OREGON

8526 Southwest Terwilliger Blvd.
Portland 97219
(503) 244-6700

PENNSYLVANIA

745 Lancaster Ave.
Strafford-Wayne 19087
(215) 688-1505

TENNESSEE

985 South Yates Rd.
Memphis 38119
(901) 767-8780

4004 Hillsboro Rd.
Nashville 37215
(615) 269-4551

TEXAS

3010 West Anderson La.
Austin 78757
(512) 467-9462

Loehmann's Plaza
11411 East Northwest Hwy.
Dallas 75218
(214) 349-6829

12370 Inwood Rd.
Dallas 75234
(214) 386-5081

6805 Green Oaks Rd.
Ridgmar Mall
Fort Worth 76116
(817) 731-4691

6271 FM 1960 West
Houston 77069
(713) 444-8002

5705 Fondren Rd.
Houston 77036
(713) 783-5499

9198 Old Katy Rd.
Houston 77055
(713) 464-8653

218 Main St.
Humble 77338
(713) 446-7576

210 Pitman Corners
1301 Custer Rd.
Plano 75075
(214) 578-1674

6413 Northwest Loop 410
San Antonio 78238
(512) 680-3406

15689 San Pedro
San Antonio 78232
(512) 496-1777

VIRGINIA

6400 Williamsburg Blvd.
Arlington 22207
(703) 536-5488

3996 Virginia Beach Blvd.
Virginia Beach 23452

WASHINGTON

210 105th Ave. Northeast
Bellevue 98004
(206) 455-2510

LIGHTING & FURNITURE

CALIFORNIA

BUDGET FURNITURE
(*chain*)
New and used furniture at good prices. They'll rent or sell.

2055 Center St.
Berkeley 94704
(415) 540-6651

3340 Ocean Park Blvd.
Santa Monica 90405
(213) 450-4006

COST-PLUS
North Point & Taylor
San Francisco 94133
(415) 673-8400
Imported Far Eastern and Mexican furniture at discount. Good selection of rattan and wicker at a good price.

COUNTRY LIVING
1133 Clement St.
San Francisco 94118
(415) 221-1414
Unpainted furniture at good prices.

CREATIVE LIGHTING
1409 Divisadero
San Francisco 94115
(415) 921-1832

SOFABED CONSPIRACY
2901 Geary Blvd.
San Francisco 94118
(415) 221-1414
Huge selection of sofa beds in attractive colors/fabrics at good discounts.

COLORADO

CLASSIC WOOD MFG.
5911 North Broadway
Denver 80216
(303) 295-0204
Thirty to 40% off butcher block and upholstered furniture.

DISCOUNT LIGHTING AND SUPPLY CO.
1735 West Forty-eighth Ave.
Denver 80221
(303) 458-8531
Fifty percent discount on every kind of lighting: table and floor lamps, track lighting, fluorescent lighting, chandeliers.

CONNECTICUT

HITCHCOCK CHAIR CO. FACTORY OUTLET
Route 7
Wilton 06897
(203) 762-9594
Fifty percent discount on Hitchcock rocking chairs, benches, dining tables, chairs, blanket chests, beds, headboards, bookcases, mirrors, desks, coffee tables.

FLORIDA

ADVANCE MANUFACTURING CO., INC.
4165 Silver Star Rd.
Orlando 32808
(305) 299-4020
Casual furniture at discount.

MASSACHUSETTS

LIGHT 'N LIVELY
1355 Beacon St.
Brookline 02168
(617) 731-2345
Twenty to 50 percent off lamps, overheads, swags, study lamps, chandeliers, and a good selection of shades.

FACTORY GIFT STORE
453 Center St. (Rt. 21)
Ludlow 01056
(413) 583-8010
Discounts on lamps, clocks, kitchen aids, crystal, small pine furniture.

MINNESOTA

LIGHTING CONCEPTS OUTLET SHOWROOM
7435 Washington Ave. South
Edina 55435
(612) 941-6410
Thirty-three percent discount on discontinued and one-of-a-kind lamps and lighting fixtures.

THE BARGAIN MART
2416 Penn Ave. North
Minneapolis 55411
(612) 521-2218
Thirty to 50% off home furnishings.

THE UNPAINTED PLACE
Cedar Lake Unpainted Furniture Co., Inc.
1601 Hennepin Ave.
Minneapolis 55403
(612) 339-1500
(612) 336-5200
Up to 40% savings on pine, birch, and particleboard. Also unfinished furniture.

GOTTLEIB FURNITURE AND CARPET CO.
2750 Johnson St. N.E.
Minneapolis 55418
(612) 781-1313
Forty percent or greater discount on furniture and lamps. Carpeting also at discount.

KOVAL'S
4317 Excelsior Blvd.
St. Louis Park 55416
(612) 920-6144
Brand name appliances at discount—dishwashers, washing machines, etc.

BUILDERS WHOLESALE INC.
1034 Lafond Ave.
St. Paul 55104
(612) 645-9315
Thirty percent discount on brand name refrigerators, dishwashers, stoves, etc.

E & G SALES
2036 Marshall Ave.
St. Paul 55104
(612) 646-3980
Up to 40% discount on name brand furniture, carpets, and mattresses. Closeouts, samples, and discontinued styles.

MUSKA LIGHTING CENTER
700 Grand Ave.
St. Paul 55105
(612) 227-8881
Lighting fixtures at 40% off.

NEW HAMPSHIRE

SPAULDING & FROST CO.
Main St.
Fremont 03044
(603) 895-3372
Planters, wine racks, baskets, barrels—all white pine. Discount: 30–50%.

NEW JERSEY

MFL INDUSTRIES
238 Thirteenth St.
Carlstadt 07072
(201) 933-3300
First-quality Tiffany-style lamps and mirrors at 35–70% off.

CHECK-O-LITE
3464 Kennedy Blvd.
Jersey City 07307
(201) 653-3161
Fifty percent off panel fixtures, overhead fixtures, imported crystal chandeliers. One-of-a-kind closeouts, samples, and discontinued styles.

IMPORT EXCHANGE CO.
173 Main St.
West Orange 07052
(201) 731-1440
Thirty to 50 percent off bamboo, wicker, and rattan furniture; also Chinese silk screens.

NEW YORK

MACY'S FURNITURE CLEARANCE CENTER
(*chain*)
Floor samples, closeouts at 20–50% off. Furniture, TVs, stereos, area rugs, lamps, bedding.

174 Glen Cove Rd.
Carle Place 11514
(516) 746-1490

1640 Broadhollow Rd.
Farmingdale 11735
(516) 293-0720

425 North Central Park Ave.
Hartsdale 10530
(914) 761-7771

2241 Central Ave.
Schenectady 12304
(518) 370-0700

SYROCO FACTORY STORE
State Fair Blvd.
Baldwinsville 13027
(315) 635-9060
Forty percent discount on Syroco plastic furniture, mirrors, sconces, etc.

MOHAWK FURNITURE, FURNITURE OUTLET
P.O. Box 488—5 Mill St.
Broadalbin 12025
(518) 883-3424
Thirty to 50 percent savings on first-quality pine and oak furniture; also college student furniture.

LAMP WAREHOUSE
1073 Thirty-ninth St.
Brooklyn 11219
(212) 436-2207
Name brand lamps, pendants, ceiling fans, track lights at 20–50% discount.

SHOWROOMS OF FINE USED FURNITURE
57 Lafayette Ave. (corner of Fulton St.)
Brooklyn 11217
(212) 834-8800
Furniture, mostly contemporary, second-hand but in good condition at a fraction of original cost.

LUCITE BARGAINS
77–35 Sixty-fourth St.
Flushing 11366
(212) 380-4829
Shelves, frames, bars (liquor), telephone stands, stackable tables, chairs. Also small accessories. Thirty to 50 percent discount.

SMART SHADES
12703 Twentieth Ave.
Flushing 11356
(212) 358-8454 or 358-9385
Custom-made lamp shades at 20–50% discount. Also repairs.

ARISTA LAMP
690 Old Willets Path
Hauppauge 11787
(516) 231-6660
First-quality lamps (all styles), chandeliers, lampshades, and fixtures at 50% off.

BLOOMINGDALE'S CLEARANCE
70 Jericho Tpk.
Jericho 11753
(516) 627-3840
Bloomingdale's model rooms at 60% off. Also other furniture at big savings.

KNOLL WAREHOUSE OUTLET
36–30 Steinway St.
Long Island City 11101
(212) 826-2405
The famous Knoll furniture at up to 50% off. Discontinued items, overstocks, showroom samples. Immediate delivery.

AID OFFICE FURNITURE
130 West Twenty-third St.
New York City 10011
(212) 924-2350
Used office furniture, including drafting tables.

ALEXANDER BUTCHER BLOCKS & SUPPLY CORP.
176 Bowery
New York City 10013
(212) 226-4021
Excellent quality butcher block furniture at very good prices.

APEX USED OFFICE FURNITURE
402 West Forty-second St.
New York City 10036
(212) 947-5260
Chairs, desks, files, office shelving at second-hand prices.

CONRAN'S—MAIN BRANCH
160 East Fifty-fourth St.
New York City 10022
(212) 371-2225
Extensive selection of sturdy, well-made, simple modern furnishings: chairs, sofas, beds, desks, tables, etc., as well as lighting fixtures and accessories. Not the least expensive, but excellent quality.

DECORATORS WAREHOUSE
665 Eleventh Ave.
New York City 10019
(212) 757-1106
Showroom furniture; overstock, discontinued styles; cancelled orders; samples. Discounts of 20–60%.

ELECTRICAL PURCHASING
302 Bowery
New York City 10012
(212) 420-1996
Wholesale distributors with limited selection at great prices. Good for simple fluorescent fixtures.

INTERNATIONAL FLUORESCENT
135 Bowery
New York City 10002
(212) 966-1096
Casual lighting at good prices. Specialize in fluorescent lights, which come in standard shapes and many colors. Many large fluorescent fixtures for kitchen and den. All prices include bulbs.

MURPHY DOOR BED COMPANY
40 East Thirty-fourth St.
New York City 10016
(212) 682-8936
Murphy beds, the famous space savers, can fold into a wall or cabinet with ease. Various sizes available.

N.Y. GAS LIGHTING CO.
148 Bowery
New York City 10013
(212) 226-2840
High-quality lighting at 60% off list. Room after room of Tiffany, Stiffel, chandeliers, poker lamps, you name it.

THE OTHER STORE
160 Bowery
New York City 10012
(212) 966-1965
Many attractive lamps, not much high-tech.

PARIS LIGHTING
134 Bowery
New York City 10013
(212) 226-7420
Large selection of Lightolier items at 50% off retail—track, recessed, etc.

STATUS FURNITURE CLEARANCE CENTER
653 Eleventh Ave.
New York City 10036
(212) 582-8627
Top-of-the-line designer furniture at 50% discount.

THUNDER & LIGHT
171 Bowery
New York City 10002
(212) 966-0757
Exquisite selection. Largest selection of high-tech lighting on the Bowery. Not the least expensive, but good prices for the quality. As much a gallery as a store.

TIMES SQUARE LIGHTING
318 West Forty-seventh St.
New York City 10036
(212) 245-4155
Stage and theatrical lighting; special effects, dimmers. Will sell or rent.

TUDOR ELECTRICAL SUPPLY CO., INC.
222 East Forty-sixth St.
New York City 10017
(212) 867-7550
A comprehensive selection: contemporary and traditional fixtures; recessed and spot lighting—all at very *competitive prices.*

THE WAREHOUSE STORE
27 Tarrytown Rd.
White Plains 10606
(914) 948-6333
High-quality furniture, name brands at 30–70% discount. Clearance center for all J.H. Harvey furniture stores.

NORTH CAROLINA

LIGHTING CENTER (*chain*)
Fifty percent discount on large selection of lighting fixtures, lamps, and some furniture.

1103 Central Ave.
Charlotte 28204
(704) 376-5648

220 Franklin Ave.
Gastonia 28052
(704) 867-7371

715 Hwy. 321 S.W.
Hickory 28601
(704) 322-2203

CARDINAL SHOWROOM
4729 High Point Rd.
Greensboro 27407
(919) 294-1123
Lamp samples direct from factory at 50% discount. Also shades.

FURNITURE OUTLET OF HICKORY
930 Hwy. 64–70 S.W.
Hickory 28601
(704) 327-2074
Showroom samples at wholesale prices.

NORTH CAROLINA FURNITURE SALES
P.O. Box 2802
1720 Hwy 64–70 West
Hickory 28601
(704) 322-7790
Brand name furniture at 40% off: Heritage, Stanley, Drexel, Century, LaBarge, Thomasville. Lamps by Stiffel, Wildwood, and Frederick Cooper. Bedding from Serta, Sealy, Kingdown, and Beautyglide.

◆ **QUALITY FURNITURE MARKET OF LENOIR**
2034 Hickory Blvd. S.W.
Lenoir 28645
(704) 728-2946
Brand name furniture at discount. All rooms and accessories.

THE FURNITURE HOUSE OF N.C. INC.
P.O. Box 1591
I-85 & Peeler Rd.
Salisbury 28144
(704) 637-1221
High-quality brand name furniture at 30–40% off. No freight charges—save an additional 10%.

OHIO

CIBON INTERIORS
526 North Cassingham Rd.
North Bexley 43209
(614) 253-6555
Furniture for all rooms at discounts up to 50%.

PENNSYLVANIA

FURLONG LAMP FACTORY OUTLET
P.O. Box 138
Furlong 18925
(215) 794-7444
Large selection of name brand and house brand lamps and shades at 40–60% off.

SCHOTT FURNITURE CO. FACTORY OUTLET STORE
215 Polar St.
Hanover 17331
(717) 632-5227
Mahogany furniture, first quality, discontinued styles and seconds at 50% discount.

SENSENICH
Airport Rd.
Lancaster 17604
(717) 569-0435
Butcher block cutting boards, tabletops, clocks. Chrome and wood bases. Discounts of 40% and more.

ALLEGHENY LAMP FACTORY OUTLET
54 Scott St.
Wilkes-Barre 18702
(717) 825-6135
Lamps and shades, repairs, spare parts, all at 40% off retail.

RHODE ISLAND

EASTERN BUTCHER BLOCK
25 Eagle St.
Providence 02908
(401) 273-6330
Forty percent discount on large selection of chairs, tables, counter tops, and living room furniture. First quality.

TEXAS

BROOKES-REYNOLDS FURNITURE
18810 Preston Rd.
Dallas, 75252
(214) 596-5439
A large selection of elegant imported furnishings; 25–45% off French writing desks, couches in cotton prints, leather chairs and ottomans, etc.

MARKET SAMPLER
1915 Greenville Ave.
Dallas 75206
(214) 826-1367
Some of everything: planters, soft furnishings and a small but good quality selection of furniture at 40% off.

LIGHTING SUPPLY CO.
128 North University
Fort Worth 76107
(817) 332-6140
Vast selection of table and floor lamps, accent lamps, chandeliers, ceiling fans, mirrors—all at big savings.

WILLIAM FINE FURNITURE
1621 North Central Expwy.
Richardson 75081
(214) 234-0871
Furniture at 50% off. Cash-and-carry on closeouts, discontinued lines. Enormous selection; stock varies.

VIRGINIA

JOSEPH M. CATALOANO CO.
929 West Broad St.
Falls Church 22046
(703) 534-8400
Forty percent discount on lighting fixtures. Table and floor lamps at 20% off. Smoke detectors, fans, intercoms, and chimes also at discount.

MONTGOMERY WARD CATALOGUE SURPLUS STORE
224 Winchester Ave.
Martinsburg 25401
(304) 263-3409
Lighting and appliances at 50% or greater discount.

FLOOR, WALL, & WINDOW COVERINGS

CALIFORNIA

CARPET CENTER
921 Parker St.
Berkeley 94710
(415) 549-1100
Good buys; good selection of contemporary carpeting.

TILE FANTASTIC SALES
2395 South Bascom Ave.
Campbell 95008
(408) 371-6747
Enormous selection in the latest patterns and designs. They are direct importers, so you save money.

HOMEWORKS
370 Park Ave.
Moraga 94556
(415) 376-7750
Shutters, Levolor blinds, wall coverings, draperies, carpeting, linoleum, hardwood flooring, furniture, lighting, and accessories—all at discount.

TILE TOWN
2525 Telegraph Ave.
Oakland 94612
(415) 893-4500
Good selection of floor coverings, including ceramic tiles at reasonable prices.

ALPHA-OMEGA
12967 San Pablo
Richmond 94805
(415) 237-7394
Wide selection at good discount. Will accept phone orders. You measure and install yourself.

CARPETERIA
2930 Geary Blvd.
San Francisco 94118
(415) 668-2234

WALLCOVERING AND FABRIC FACTORY OUTLET
2660 Harrison St.
San Francisco 94110
(415) 285-0870
Coordinating wallpaper and fabric, vinyls, suedes, Mylars, foils, grasscloth, prepasted and kraft. Almost-perfects, mill ends, discontinueds and overstocks—all at discount prices.

INNER LIGHT
980 Seventeenth Ave.
Santa Cruz 95062
(408) 462-3144
Garden windows, custom glass, windows and doors, roof windows, glass and acrylic skylights—all at factory direct prices.

COLORADO

AMERICAN BLIND CO.
3102 South Parker Rd.
Parker Landing Center
Aurora 80014
(303) 755-0923
Fifty percent discount on an enormous selection of vertical blinds, woven wooden blinds, decorator mini-blinds, etc.

FLORIDA

FAMOUS WALLCOVERINGS (*chain*)
Vinyl, foils, Mylars, hand printed overruns, closeouts, seconds, etc. Cork, burlap, and grasscloth at 50–80% off!

3282 North State Rd. 7
Lauderdale Lakes 33313
(305) 484-1444

3425 North Federal Hwy.
Pompano Beach 33064
(305) 943-4405

ILLINOIS

ELENHANK DESIGNERS, INC.
347 East Burlington St.
Riverside 60546
(312) 447-5344
Elenhank hand screen-printed, custom-designed draperies and wall hangings, seconds and overruns—all at discount.

MARYLAND

BILL'S CARPET WAREHOUSE (*chain*)
Overstocks, discontinued colors, remnants; runners and carpets at discounts up to 50%. Large selection.

12 New Ordinance Rd.
Glen Burnie 21061
(301) 768-7717

Route 1
Laurel 20707
(301) 498-4400

11411 Reisterstown Rd.
Owings Mills 21117
(301) 356-7266

11800 Rockville Pike
Rockville 20852
(301) 468-0505

2135 Green Spring Dr.
Timonium 21093
(301) 252-7530

MASSACHUSETTS

OLD STONE MILL CORP.
Route 8—Grove St.
Adams 01220
(315) 743-1015
Discounts to 60% on hand- and machine-printed wallpaper. Factory overruns, overstocks, seconds. Also stock wall covering fabrics.

WALLPAPER HANG-UPS, INC.
Campus Plaza, Rt. 18
Bridgewater 02324
(617) 697-3311
Brand name wall coverings at discount.

◆ **HARMONY SUPPLY, INC.**
18 High St. (Medford Sq.)
Medford 02155
(617) 395-2600
Brand name wall coverings at discount.

THORNDIKE MILLS, INC.
Ware Rd.
Palmer 01069
High-quality, machine-made rugs at discount.

MINNESOTA

CARPET WORLD
8017 Nicollet Ave.
Bloomington 55420
(612) 888-9205
Fifty percent off remnants; 30% off slightly irregular rolls.

BUDGET PAINT AND WALLPAPER
4009 Minnehaha Ave.
Minneapolis 55406
(612) 724-7676
Sixty to 80% off first-quality, brand name, discontinued patterns. Enormous selection. Paint at 10% discount.

NEW JERSEY

FABULOUS WALLCOVERINGS (*chain*)
Huge selection at 50% off. Cork, grasscloth, burlap, vinyl, foil, Mylar, cloth backed, etc. Overruns, closeouts, hand prints, and seconds.

1199 Amboy Ave.—Tano Mall
Edison, N.J. 08846
(201) 548-0044

300 South Ave.—Garwood Mall
Garwood 07027
(201) 789-2211

65 East Ridgewood Ave.
Paramus 07652
(201) 967-9680

179 Main St.
West Orange 07052
(201) 673-2220 or 673-2221

BUDGET WALLS/ WALLCOVERING FACTORY OUTLET
85 Lincoln Hwy.
South Kearny 07032
(201) 589-6232
Forty to 90 percent off large selection first-quality wall coverings and matching fabrics for bedspreads and drapes. Also wallpaper tools available.

NEW YORK

WEBSTER WALLPAPERS
2737 Webster Ave. (near 197th St.)
Bronx 10458
(212) 267-0055
Name brand wallpaper and vinyls at up to 50% discount, also available from sample books.

ODD LOT WALL COVERING SUPERMARKET
10-19 Jackson Ave.
Long Island City 11101
(212) 729-9553
Immense selection of patterned wall coverings. Discount from 30–50%. Accessible by subway.

A. A. HEAVY TRAFFIC CARPET
(Division of Whistle for Service)
19 West Thirty-fourth St.
New York City 10001
(212) 749-0500
Industrial carpeting at competitive prices.

ABC CARPET
881 Broadway
New York City 10003
(212) 677-6970
Huge selection of rugs and carpeting, including industrial carpeting. Mill ends and overruns available. Good prices, but check quality carefully.

THE CARPET LOFT
161 Sixth Ave. (near Spring St.)
New York City 10013
(212) 924-2400
A wide selection of residential and industrial/commercial carpeting at discount.

CENTRAL CARPET
426 Columbus Ave.
New York City 10024
(212) 787-8813
Great prices on all kinds of carpet. Second-hand Orientals in excellent condition.

SHEILA'S WALL STYLES
273 Grand St.
New York City 10002
(212) 966-1663
Wallpaper, fabrics, draperies, blinds, shades, spreads, woven woods, upholstery at 75% off. Decorators on premises to advise.

OHIO

LAZARUS
562 West Whittier
Columbus 43215
(614) 463-2121
Warehouse store for carpets and furniture at discount.

PENNSYLVANIA

BEST BROTHERS PAINT AND WALLPAPER OUTLET (*chain*)
Forty percent off discontinued wallpaper, 10% off current patterns.

615 East Walnut
Lebanon 17042
(717) 272-0311

4900 Fifth St.
Temple 19560
(215) 921-3566

38 Memory La.
York 17402
(717) 755-8244

PAINT AND WALLPAPER OUTLET
1128 Walton St.
Lebanon 17042
(717) 272-0311
Forty to 80 percent discount on name brand vinyls and wallpaper. Paint at $4 off per gallon.

AMERICAN DISCOUNT WALLCOVERINGS
1411 Fifth Ave.
Pittsburgh 15219
(412) 471-6941
Fifty percent off closeouts. Hand prints, photo murals, and first-quality name brands at 15–33% discount. Mail and phone orders okay, but you need the manufacturer's name, book name, and pattern number.

TEXAS

MILLCO INTERIORS
5223 Military Pkwy.
Dallas 75227
(214) 388-5447
Carpets and other floor coverings; 33–50% off first-quality floorings.

THE CARPET WAREHOUSE
3317 Garden Brook Dr.
Farmers Branch 75234
(214) 247-4545
Up to 70% off brand name carpet and floor coverings. Brands include: Lee's Philadelphia, Armstrong, Galaxy, Georgian, Salem, Landmark, and Hollytex.

THE BLIND SPOT
2067 North Central Expwy.
Richardson 75080
(214) 669-1383
Name brand blinds at 30–50% discount—wooden, mini, vertical, louver, etc.

UNIQUE RUG OUTLET
201 West Main
Richardson 75208
(214) 680-0494
Oriental rugs at 20–40% off.

MISCELLANEOUS GOOD BUYS

CALIFORNIA

RED VICTORIAN SALVAGE
1665 Haight St.
Alameda 94117
(415) 864-1978
Used building materials: plumbing fixtures, tongue-and-groove flooring.

THE WHOLESALE HOUSE
232 Santa Cruz Ave.
Aptos 95003
(408) 688-6485
Appliances, floor coverings, bedding, indoor and outdoor furniture, lighting, wallpaper—you name it, they sell it at discount.

FRAME-O-RAMA
3167 College (at Alcatraz)
Berkeley 94705
(415) 653-4852
Do-it-yourself picture framing. Silver, bronze, and gold frames cut to any size. Easy, fun, and cheap.

OHMEGA SALVAGE
2407 San Pablo Ave.
Berkeley 94702
(415) 843-7368
One of the cheapest around. They sell anything that comes their way, from tin coffee pots to stone cornices.

PLUMBING 'N THINGS
1808 Fourth St.
Berkeley 94710
(415) 549-3720
Discount prices on Waterjet, Jacuzzi, American Standard, Kohler, Pozzi Ginore, Florestone, Phylrich, and accessories.

◆ **SUNRISE SALVAGE CO.**
2210 San Pablo Ave.
Berkeley 94702
(415) 845-4751
Large selection of Victoriana salvage items. Many brass shower assemblies, faucets, beveled glass, oak-framed windows. Sixteen-page color catalog.

NEW RENAISSANCE GLASS WORKS
5151 Broadway
Oakland 94611
(415) 653-1231
Do-it-yourself stained glass. Classes, tools, materials, estimates, kits, and already-made windows and lamps.

PLUMBING 'N THINGS
1620 Industrial Way
Redwood City 94063
(415) 365-3150
Discount prices on Waterjet, Jacuzzi, American Standard, Kohler, Pozzi Ginore, Florestone, Phylrich, and accessories.

SAN FRANCISCO VICTORIANA
2245 Palou
San Francisco 94124
(415) 648-0313
Large selection of moldings and building materials for quality home improvement. Reasonable prices for excellent quality.

CONNECTICUT

BASKET PEOPLE FACTORY STORE
Across from Mystic Seaport
Mystic 06355
(203) 536-6191
Discounts of 20–80% on baskets and decorating accessories.

NORWALK FOAM RUBBER INC.
22 Raymond St.
South Norwalk 06854
(203) 853-3220
Discounts of 50% on odd pieces of foam. Also, polyester batting for quilting and polyester fiber for stuffing.

HARVEY MFG. CO.
1122 North Silver Lake Rd.
Cary 60013
(312) 639-2166
Wicker accessories at discount. Also 52-inch vinyl fabrics.

MASSACHUSETTS

AKKO INC.
300 Canal St.
Lawrence 01840
(617) 685-3888
Savings to 50% on Lucite magazine racks, plant stands, telephone stands, record racks, planters, etc.

BUILDING #19⅞
810 The Lynnway
Lynn 01905
(617) 593-4445
Buys merchandise from insurance companies. Potluck.

SPAG'S SUPPLIES
193 Boston Tpk., Rt. 9
Shrewsbury 01545
(unlisted phone)
Odd lots of electrical supplies, housewares, paint, tools, furniture, appliances, garden supplies, etc. Potluck. Phone number is unlisted because of the immense volume and overwhelming daily flow of stock.

CAMEO FACTORY OUTLET
16 Ionia St. S.W.
Grand Rapids 49503
(616) 451-2759
Feather, dacron, decorator, bed pillows at 25–70% off retail.

MERILLAT INDUSTRIES INC.
21755 Cedar Avenue South
Lakeville 55044
Up to 40% off kitchen cabinets in several styles and finishes. Also stacking units. All first-line quality.

WATERBED WAREHOUSE
505 First Ave. N.E.
Minneapolis 55413
(612) 379-0504
Discounts of 50% on water beds and accessories with full factory warranties. Good selection.

NEW JERSEY

METALTEX OUTLET
70 Ave. A (N.J. Tpk. exit 14A)
Bayonne 07002
(201) 436-4734
Bath accessories—wicker, metal, ceramic—at 40–70% discount.

WOOD LOFT
222 Tappan St.
Kearney 07032
(201) 991-9088
Reasonably priced stripping of wooden furniture, also in-home stripping of woodwork, trim, windows, etc. Will pick up and deliver in New York City.

ALTO PALLETS
Route 1
Rahway 07065
(201) 382-3311 or 272-4040
This place usually sells pallets by the truckload, but see if you can bargain with the owner for the quantity you need. Singly, about $10.

NEW YORK

◆ **AMERICAN PRESSED STEEL**
3175 Fulton St.
Brooklyn 11208
(212) 235-4440
Gym-style 12" × 12" × 12" box lockers available stacked five or six cubes high (bottom locker is on short legs). Gray only, but easy to paint. Mail orders accepted. Free catalog.

ACADEMY GLASS AND MIRROR CO.
26 Bruckner Blvd.
Bronx 10454
(212) 288-3673
An enormous range of tabletops available in any size or thickness. Competitive prices.

JARRETT WOODWORKING
1314 Blondell Ave.
Bronx 10461
(212) 931-8333
Will build beds, storage units, multipurpose units, shelving, etc., to fix any space.

L & B PRODUCTS
3232 Lurting Ave.
Bronx 10469
(212) 882-5400
Good prices on bases for luncheonette tables. Prices vary with finish. Many styles to choose from.

RAW EQUIPMENT CORP.
28–21 122nd St.
Flushing 11354
(212) 461-2200
Sonotubes are available here in diameters from 4" to 48". Prices depend on quantity.

ASSOCIATED MARBLE
101 West End Ave.
Inwood 11696
(516) 371-4307
(212) 297-8401
Varied colors at varied costs. Wide selection of colors and thicknesses.

AAA RESTAURANT EQUIPMENT
284 Bowery
New York City 10012
(212) 966-1891
Good prices on restaurant supplies.

◆ **AA-ABBINGDON CEILING CO., INC.**
619 Second Ave.
New York City 10016
(212) 477-6505
Twenty-five different patterns of pressed metal ceilings. Also acoustical suspended ceilings. Good prices. Catalog available. They ship all over the United States and Canada.

AD-HOC HOUSEWARES
842 Lexington Ave.
New York City 10021
(212) 752-5488
Metro shelving system available here in many sizes and combinations. Also high-tech furniture, drafting tables, dining tables, chairs, and accessories.

ALEXANDER'S HARDWARE STORE
60 Reade St.
New York City 10007
(212) 267-0336
Job lots of artists' supplies, tools, fireplace equipment. Discount from 25%.

◆ **BARI RESTAURANT & PIZZA EQUIPMENT**
244 Bowery
New York City 10012
(212) 925-3786
Restaurant supplies at good prices. Free catalog doesn't list prices. Discounts vary with quantity. Mail order with certified check only.

BOWERY AUCTION OUTLET
263 Bowery
New York City 10002
(212) 533-8963
Used bar and restaurant equipment. Stock varies according to the auctions. Some of this is pretty beat-up, but there are good finds here.

DIXIE FOAM
20 East Twenty-ninth St.
New York City 10016
(212) 777-3626
All sizes and thicknesses of foam for cushions and mattresses; good prices, huge stock.

M. EPSTEIN'S SON, INC.
809 Ninth Ave.
New York City 10019
(212) 265-3960
Wooden doors and shutters with movable louvers; also blinds, paints, vinyl tiles, carpet tiles, and broadloom at discount prices.

FEDERAL RESTAURANT SUPPLY CORP.
202 Bowery
New York City 10012
(212) 226-0441
Flatware at $4–$6 for a dozen pieces.

FRAMER'S WORKROOM
1484 Third Ave.
New York City 10028
(212) 570-0919
Do-it-yourself framing in many styles and a wide choice of woods and plastics. Inexpensive alternative and fun!

◆ **MAC LEATHER INC.**
428 Broome St.
New York City 10013
(212) 964-0850 or 431-9440
A complete selection of leather and suede skins, starting at $1 per square foot. Also leathercraft supplies. Catalog: $3.

THE PROFESSIONAL KITCHEN
18 Cooper Sq.
New York City 10003
(212) 254-9000
Here they sell the versatile high-tech Super Erecta shelving system in chrome-finish steel, which can be wall-mounted or freestanding.

RENNERT CO.
93 Greene St.
New York City 10012
(212) 925-1463
They specialize in movers' pads. Colors vary by lot; usually black, blue, green, gray, rose. All pads reversible; most reverse to khaki.

TOP EQUIPMENT CORP.
222 Bowery
New York City 10012
(212) 925-1998
Enormous stock of restaurant tables, chairs, and stools. Table bases in all styles from sculptured classical Greek to regular soda shop.

THE VILLAGE STRIPPER ANTIQUES
519 Hudson St.
New York City 10014
(212) 929-4180
Movers' pads in reversible colors: olive/beige, purple/pink, brown/beige, black/beige, dark blue/light blue, and red/beige. Also, good used furniture and some antiques at reasonable prices.

ZABAR'S
2245 Broadway
New York City 10024
(212) 787-2000
Vast selection of kitchen supplies at the best prices in town.

ZECCA MIRROR & GLASS
1180 First Ave.
New York City 10021
(212) 758-0639
Wide selection of glass and mirrors at good prices.

SEARS ROEBUCK SURPLUS STORE
Rt. 25A Westchester Dr.
Rocky Point 17778
(516) 821-1800
Surplus Sears catalog and retail items at 20–75% off. Stock changes frequently. Furniture, power tools, rugs, light fixtures, file cabinets.

OHIO

J.C. PENNEY OUTLET STORE (*chain*)
Discount household needs.

8770 Colerain Ave.
Cincinnati 45239
(513) 385-9700

2361 Park Crescent
Columbus 43227
(614) 868-0250

◆ **FACTORY OUTLET WHOLESALE**
2171 East Fourth St.
Cleveland 44115
(216) 621-0960
Housewares, kitchen equipment, hardware, and restaurant, and bar supplies at discount.

PENNSYLVANIA

CAPE CRAFTSMAN
Route 73 & 202
Center Square 19422
(215) 279-2227
Pine kitchen accessories, stoneware, baskets, mirrors at discount.

READING HOME FURNISHINGS MARKET
Eighth & Hill Ave.
Wyomissing 19610
(215) 376-7138
Upholstery fabrics and large selection of furniture at discount. Oriental rugs at 30–50% off.

NORTH CAROLINA

HYALYN, LTD. FACTORY OUTLET
585 Old Lenoir Rd.
Hickory 28601
(704) 322-3400
Ceramic lamps, planters, bath accessories, vases, lampshades at 40–50% discount.

OKLAHOMA

WALL'S BARGAIN CENTER (*chain*)
Job lots of housewares and hardwares at discount.

4011 S.E. 29th St.
Del City 73115
(405) 672-4438

4640 South Pennsylvania Ave.
Oklahoma City, 73119
(405) 681-2396

521 West Archer Ave.
Tulsa, 74103
(918) 582-5437

VIRGINIA

WILLIAMSBURG POTTERY
Rt. 60, west of town
Williamsburg 23187
(804) 564-3326
Enormous sprawling discount complex. Lamps, pewter, brass, frames, candles, plants, baskets, pottery, glassware—at big discounts.

WEST VIRGINIA

BLENKO GLASS CO.
P.O. Box 67, Henry Rd.
Milton 25541
(304) 743-9081
Stained glass for church windows at up to 50% discount. Also discount glassware.

INDEX

A

Acrylic paint, 73
Adjustable shelves, bookcase with, 123–24
Alkyd paint, 73
Allen, Gerald, 42–43, 86
Anchors, 107
Antique shops, 143
Antiquing furniture, 145–46
Antiquing wallpaper, 82

B

Babington, Colleen, 146–47
Backsaw, 107
Baffle, 97, 107
Bakelite, 97
Baker, Douglas, 97
Basic bookcase, 121
Basic box, 110
Basic platform, 115–16
Basic wall shelving, 126–27
Bathroom lighting, 100, 102
Battelle, Kenneth, 66, 91
Beds, platform, 118–19
  modular system, 142
  open storage space, 120
  variations, 119
Berke, Deborah, 70
Bevel, 107
Bierman, Bruce, 46–47, 85
Blaustein, Peter, 71, 115
Bleaching floors, 90
Bolt, 107
Bookcases and shelved units, 121–28
  with adjustable shelves, 123–24
  basic, 121
  basic wall shelving, 126–28
  kitchen storage closet, 127
  not-so-basic, 122–23
  pedimented wall, 125–26
  salvage bookcase, 128
  stepped divider, 124–25
Bottle table lamp, 98
Bourne, Odessa and Bill, 64
Bowyer, Caroline, 44–45
Boxes, 110–15
  basic, 110
  coffee table with legs, 113
  with a lid, 112
  mirrored, 111
  storage, with drawers, 114–15
Bulbs, designers' tricks with, 105
Butt joint, 107

C

Can lights. *See* Uplights
Canopy, 97
Canvas dressing room, 128–29
Canvas lining, 73
Canvas partition "doors," 131
Carpentry and wood working, 107–42
  bookcases and shelf units, 121–28
  boxes, 110–15
  buying lumber, 108
  fireless fireplace, 136–37
  kitchen counter, 135
  modular system, 139–42
  multipurpose L-unit, 136–37
  nail sizes, 109
  partitions, 128–33
  platforms, 115–20
  tables, 133–34
  terms, 107–9
  See also Furniture
Carriage bolt, 107
Casein paint, 87
Ceilings, 64–65, 73–86
  mirror tiles, 86
  painting, 74–81
  paint terms, 73–74
  tin, 86
  See also Walls
Cement-coated box nail, 107
Chamfer strip, 107
Chapell, Don, 70
Chinn, Austin, 40–41, 105
Chipboard, 107
Circular saw, 107
Cleat, 107–8
Coffee table
  with boxy legs, 113
  modular system, 139–40
Coilcord chandelier, 103
Color run, 73–74
Colors, tinting, 74
Combed squares floor "tiles," 92
Combing technique, 67
Common nail, 108, 109
Con-tact, 82–83
Contact cement, 108
Countersink, 108
Crosscut saw, 108
Crozer, Veva, 64, 65, 67, 80–81, 94
Curved kitchen counter, 135

D

Dabbing technique, 77
Dado joint, 108
Dimmer switches, 106
Donghia, Angelo, 82
Downlight, 98
Dragging the glaze, 72, 76–77
Drain tile uplights, 99
Drill stop, 108
Drop match, 74
Drywall, 108
Drywall screen, 130–31
Drywall tape, 108
Dutch metal leaf, 146–47

E

Edgemate tape, 108
Engel, Bill, 22–23, 48–49, 69, 79

F

Fabric on walls, 84–86
  linen panels, 85–86
  pleated, 85
  shirring, 84
  stapling, 84
Fillers, 108
Finish
  paint, 74
  polyurethane, 95
Finished lumber, 108
Finishing nails, 108, 109
Fireless fireplace, 137–38
Fitzgerald, Robert, 40–41
Flat (paint) finish, 74
Flea markets, 144
Floorcloths, 67, 94
Floors, 66–68, 87–96
  bleaching, 90
  how to use a grid, 96
  lightening, 90
  marbleized, 93
  painting, 90–93
  polyurethane finish, 95
  quick fix for, 92
  sanding, 88
  staining, 89
  stenciled, 94
  terms, 87
  "tiles," 91–92
Fluorescent lights, 103
Frazer, Nick and Charlotte, 62
Furnishing space, 143–52
  finding furniture, 143–44
  refurbishing furniture, 145–47
  tables, 149–52
  transforming castoffs, 148
Furniture, 69
  antiquing, 145–46
  dealing with space, 147
  finding, 143–44
  glass-top tables, 149
  glazing and marbleizing, 144
  gold leafing (Dutch metal leaf), 146–47
  painting, 145
  pallet sofa, 148
  revolving storage wall, 151
  small pedestal table, 152
  sonotubes, 150
  See also Carpentry and woodworking
Furring strips, 108

G

Garage sales, 144
Gewirtz, Janice, 34–35
Gillis, John, 26–27, 71
Glass-top tables, 149
Glazes and glazing, 72, 75–76
  basics, 76
  dragging, 72, 76–77
  furniture, 144
  stippling, 77
  tinting, 75–76
Glossy (paint) finish, 74
Glue block, 108
Gold leafing (imitation), 146–47
Graduated paint technique, 72, 78
Grasscloth wallpaper, 83
Grid, how to use, 96
Grout, 108

H

Hacksaw, 108
Halsband, Frances, 17
Hand-blocked wallpaper, 82
Hardwood, 87
Hector, Denis, 70
Homosote, 108
Household liquidation sales, 144
Hughes, Charles, 30–31, 110
Hulla, Mark, 18–20, 148

I

Industrial bathroom lighting, 102
Interspace Design, Inc., 34–35

J

Japan colors, 74
Jig, 108
Jigsaw, 108
Joint compound, 108
Joist, 108
Jug or bottle table lamp, 98
Junk shops, 144

K

Keyless socket, 98
Kitchen storage closet, 127
Kliment, Robert, 17

L

Lacquering, 79
Laminate router, 109
Laminate trimmer, 108–9
Lamley, Richard, 54, 71
Latex paint, 74
Lath, 109
Lawn sales, 144
Lead anchor, 109
Lid, box with, 112
Lightening floors, 90
Lighting, 70–71, 97–106
  bathroom, 102
  coilcord chandelier, 103
  designers' tricks with bulbs, 105
  dimmer switches, 106
  drain tile, 99
  experiments, what works best, 100
  fluorescence, 103
  jug or bottle lamp, 98
  mirror, 100
  Plugmold Systems, 104
  terms, 97–98
  track, 101
  wok-lid fixture, 104
Lighting Your Home: A Practical Guide, 97
Linen panels, 85–86
Lining paper, 74
Lumber, buying, 108
L-unit, 136–37

M

McFarlane, Julia, 28–29
Machado, William, 16, 55, 85–86
McHugh, Tom, 36–38, 86, 114
Marbleizing, 72
  floors, 93
  furniture, 144
Masonite, 109
Matching, 74
Mineral spirits, 74
Mirrored box, 111
Mirror lights, 100
Mirror tiles, 86
Miter, 109
Miter box, 109
Modular system, 139–42
  bed, 142
  coffee table, 139–40
  wardrobe, 140–41
Molly bolt, 109
Moving and storage companies, 144
Muller, Louis, 24–25, 66, 71
Multipurpose L-unit, 136–37
Murphy, William, 24–25, 71

N

Nails, sizes of, 109
Neas, Richard, 67, 68, 91, 92
Neustadt, Samuel, 12–13, 21, 139–42
Not-so-basic bookcase, 122–23

O

Oil paint, artists', 73
Oliver, Richard, 56–57

P

Paint and painting, 73–81
  dragging the glaze, 76–77
  floors, 90–93
  furniture, 145
  glazes and glazing, 75–76
  graduated or shadow, 72, 78
  how to calculate quantity, 77
  lacquering, 79
  meaning of, 74
  popular techniques, 72
  rag rolling, 78
  stenciling, 65, 80–81
  stippling, 77
  terms, 73–74
  wall and ceiling preparation, 75–76
Pallet sofa, 148
Panhead screw, 98
Parquet, 87
Partitions, 128–33
  canvas "doors," 131
  canvas dressing room, 128–29
  drywall screen, 130–31
  ways to use stretcher bar partitions, 129
Partition wall with window, 132–33
Pedimented wall bookcases, 125–26
Peskett, Stan, 52–53
Pigmented polyurethanes, 74
Pivot hinge, 109
Plastic anchor, 109
Plastic laminate, 109
Platforms, 115–20
  basic, 115–16
  bed, 118–19, 120, 142
  ramp, 116
  triangular, 117
Pleated fabric, 85
Plugmold Systems, 100–102, 104
Plumb, Barbara, 66
Plywood, 109
Polyurethane finish, 95
Polyurethane varnish, 74
Porch sales, 144
Priming, 74

R

Raceway, 98
Radius, 109
Rag rolling (burlap), 72, 78
Rag rubbing (gauze), 72
Ramp, platform, 116
Random match, 74
Regenbogen, Joan, 32
Repeat, 74
Revolving storage wall, 151
Roberts, Leslie, 14–15, 137–38
Roller stippling, 77
Romanello, Tim, 33, 50–51, 118
Roper, Jamie, 11, 112
Router, 109
Rummage sales, 144

S

Saber saw, 109
Salasky, Franklin, 58–59
Salvage bookcase, 128
Sanden, Ken, 39, 124
Sanding floors, 88
Seamless paper, 82
Second-hand shops, 144
Seconds, 74
Semigloss (paint) finish, 74
Set, 109
Shadow painting, 78
Shirred fabric, 64
Shirring walls with fabric, 84
Small pedestal table, 152
Softwood, 87
Sonotubes, 32, 134, 150–152
  console table, 150
Source guide, 153–162
Spaces, 11–62
  Ad Hoc at home, 28–29
  airy and loftlike, 36–38
  all-in-one living, 11
  ambience of 1950s, 30–31
  artist's fantasy, 52–53
  Art Moderne, 40–41
  basic black and white, 46–47
  breaking out of the box, 12–13
  dark elegance, 54
  dress circle, 58–59
  dual-purpose, 16
  18-by-13-foot apartment, 33
  eye for bargains, 14–15
  family planning, 17
  greenery and plants, 39
  high tech, 62
  illumination effect, 48–49
  Manhattan loft, 18–20
  modularity, 21
  pump house (Brooklyn Heights), 26–27
  raised or stepped up, 24–25
  room for all reasons, 50–51
  separate living and sleeping quarters (20-by-30-foot apartment), 34–35
  simple harmony, 56–57
  sleeping and working area (7-by-14-foot room), 42–43
  sonotubes, 32
  three-dimensional painting, 22–23
  variety of lost and found treasures, 60–61
  writers' retreat, 55
  See also names of architects; designers
Spackle. *See* Fillers
Staining floors, 89
Stapling fabric, 84
Stenciled floor, 94
Stenciling, 65, 80–81
Stepped divider bookcases, 124–25
Stippling, 77
Storage box with drawers, 114–15
Stove bolt, 109
Straight match, 74
Streets, finding furniture, 144
Supergraphics, 77
Suspended track lighting, 101
Sygar, Richard, 70

T

Tables, 133–34, 149–52
  glass-top, 149
  sonotubes, 150
  three-piece, 133
Table saw, 109
Tag sales, 144

Three-piece table, 133
Thrift and consignment shops, 144
Tiles, "floor" (painted), 91–92
Tin ceiling, 86
Tinting colors, 74
Toggle bolt, 109
Track and bracket shelving, 126–27
Triangular platform, 117
Tussah silk weave, 83
Two-conductor wire, 98

U

Uplights, 98
    drain tile, 99

V

Valance, 98
Varnishes, 74
    polyurethane, 74

W

Wall-and-pedestal table, 134
Wallpaper, 81–83
    antiquing, 82
    Con-tact, 82–83
    grasscloth, 83
    hand-blocked (do-it-yourself), 82
    how to order, 83
    how to put up, 81–82
    price factors, 81
    Rollerwall, 82
    seamless, 82
    trompe l'oeil effects, 83
    tussah silk weave (imitation), 83
    wastepaper as, 83
Walls, 64–65, 73–86
    collectibles on, 64
    country warmth, 64
    covering with fabrics, 64, 84–86
    painting, 74–81
    paint terms, 73–74
    papering, 81–84
    See also Ceilings
Wall shelving, 126–28
Wardrobe, modular system, 140–41
Wastepaper as wallpaper, 83
Weymouth, Yann, 28–29, 71
White glue, 109
Winchester, Elizabeth, 71
Winthrop, Lewis, 34–35
Wiring a socket, 106
Wok-lid light fixture, 104
Wood, Peter and Shirley, 64
Woodworking. *See* Carpentry and woodworking
Wrecking companies, furniture from, 144

Y

Yard sales, 144

Z

Zevon, Susan, 12–13, 21, 54, 117